WOMEN, THEATRE

AND PERFORMANCE

MANCHESTER
UNIVERSITY PRESS

WOMEN, THEATRE
AND PERFORMANCE

SERIES EDITORS

MAGGIE B. GALE AND VIV GARDNER

This series, *Women, Theatre and Performance*, has its origins in the work of a number of feminist theatre academics from the 1980s and 1990s – a period when interest burgeoned in the part that women have played in theatre over the centuries. That interest was in its turn the daughter of the 'Second Wave' women's movement, the women's theatre movement and the women's history movement from the previous two decades. It was with some delight that women theatre workers, spectators and scholars alike discovered that women *did* have a significant history in performance, and these women – and some men – have continued to investigate, interrogate and work with their histories. Feminist performance analysis and women's theatre history has now become an established part of performance practice and theatre studies at both a university and a more popular level.

In the 1990s, the journal, *Women and Theatre Occasional Papers*, became the host for the documentation and dissemination of contemporary research and innovation in theatre practice and scholarship in Britain. The emphasis on history and historiography was a considered decision. It was felt that at that time no consistent outlet existed for all the work that carried on the feminist retrieval project of the 1980s which was emerging from theatre and drama departments in Britain and elsewhere. This emphasis on history did not – and does not – preclude engagement with contemporary practice. On the contrary, it was felt that our history was very much part of our present and that the two could, and should, be studied side by side. This series seeks to continue that original project and to make the research and debate available on a more than 'occasional' basis. The series will consist of themed volumes that consider theatre as part of a wider nexus of social and cultural practices. Women's contribution to all areas and types of theatre and performance will be included, from opera and acrobatics to management and dramaturgy. Continuities and consistencies will not be sought, though they may be found within the transhistorical and transcultural organisation of the material.

The series is designed for students at all levels, teachers and practitioners, as well as the interested enthusiast who wishes simply to 'fill in the blanks' where women have been hitherto 'hidden' in theatre histories.

Forthcoming title:

Autobiography and identity
EDS MAGGIE B. GALE AND VIV GARDNER

WOMEN, THEATRE AND PERFORMANCE

New histories, new historiographies

EDITED BY
MAGGIE B. GALE AND VIV GARDNER

Manchester University Press
Manchester and New York

distributed exclusively in the USA by Palgrave

Published by Manchester University Press
Oxford Road, Manchester M13 9NR, UK
and Room 400, 175 Fifth Avenue, New York, NY 10010, USA
http://www.manchesteruniversitypress.co.uk

Distributed exclusively in the USA by
Palgrove, 175 Fifth Avenue, New York, NY 10010, USA

Distributed exclusively in Canada by
UBC Press, University of British Columbia, 2029 West Mall,
Vancouver, BC, Canada V6T 1Z2

British Library Cataloguing-in-Publication Data
A catalogue record for this book is available from the British Library

Library of Congress Cataloging-in-Publication Data applied for

ISBN   0 7190 5712 4   *hardback*
       0 7190 5713 2   *paperback*

First published 2000

07 06 05 04 03 02 01 00   10 9 8 7 6 5 4 3 2 1

Typeset by
D R Bungay Associates, Burghfield, Berks

Printed in Great Britain
by Biddles Ltd, Guildford and Kings Lynn

This volume is dedicated to our four boys,
Matti and Wilf Gardner, and
Oscar and Sol Partridge.

CONTENTS

Notes on contributors

Susan Bennett is Professor of English and Associate Dean (Development & Research) in the Faculty of Humanities at the University of Calgary. She is the author of *Theatre Audiences* (London, Routledge, 1990) and *Performing Nostalgia* (London, Routledge, 1996). She is also editor of *Theatre Journal*.

Jacky Bratton is Professor of Theatre and Cultural History at Royal Holloway College, University of London. She is editor of *Music Hall: Performance and Style* (Milton Keynes, Open University Press, 1986) and has published extensively on gender and the eighteenth- and nineteenth-century British and American stage. She is currently editor of *Nineteenth Century Theatre*.

Charlotte Canning is Associate Professor of Theatre History and Theory in the Department of Theatre and Dance at the University of Texas at Austin. She is the author of *Feminist Theatres in the USA: Staging Women's Experience* (London, Routledge, 1996) and numerous articles on feminism and theatre history. She was President of the Women and Theatre Program from 1998–2000.

Susan Carlson is Professor of English at Iowa State University where she teaches courses in drama, British and women's literature, and literary criticism. She has published two books, including *Women and Comedy* (Ann Arbor, University of Michigan Press, 1991) and has recently published essays on Aphra Behn, Shakespeare, Timberlake Wertenbaker and nineteenth-century women playwrights. She is currently working on a book entitled *Shakespeare and the Suffragettes*, a study of British suffrage theatre and its connections to Edwardian productions of Shakespeare's work.

John Deeney is Lecturer in Theatre Studies in the School of Media and Performance Arts at the University of Ulster at Coleraine. He is editor of *Writing Live: An Investigation of the Relationship Between Writing and Live Art* (London, New Playwrights Trust, 1998). His most recent work is on censorship and 'other' sexualities in British theatre between the two world wars.

Maggie B. Gale is Senior Lecturer in Drama and Theatre Arts at the University of Birmingham. She is author of *West End Women: Women on the London Stage 1918–1962* (London, Routledge, 1996), and is editor with Clive Barker of *British Theatre Between the Wars 1918–1939* (Cambridge, Cambridge University Press, 2000). She is joint series editor with Viv Gardner of the *Women, Theatre and Performance* series for Manchester University Press.

Viv Gardner is Professor in Theatre Studies at the University of Manchester. She is editor with Susan Rutherford of *The New Woman and Her Sisters: Feminism and Theatre, 1850–1914* (Hemel Hempstead, Harvester Wheatsheaf, 1992) and with Linda Fitzsimmonds of *New Woman Plays* (London, Methuen, 1991). She has published extensively on late nineteenth- and twentieth-century theatre and with Maggie B. Gale is joint series editor of the *Women, Theatre and Performance* series for Manchester University Press.

Ros Merkin is Senior Lecturer in the Department of Drama at Liverpool John Moore's University. She is the editor of *Popular Theatre?* (Liverpool, Liverpool John Moores University, 1996) and has published articles on the Independent Labour Party and the Arts Guild. Her current research is in the area of Musical Theatre.

Susan Rutherford is Lecturer in Performance Studies at the Department of Drama in the University of Manchester. She is editor with Viv Gardner of *The New Woman and Her Sisters: Feminism and Theatre, 1850–1914* (Hemel Hempstead, Harvester Wheatsheaf, 1992) and her forthcoming publications include *Sirens, Songbirds and Superwomen: The Female Singer, Opera and Theatricality 1800–1930*.

Catherine Schuler is Associate Professor in the Department of Theatre at the University of Maryland, College Park. She has published on performance art and Russian theatre in *The Drama Review, Theatre History Studies, Theatre Survey* and *Theatre Topics*. Her book, *Women in Russian Theatre: The Actress in the Silver Age* (London, Routledge, 1996) won the Hewitt Prize in 1997. She is currently working on acting theory and practice in Russia before Stanislavsky and on Russian actresses' memoirs.

John Stokes is Professor of Modern British Literature in the Department of English at King's College, London. His most recent book is *Oscar Wilde: Myths, Miracles and Imitations* (Cambridge, Cambridge University Press, 1996). He has written widely on nineteenth-century French Actresses, on nineteenth and twentieth-century theatre and reviews for the TLS and other journals.

Joanna Townsend is Lecturer in Drama in the School of English Studies at the University of Nottingham. Her recently completed thesis, 'Speaking the Body, Representing the Self: Hysterical Rhetoric on Stage', revisits the history of hysteria in order to re-centre attention on the symptomatic acts of the performing body on stage. She is currently pursuing her research on Elizabeth Robins.

Acknowledgements

Every effort has been made to trace and seek permissions from copyright holders. All authors would like to thank those who have given consent to publish copyright material. Special thanks to the Theatre Museum, London, the Mander and Mitcheson Theatre Collection, the Fales Library, New York University and The British Newspaper Library at Colindale. Catherine Schuler's research was made possible by the provision of an IREX grant and Joanna Townsend is grateful for the enthusiastic granting of permissions to quote for Elizabeth Robins's work from Mabel Smith, Trustee of the Backsettown Estate. Maggie B. Gale would like to thank Joel Kaplan and Sheila Stowell for giving access to research funding for this project. The editors would particularly like to thank Helen Day-Mayer and David Mayer for permission to use their delightful De Wilde painting of Eliza Vestris as Mrs Page.

INTRODUCTION

We cannot understand the present if we isolate it from the past. If we want to understand what it is that [we] are doing now ... [w]e must forget that we are, for the moment, ourselves. We must become the people that we were two or three generations ago. Let us be our great grandmothers. (Virginia Woolf, *The Pargiters*[1])

Between 1991 and 1997 four editions of *Women and Theatre Occasional Papers* were published, the first three edited by Maggie B. Gale and Susan Bassnett and volume four by Maggie B. Gale and Viv Gardner. The journal, hosting many articles from British conferences, was dedicated to 'documenting and providing a forum for discussion on research and innovations both in theatre practice and academia, which are current in the field of "women and theatre"', with an emphasis on historical research rather than the theoretical research which had a particular currency at the time. These journals were the foremothers of this volume of essays, which in its turn launches this new series – a series dedicated to the investigation of women's work in theatre and performance. The series is thematically based, with further volumes on 'Auto/biography and Identity', 'Women and Theatre Design', 'Women Theatre Managers' and 'Women Directors' in preparation.

In the introduction to the 1992 volume of essays, *Gender and Performance*, Laurence Senelick makes no apology that,

> The image of woman dominates this book, because, in most cultures until very recently, to be human meant to be male. Man was taken as the generic form, and woman as a subspecies, a somehow imperfect version or soluble problem.[2]

We too make no apology that women dominate this series – they are the reason for its existence. The questions raised by women's exclusion and occlusion in theatre practice and theatre studies until recently are the conduit by which we begin to understand not just theatre and performance practice but social and cultural practice.

Feminist studies underpin the project – from its inception, feminist studies and feminist practice has radically revisioned the discipline and practice of theatre. It has raised ontological as well as epistemological questions. The feminist project that emerged from the so-called Second Wave was, in Jill Davis's words, 'the instigator of the questioning of gender, the place where the operation and limitation of a binary gender system – and indeed its instability and fictionality – was theorised'.[3] Our project, by separating out women and theatre, women and performance, does not seek to reinstate the binaries but to further that questioning of gender. Feminism itself is, and always has been, pluralist; feminist studies within the academy, interdisciplinary. The 'absence of an all-embracing manifesto or methodological design for research' in feminist theatre history, identified in 1989 by Tracy C. Davis,[4] is a guiding principle in this series. There is no single agenda that binds the contributors, there is no common theoretical position. However, the series does pursue what might loosely be called a 'materialist' position, and will concentrate on the retrieval and analysis of data, the observation and documentation of performance and theatrical text rather than engage in,

> the bravura theoretical display [that] is not untypical in feminist theatre scholarship of the past decade, but [which] contains, or rather masks, some serious contradictions ... [and results in] the domination of a theoretical agenda over performance practice.[5]

Our wish is to identify performance and historiographical practice and to develop new methodological approaches and theoretical models that serve our purpose.

This first volume in the series addresses issues of histories and historiography. Feminist theatre scholars have consistently seen 'archaeology' as an important part of the feminist project. As Susan Bassnett notes:

> By re-assessing the history of women in theatre we may well come to rethink many of the premises on which current research into the history of culture has been founded. And then we may well find that our practcal theatre work today moves forward onto a new, as yet undiscovered plane.[6]

And Elaine Aston has argued that, 'examining the material conditions of theatre as a cultural form ... furthered an understanding of the theatrical and social conditioning of a cultural past to be seen as a continuum of a materially-conditioned cultural present.'[7] The archaeological process continues in this volume with the unearthing of 'new histories', but again as Tracy C. Davis has argued, the feminist theatre historian's task is not simply to recreate and document hitherto 'lost' women, texts or performances, but 'to address the censoring impulse, to validate the experience, and to connect the woman with the work and the work with the world at large.'[8] The new histories open up the historiographic questions, sometimes explicitly, sometimes implicitly.

Many of the chapters in this volume offer possibilities of revisioning the theatrical past both transculturally and transhistorically. Jacky Bratton explores the critical reception of Susanna Centlivre, whose plays, amongst the most popular of her day, have now all but been forgotten. Bratton points to the way in which Centlivre's success was the 'entertainer's success, in matching her offering to the taste of the time'. Paradoxically it was this success which inhibited critical re-evaluations of her work, where even feminist critics have found it difficult to position her within a canon of women playwrights. For Bratton an approach to re-evaluation which places 'intertheatricality' in a central position is vital. Thus the gender-biased accusations of a lack of theatrical wit and literary originality which have plagued Centlivre's critical career need to be re-contextualised by locating her plays in relation to both the theatre of her day and the complex layers of theatrical codes at work at any one time in that theatre. In a similar vein, Viv Gardner approaches London's late nineteenth-century West End theatreland from the perspective of gendered geographical, architectural and social spaces. Borrowing from recent interdisciplinary feminist theoretical explorations of 'place and space', Gardner proposes that the gentrification and 'domestication' of theatres during the late nineteenth century held a paradoxical significance for women, who were at one and the same time given more freedom as spectators yet rendered invisible.

Susan Bennett moves away from the specifics of one particular practitioner or theatrical era to look at the ways in which women playwrights, through new anthologies and new higher education courses, have been accommodated by the academy. Bennett acknowledges the problematics of 'canonisation' but uses it as a starting point for an examination of how we might use such practice as a means of questioning what exactly it is that we mean by theatre history – what are the terms of inclusion and exclusion. Bennett sees historiography as both a 'road block and a means to reinvigorating theatre history'. It is this desire for a reinvigoration of theatre history as a discipline which reverberates in a number of other chapters in this collection.

Susan A. Rutherford, John Stokes and Joanna Townsend all focus on one practitioner with the intention of reinvestigating the relationship between the contemporary and a historically-based reception of their work. Rutherford assesses the way in which the German soprano Wilhemine Schröder-Devrient influenced the 'broader personal and cultural development' of Richard Wagner. Rutherford suggests that a revisioning of the complexity of the term 'muse' allows for a more thorough reading of the way in which Schröder-Devrient developed the roles written for her by Wagner, through performance. Thus the muse, and in this case performer, moves into the position of a working partner who, through her ability to absorb herself and play with the notion of 'self' in her performance, helps the composer to develop his understanding of the performative possibilities of the roles which he composes.

John Stokes, in his analysis of Madame Arnould Plessy's career, places her acting style, that of *la grande coquette,* in the context of the changing fashions and techniques of the French theatre of her day. Using Henry James's *The Tragic Muse* as an accompanying narrative, Stokes discusses Plessy in relation to the new *nerveuse* style (much influenced by notions of hysteria) of the young Bernhardt, and suggests that we should reassess Plessy in the light of the way in which her studied technique linked her to the French theatre of the past and provided a model from which future actresses might work. Joanna Townsend's chapter on Elizabeth Robins links the trajectory of the actress and playwright's career to her growing awareness of Freudian ideas and her developing political consciousness. Drawing a line from her playing of Hedda Gabler through to her radical *Votes For Women,* Townsend makes detailed reference to Robins's prompt copies and writings to look at the ways in which Robins the actress was integral to the development of Robins the writer.

The three chapters that follow are all concerned with the retrieval or reconstruction of the past or recent past, either that of an individual or that of a particular movement of individuals. Maggie B. Gale's work on Clemence Dane is an attempt to construct an autobiographical picture of this prolific and popular writer and important theatrical figure from the mid-twentieth century. Charlotte Canning uses two texts to examine the various strategies used by playwrights to rewrite an experience-based history of Second Wave feminism. John Deeney, on the other hand, problematises what we have often taken as easy dichotomies between the areas of mainstream, commercial and subsidised theatres, in order to question the ways in which we categorise women playwrights. Arguing that our refusal to acknowledge the complexities of such terms leads to an undermining of the achievements of recent women playwrights,

Deeney proposes that theatre historians still locate women's work in relation to so-called crises in male-dominated theatre. The last three chapters return to established areas of theatre history research and reinvest them with a female presence in the work of Ros Merkin and Catherine Schuler, or with a different perspective on women's contributions to a particular genre of theatre. Ros Merkin looks at three playwrights whose work was produced by the Independent Labour Party's Arts Guild in the context of socialist rather than feminist politics. Susan Carlson, in her chapter on 'comic militancy' and the suffrage drama, directs us towards those suffrage plays which made a positive use of humour and comedy as a political strategy. And Catherine Schuler ends this volume with a return to the years of serf theatre in Russia to examine the ways in which women were forced to engage with and suffered under the serf system of theatre.

This volume deliberately seeks to disturb the notion of progression, a 'rise' from absence to presence, from mute to 'motormouth', from prostitute to artist, in women's engagement in theatre and performance propagated by the periodisation of traditional theatre histories, by juxtaposing historical and contemporary subjects. It also seeks to avoid the valorising of textual over non-textual performance, a 'mission' identified as key by many theatre scholars in feminism's revisionist theatre history.[9] Instead it tries to concretise the notion of a continuum in women's involvement in theatre, to demonstrate that absence from the histories is not an indication of an absence from history.

Notes

1 Virginia Woolf, 'The Pargiters': The Novel-Essay Form of THE YEARS (London, The Hogarth Press, 1978), p. 8.

2 Laurence Senelick, ed., Gender and Performance: The Presentation of Difference in the Performing Arts (Hanova, University Press of New England, 1992), p. xiv.

3 Jill Davis, 'Goodnight Ladies … on The Explicit Body in Performance', New Theatre Quarterly, 58, XV, 2 (May 1999), p. 187.

4 Tracy C. Davis, 'Questions for a Feminist Methodology in Theatre History', in Thomas Postlewait and Bruce McConachie, eds, Interpreting the Theatrical Past: Essays in the Historiography of Performance (Iowa City, University of Iowa Press, 1989), p. 59.

5 Davis, 'Goodnight Ladies', pp. 183–4.

6 Susan Bassnett, 'Struggling with a Past: Women's Theatre in Search of a History', New Theatre Quarterly, V, 18 (May 1989), pp. 107–12, p. 112.

7 Elaine Aston, *An Introduction to Feminism and Theatre* (London, Routledge, 1995), p. 2.

8 Davis, 'Questions for a Feminist Methodology in Theatre History', p. 66.

9 Including: Bassnett, 'Struggling with a Past'; idem, *Magdalena: International Women's Experimental Theatre* (Oxford, New York & Munich, Berg, 1989), Jacky Bratton, 'Working in the Margin: Women in Theatre History', *New Theatre Quarterly*, 38, X (May 1994), pp. 122–240; Davis, 'Questions for a Feminist Methodology in Theatre History'; Lesley Ferris, *Acting Women: Images of Women in Theatre* (Houndmills, Macmillan, 1990).

1

Reading the intertheatrical, or, the mysterious disappearance of Susanna Centlivre

Jacky Bratton

The disappearance

Susanna Centlivre (1667–1723) published twenty plays and had nineteen of them staged between 1700 and 1720; adding up the number of years in which each of her plays was produced in London during the eighteenth century, Judith Phillips Stanton arrives at the remarkable figure of 289. They were published or republished 122 times.[1] The popularity of Centlivre's three most acted comedies, *The Busie Body* (1709), *The Wonder! A Woman Keeps a Secret* (1714) and *A Bold Stroke for a Wife* (1718) extended well into the nineteenth century; so that in terms of stage success, before the twentieth century, Centlivre is second only to Shakespeare.[2]

And yet she is more or less forgotten by modern audiences. In 1997 there was a website entitled 'Susanna Centlivre, The Forgotten Playwright of the Eighteenth Century', which has itself now disappeared.[3] She wrote Garrick's favourite role, Don Felix in *The Wonder!*, in which he chose to take his farewell of the stage;[4] but, according to the critics, she never wrote a witty line. When her plays are mentioned in mainstream critical discourse,[5] it is as Whiggish Restoration-and-water, harmless but ultimately dreary fun, part of the deplorable reaction and decline initiated by Collier's attack upon the stage. His *Short View of the Immorality and Profanity of the Restoration Stage*, published two years before her first play was produced, was long supposed to have corrupted the sensibility and the playgoing habits of London society: the result was said to be an audience so misled as to prefer Mrs Centlivre, while the more sensitive genius of Congreve was driven from the stage. Critics from Elizabeth Inchbald in 1808 to Bonamy Dobree in 1924 attributed Congreve's failure, and Centlivre's success, to 'the degraded taste of the public'.[6] It was Byron who actually blamed Centlivre for Congreve's rout:

'I ... know that Congreve gave up writing because Mrs Centlivre's balderdash drove his comedies off.'[7]

During the ensuing century her plays gradually ceased to be produced, at least in a form that had to be attributed to her. The critical exercise of canon-formation was able to exclude her work; in the twentieth century, accounts of the drama of the eighteenth century began to dismiss it completely, to extraordinary effect. The convention amongst summarising literary critics until the 1960s was to refer their readers only to Farquhar, who died in 1707, or straight to the unplayable sentimental comedies of Cibber and Steele, leaving the student of theatre baffled as to what the early eighteenth century thought was funny.[8] It is striking that the feminist recuperation of the female dramatists of the Restoration has focused on the work of Aphra Behn, who now finds a leading place in the literary canon; Centlivre does not. Many feminist commentators echo the emphasis on Centlivre's conformity to Whig, mercantile values and seem disappointed to discover her supreme technical skills: they prefer Behn, a complex writer whose work can be compared with that of male contemporaries, and discovered to be great literature.[9] Laura Rosenthal, in her book on the development of literary property as part of the commodification and professionalisation of Early Modern culture,[10] sees Centlivre as deliberately setting herself up to fail as a contender for literary honours. Pointing out that 'dramatic writing raises particular ambiguities of intertextuality and originality', she argues that Centlivre was acutely aware of the challenge her success might present to the male literary establishment. Rosenthal suggests that she deliberately avoided claiming originality or genius for her work, publishing her most popular, intertextual pieces anonymously or under a male name, and where she wrote as herself deliberately characterising her plays as trivial entertainments. She refrained from the publication of her collected plays so as to avoid any claim to literary prestige. The consequences of this gendered negotiation of power and submission were, I would argue, perpetuated in the emergent discourse of Romantic and post-Romantic aesthetics, and are still operative today; Centlivre is only one woman theatre worker to suffer from them.

Centlivre is heavily disadvantaged by hegemonic ideology. Her work can be – indeed, has to be – condemned as inferior three times over. In the first place, Centlivre's plays fail to fulfil the basic requirement of art in bourgeois society, that it be the unique product of the autonomous artist, the individual 'genius' at work alone, challenging and expanding the horizons of human experience.[11] Extending Rosenthal's observation, we may say that this is the case with all dramatists: none can operate fully without the co-operation of other creative artists, and their work will be not only added to, but transformed, by the actor, the scene-painter and others. When the aesthetic of autonomy was first articulated in Western literary and philosophical thought around 1800, there was a strong move to free the dramatic writer from what was perceived as the impediment of theatrical realisation. Coleridge and Charles Lamb insisted that the work of the great dramatists, especially Shakespeare, was best appreciated as literature, by the solitary reader. In the closet, Centlivre's work reads as incomplete, as indeed it is; she wrote for performance. Wrested from its context, it is impoverished and compromised, shown to be reliant upon what she takes from and gives to others. In artistic practice, as the aesthetic of autonomy gained ground in England, writers for the stage struggled to assert exclusive possession of their work and repudiate all theatrical involvement, until by the 1880s Arthur Wing Pinero could write his drama, having it 'laboriously thought out, every detail of it' and printed, complete with stage directions, before he entered the theatre, where, he said, 'rehearsal is not – or certainly should not be – a time for experiment'.[12]

Centlivre's failure to create literature is expressed from the first as a lack of 'wit', an essential tool for neutralising and converting theatrical pleasure to an acceptable aesthetic response. Wit is the rationalising abstraction of laughter by the exercise of mind, converting human relations into a play of language. Critics, from the writer who composed a study of her work for the *Morning Chronicle* in 1758 onwards, have agreed that Centlivre's language did not do this. Reviewing a production of *The Wonder!* he pronounces that 'the language is contemptible to the last degree'.[13] Most subsequent writers have agreed with him. Bertram Shuttleworth in 1953 speaks of her 'rather flat, but unexpectedly natural dialogue';[14] Nancy Cotton, who uses many superlatives in her discussion of Centlivre, is apparently self-contradictory over this issue. She says Centlivre 'is a writer of small verbal distinction. She did, however, have a good ear for jargon, slang, religious cant, dialect, and foreign accent.' In other words she can write interesting realistic dialogue; what is lacking is the literary quality of wit. Even for Nancy Cotton, therefore, *A Bold Stroke for a Wife* 'has no depth but is an excellent stage play'.[15] Douglas R. Butler spells out the implications of this in the eyes of the literary critic. Writing in 1991 about the same play (under the extraordinary heading of

'Closet Drama'), he claims Centlivre has 'little wit', and deduces that she 'does not have a serious vision' because her ideas are 'not conveyed most effectively through her language'.[16] The second barrier to Centlivre's being taken seriously is succinctly expressed by F. W. Bateson, in 1927. He states that all but six of her plays are 'almost completely worthless', but that these six comedies,

> all have a certain vitality and technical *finesse*, and are as good examples as one can hope to find of the work of the professional dramatist of the eighteenth century. They have, it must be admitted, no intellectual or literary significance; the writing is never distinguished and the characterization, with the single exception of Marplot in *The Busie Body*, is conventional and superficial. But the purpose for which they were written is fulfilled, to a greater or lesser extent, in all of them. They amuse, they distract the mind. Mrs Centlivre's comedies occupy the position in the literature of the eighteenth century that is now filled by the detective story. They are the railway reading of Georgian England.[17]

This attractive passage captures the evaluation of her work as 'entertainment' that asserts its essential difference from art. Such work amuses and distracts, serving to pass time when one has an excuse for self-indulgent avoidance of intellectual pursuits. It has no literary significance, however good of its kind it might be, because it has only the technical vitality of professional (paid) work, which can never be the life of art. Again, this remains an assumption in the work of recent critics. F. P. Lock, in the only current monograph about Centlivre, speaks dismissively of hers as 'the representative career of a prolific, professional dramatist'. Pointing out John Loftis's false opposition in calling Centlivre 'thoroughly professional, much concerned with the money to be made from her plays'. rather than with 'artistic consistency', even Jacqueline Pearson hastens to claim that *despite* being an 'accomplished practical playwright' Centlivre had 'her own consistent vision as an artist'.[18]

Pearson's anxiousness as a feminist to make the 'larger claim' of artistic integrity for Centlivre, like Bateson's vehement, sneering dismissal sixty years before, signals the third and most important ideological issue. The process of the elevation of plays into literature is part of a hegemonic move upon the theatre. To take Centlivre's work seriously, as we take that of her only theatrical rival, Shakespeare, would challenge the way in which plays are read as literature, and undermine the division between art and entertainment that protects literature from the market-place; it would also allow a woman's work to undermine the fundamental binary, the distinction between mind and body, upon which Western patriarchal culture rests. The feminist writer prefers the less radical option of asserting the literary value of her female subject; the masculine discourse, however, knows that this claim cannot be made without undermining the whole structure.

The purity of the aesthetic is guaranteed by its lack of *function*, and thus its distinction from the material and the mortal. Through our grasp of the aesthetic, our recognition of beauty in pure art, the power of Reason can be applied to the physical world that so delights our senses and bring the bodily under moral control. This has amounted to a 'programme of spiritual hegemony' whereby 'sensibility' became the foundation of moral life and the rational education of desire became 'an active, transformative force' that teaches us pleasure in the material world is wrong.[19] The peculiar dangers involved in finding art in the setting of the theatre are vividly described by Centlivre's contemporary, Jeremy Collier:

> The business of Plays is to recommend virtue ... This design has been oddly pursued by the English Stage. Our poets ... have in a great measure the Springs of Thought and Inclination in their Power. Show, Musick, Action and Rhetorick, are moving Entertainments ... But ... If delight without Restraint, or Distinction, without Conscience or Shame, is the supream Law of Comedy, 'twere well if we had less on't. Arbitrary Pleasure, is more dangerous than Arbitrary Power. Nothing is more Brutal than to be abandon'd to Appetite.[20]

Collier is less direct, but even more extreme, about the role of women in this dangerous business of theatre. He cites Dryden as censuring the Roman dramatists for 'making Mutes of their single women', not allowing them to speak. He himself feels this 'old Discipline would be very serviceable upon the Stage' in his own time.[21] He does not want to hear the voices of women. In the English theatre after the Restoration, the novel presence of women on stage contributed to the imperative that aesthetic distance be preserved, and that first wit, and later sensibility (the intellectualised response to feeling), should police the bodily. The outstanding and enduring success of a woman as writer is an unmanageable challenge to the masculine aestheticisation of the theatre's public space. Bateson begins his chapter on Centlivre with a quotation from an eighteenth-century source: 'What a Pox have women to do with the Muses?'[22]

The intertheatrical

To make a valuation of Centlivre's work that explains its success without simultaneously condemning it as dangerously second-rate we have, I would argue, to free our consideration of all plays in the theatre from the ideologically-driven aesthetics I have outlined. Rejecting these three grounds of condemnation – that her work is not literature because it is collaborative, that it is compromised by the populist and commercial creative processes of the theatre, and that it is morally and aesthetically suspect because it provokes and includes rather than suppresses bodily response from an audience – I want to offer a conceptualisation of her work that addresses and analyses its theatrical success. By analogy with a range of accepted terminology I want to call this concept 'intertheatricality'.

Some modern writers have begun to move towards reading Centlivre's work in its context. Her theatrical success is noted, sometimes quite enthusiastically, by modern writers. Nancy Cotton begins by announcing that she was 'the most successful of England's early women playwrights, perhaps the best comic playwright between Congreve and Fielding'[23] (this is not actually a very large claim). Jacqueline Pearson is self-consciously bolder: 'Her best comedies are the most brilliant of the century: I would not myself exclude even Goldsmith or Sheridan from this. [Their] disappearance from the stage … is a serious loss.'[24] Her theatrical artistry is suggested when Fidelis Morgan points out that in *The Wonder!* Centlivre achieved a 'brilliant compromise', a play with 'one foot in each century', 'finding a way to please the new and more po-faced audience with a distressing degree of vitality'.[25] I would argue that, in the first place, at the moment Centlivre was writing her ability to match the feeling of her audience was an outstanding, and a unique, achievement. The early eighteenth-century stage was reeling under the loss of fashionable patronage, the assaults of Collier and his followers, and the influx of audiences with different cultural imperatives and agendas; the successful dramatist had to negotiate and reconcile contradictory audience demands, delivering the bodily pleasure of laughter within the grip of repressive sensibility. What Fidelis Morgan sees in *The Wonder!* is an instance of this, an ingenious compromise between moral sentiment and rakish attitudes. Richard Frushell prefaces his edition of her plays – the first complete edition, published in 1982 – with the confident assertion that 'there can be no doubt that Mrs Centlivre is one of the most … savvy playwrights of the first quarter of the eighteenth century. She was at once actively regardful of the Restoration comic traditions of plot and theme, mindful of textual and tonal fashions of her own day, and unwittingly prescient of what would please in generations after her.'[26]

Her success, then, is the entertainer's success, in matching her offering to the taste of the time. But Frushell's final clause troubles this simple formulation. It signals that there is a dimension of her success – its long duration – that cannot be accounted for as merely shrewdness and observation of her market; he is content to ignore the challenge this presents to his account, and dub her 'unwittingly prescient'. But performers and indeed writers whose skill is in echoing contemporary vibrations are just those whose work goes out of date. There are many examples of such transient success amongst Centlivre's contemporaries, including all the writers of the comedy of sensibility, and most of the satirists and poets of the time. But her best work requires no footnotes. It did not only succeed in those circumstances for which it was written: on the contrary, the extensive stage histories which Frushell provides demonstrate that her plays have an astonishing degree of flexibility and transferability across both space and time.

The huge figures for years of performance given at the head of this essay were computed by Judith Stanton from *The London Stage*, which details recorded performances in the capital. Frushell's net is cast more widely. He shows that even Centlivre's minor work had a busy life on the theatrical fringe; *The Man's Bewitched* (1709) was turned into a har-lequinade and given at Bartholomew Fair, for example, and *Love's Contrivance* (1703), a pastiche of three plays by Molière, was a favourite in the tavern theatres of the day. Centlivre herself claimed a hundred performances for this play.[27] Her major plays were staged from Covent Garden to the Crown Inn, Islington, and then across Britain and the world. Sybil Rosenfeld records them as the staple of British provincial circuits and strolling companies;[28] Frushell documents that General Burgoyne's soldiers played her first in America, and the theatre in Sydney mounted her work as early as 1796; the records of theatres large and small in Ireland, Canada, Australia and the USA show her plays as standard repertoire well into the next century. Such a record is not simply accounted for as a capacity to respond to the passing fashion at the time the plays were first written; these texts are alive in stage enter-tainment.

Frushell's evidence offers some suggestive leads from which to begin a revaluation of Centlivre's work according to a different perspective. He remarks an extraordinary number of adaptations, shortened versions and rewritings of her plays. Some are selections or cut versions for small playhouses, some open adaptations by actors, while others are by dramatists who tried to pass off the results as their own, as in the case of Colley Cibber's *The Double Gallant* (1707), which is clearly taken from Centlivre's *Love at a Venture* (1706), which he had read and rejected in his role as manager. Her texts lived on in twenty new versions, as well as in their original shapes. Bowyer's exhaustive work on the derivations and analogues of her writing similarly demonstrates that the plays had an ancestry as well as a rich and varied posterity.

They also existed in close relationship with their own generation of entertainments. All eighteenth-century plays were presented within a programme of entertainments, framed and punctuated by interludes of various kinds. F. P. Lock, producing a purely literary reading of Centlivre, explicitly chooses to pretend the plays did not suffer from such destructive interruptions.[29] Frushell reports, with a note of surprise, that 'Success in the theatre came also because her plays often had the good fortune to be accompanied by popular afterpieces, vocal and instrumental music, dancing, and interesting para-dramatic entertainments otherwise – the total theatrical evening as much a draw as the plays that mainly constituted it.' He also shows that these theatrical successes were often command or benefit nights[30] – moments when someone, either powerful members of the audience, who could choose what would please them most, or a working performer who could predict what would bring in the biggest audience receipts, put together the best possible bill.

I suggest that the choice of Centlivre on these nights is not a matter of her good fortune; that her plays have a quality that made them especially suitable and likely to be selected for galas, benefits and evenings of choice entertainment, just as they were fruitful ground for the adapter and the theatrical thief. The last clue to the special value of Centlivre's work to be found in Frushell's stage history is that his account of their productions reads like a roll-call of major actors, all of whom founded a reputation on roles in these plays. They seem to have made the careers of a long succession of men. Frushell, in noting this, quotes Edward Shuter's critique of the dramatist from a performer's point of view:

> Mrs Centlivre's Comedies have a vein of pleasantry in them that will always be relish'd. She knew the Genius of this nation, and she wrote up to it; her Bold Stroke for a Wife, was a masterpiece that much

increased her reputation: it establish'd that of Kit Bullock ... a smart
sprightly actor ... [31]

The plays, then, belong to the theatre – they support it and are
supported by it. They are precisely the kind of writing that refuses to be
understood on the page, as 'Drama'; their capacity to please must therefore be challenged or obscured, lest the autonomy of art be undermined
by it. Their excellence is not in spite of, but because of their multiple
strands of connection, their place *within* their milieu, meshed to writing
past and present, to actors and their strengths and needs, to music, dancing the audience's pleasures. They have to a high degree the quality of
'intertheatricality'.

By intertheatricality I mean that mesh of connections between theatre texts and between texts and their creators and realisers that makes
up the moving, multi-dimensional, cross-hatched background out of
which individual performances, nights at the theatre, regularly crys-
tallise. The plays written and performed within a single theatrical tradition are all more or less interdependent. They are uttered in a theatrical
code shared by writers, performers and audience which consists not
only of language, but of genres, conventions and memory – shared by
the audience – of previous plays and scenes, previous performances, the
actors' previous roles and their known personae on and off stage. There
is a collaboration, taking place not only over the period of the creation
of a play in rehearsal, but anew, live, each night of its performance in
front of an audience, that creates shared meaning out of the concatena-
tion of theatre systems that is far more complex than any set of conventions deployed by a writer whose medium is print.

The extent to which this quality, especially when it is presented in the
work of a woman, is perceived as threatening and needing to be critically
put down is signalled by the charges brought against Centlivre. After she
is denied the literary quality of wit, she is denied the other literary
marker, originality; indeed she is accused of plagiarism. John Wilson
Bowyer, writing in 1952 in a critical tradition that made the identification
of sources and analogues its primary method, was nevertheless surprised
at '[t]he extent to which scholars have sought sources for *The Busy
Body* ... They seem to have assumed that Mrs Centlivre could not write a
play of her own. Except for the two scenes from Jonson, her borrowings
are general and no discredit to her'.[32] The issue is control, integration and
integrity: women lack integrity, they and their works are permeable,
inadequately bonded and bounded; this is deprecated by classic

dramatic theory which demands a defined shape, an integration of all parts subordinated to whole, a single forward drive, climax and closure. Feminist writers have sought to discover a female counter-tradition at work within the literary, tracing a line from Aphra Behn to Centlivre to Hannah Cowley, whose play *Who's the Dupe?* (1779) is based upon the subplot of Centlivre's *The Stolen Heiress* (1702). It would be more effective as a recuperative strategy to see these female writers as central to a different tradition – that of intertheatricality. They could be said to be leaders in a practice that they shared with countless other women and men, of making plays within, instead of at odds with, the context in which the theatre artist works. Centlivre explicitly acknowledged this when she dismissed literary prescriptions in her preface to *Love's Contrivance*, saying 'the criticks cavil most about Decorums, and cry up Aristotles Rules'. Tongue in cheek she owns they are in the right, but that 'the Town' – audiences – do not agree; so while 'the Unity of Time, Place and Action' are no doubt 'the greatest Beauties of a Dramatick Poem', successful *plays* are created by 'the other way of writing'. And this other, or Other, way is the procedure of the person who crystallises the successful moment – or string of moments – out of the intertheatrical chemistry of plots, players and expectations. The differences between Shakespeare's use of earlier dramatic sources, Cibber's casual appropriation of Centlivre's play as so much 'Poetical Lumber' handy for his use, the actors' conversion of *A Bold Stroke for a Wife* into a fairground droll, and Centlivre's translation and condensation of three plays by Molière, lie in the politics of public utterance and the construction of critical control.

Centlivre encapsulates a salient feature of her method when she goes on, in this same preface, to describe her construction of plays in a metaphor from her husband's realm, the kitchen.[33] She says her audience 'relishes nothing so well as Humour lightly tost up with Wit, and drest with Modesty and Air …'. The ingredients of a salad are not fixed; we may pick out the bits we like better, or tip the whole thing into a sandwich and add a piece of cheese. Entertainment is created like a salad, which may contain variable amounts of lettuce; *The Busie Body* may please one day as a main course, another as a three-act snack. Thalia Stathas is troubled by the 'tonal shifts and shifts in characterisation' that abound even in Centlivre's best plays. She prefers for that reason *A Bold Stroke for a Wife* which provides a fairy-tale structure, the wooing of four guardians who are strongly contrasting cartoonish humorous characters, to justify the comic shifts 'without making them incredible'. But it is this characteristic structuring to convince and amuse scene by scene, rather than according to an integrated unity of plan, that gives the plays their powerful malleability, and makes them – as Stathas herself concedes – ideal vehicles for the actor. Seeking the reason for Garrick's love of *The Wonder!*, she says 'The changing moods of Don Felix are said to have been a perfect vehicle for Garrick's skills, and the rapidity with which these changes occur itself demands a virtuosity in characterisation which few actors can achieve convincingly.'[34] Perhaps not, today; but for many decades such virtuosity was the actor's stock-in-trade. That is why the role of Fainwell in *A Bold Stroke for a Wife* was chosen by the great comic actors – Shuter, Woodward, Bannister, Charles Kemble, Charles Mathews, Robert Elliston – and by all the barnstormers of the provincial circuits, and of Ireland, Scotland, Australia and colonial America. It is a play that is about acting your way to success, the trickster's triumph, the apotheosis of impersonation; and every man who believed in the power of the stage – which must needs have been a powerful belief, to keep the strolling player on the flinty and unresponsive road, convinced of his personal ability to charm money out of Philistine pockets – would want to see himself in it.

The Busie Body

The best demonstration of the intricate mesh which is intertheatricality is a consideration of one play. Centlivre's most popular production was *The Busie Body* (1709), which Hazlitt said had been played a 'thousand times in town and country, giving delight to the old, the young, and the middle-aged'.[35] It was staged in London during eighty-seven years of the eighteenth century, with 475 known performances. There were doubtless many more, not only at unrecorded little theatres, but at the main houses, where it was the play of all others to be put on when the advertised piece for some reason failed: an actress ill, an actor detained in the country, and at an hour's notice Covent Garden could stage a successful performance of *The Busie Body*.[36] Into the next century this was still the case: John Philip Kemble kept a production in reserve, always ready in case of accidents.[37] From London the play was carried across the world by strollers, professionals and amateur gentlemen; it was a stock piece at the foundation of most anglophone theatres. Any pile of old playbills, from Devon to Virginia, will probably contain its name.

The rapid success of the play, despite the hostility of its original performers and a thin attendance on the first night, caused considerable critical unease. Richard Steele wrote a favourable notice in *The Tatler*, for which, according to Bowyer, Centlivre was for ever grateful. To the modern eye Steele's praise is lukewarm and patronising, and chiefly concerned, as most critics have been, to explain away a moral impossibility – the success of a woman dramatist:

> On Saturday last was presented *The Busie Body*, a comedy, written (as I have heretofore remarked) by a woman. The plot and incidents of the play are laid with that subtilty of spirit which is peculiar to females of wit, and is very seldom well performed by those of the other sex, in which craft in love is an act of invention, and not, as with women, the effect of nature and instinct.[38]

It is significant that Bowyer should assert that Centlivre was eternally indebted to Steele for disempowering her and allaying audiences' fears of an unnatural success by reducing her writing to 'the effect of nature and instinct'.

Many critics have since worked hard at explaining away her success by seeking to show which men she borrowed the play from. The first suggestions of sources appear in an early critical account of her work, David Baker's *Biographia Dramatica 1782*, and by the time Bowyer wrote borrowings from Francis Fane's *Love in the Dark* (1675), Dryden's *Sir Martin Mar-all* (1668), Molière's *L'Étourdi* (1653), John Dryden Jnr's *The Husband His Own Cuckold* (1696) had all been suggested as her sources. None of them bears anything but a slight general resemblance to her work. There is one significant analogue, however, and that is a scene in Ben Jonson's *The Divell is an Asse* (1616). This is clearly a rewriting on her part, interesting in the way in which Centlivre changed the balance of power in the important scene she borrowed from the male characters to her heroine Miranda. Modern feminist critics like Jacqueline Pearson and Suz-Anne Kinney find the controlling power of Miranda throughout the play attractive, reading her as a stand-in for the writer.[39] But theatre audiences have been less interested in her than in the eponymous Busy Body, Marplot, the one character in all Centlivre's writing that Bateson allowed to be original. (Even this is disputed by the source hunters, who find a tenuous resemblance to the ineffectual servant Pug in Jonson's play.) But the original creation Marplot is still strikingly successful because of his intertheatricality. Like many iconic creations – Falstaff, Pickwick, Dracula, James Bond, Superman – he takes on a life of his own, and exists within and beyond the play in his own right. Centlivre wrote a sequel to feature him again,

Marplot, or the Second Part of the Busie-Body (1710). Woodward, for whom Marplot was a signature role, then adapted this into a farce afterpiece, *Marplot in Lisbon* (1755), which found its way into the first collected edition of Centlivre's works in 1760–61. By the early nineteenth century the character was ripe for further updating, and was transmogrified into Paul Pry, in a play written first by John Poole and then by Douglas Jerrold.[40] Poole acknowledged a French source for his subplot, but insisted the rest was all his own. It 'became one of the greatest theatrical hits of the age: it had one of the longest runs recorded since *The Beggar's Opera*'.[41] The farce was a star vehicle for John Liston, in which he was known to thousands and modelled in china by the Bloor Derby works.

So the text, transformed and redirected by Centlivre's work, was also deeply embedded in other writings; and on a second axis, in the performances of actors. Even more than Fainwell and Don Felix, Marplot was a comic actor's vehicle; the play was staged so that Edward Shuter could repeat his much-loved creation of the role, Henry Woodward could inject funds into the Covent Garden box office, or Garrick could challenge him in it.[42] The text became not only a pretext for the character, but a malleable vehicle for him. It was changed around him, giving him more prominence, presumably by the actor playing the role. Beginning as a five-act comedy, the play was cut to three acts by the exclusion of the second love intrigue, without cuts to Marplot's appearances or lines; and even the printed editions hint at the nature of the role, the spaces that were given to its performer for extemporisation and extra business. In 1776, after Woodward performed his famous Marplot for the last time, the printed editions[43] change markedly; one might speculate that they are changed to show or suggest his alterations to the text, now that they had ceased to be a trade secret of his. At the end of Act II, for example, the editions of 1776 onwards show a changed order of speeches, and violence is done to the sensible sequence of exits in order to give Marplot the tag, and a moment on stage when he is alone with the audience. No doubt these changes happened even more in the theatre than is recorded in print; Marplot is allowed out of the frame of the plot, into direct and conspiratorial relationship with the audience.

If Miranda is a surrogate for the writer, Marplot is perhaps the opposite: he is a kind of anti-dramatist; he conspires with the actor and the audience to disintegrate the play. His interference, with the best of intentions, spoils plots and ruins closures; he is not a gull, or the foppish, would-be wit of earlier plays, for he has no vanity or covetousness or sense of envy or emulation towards the lovers. He is indeed a virgin, a point which is more stressed in *Marplot* than the earlier play; and he is a coward, a desexualised innocent, a kind of wild child who just wants *to know what they are all doing*. A well-trained audience, with a proper sense of how a love-intrigue plot should be conducted, watches with horrified amusement as his well-meaning interference lays it in ruins over and over again.[44] He is in that sense an unruly member of the audience taking control, the disintegrative force outside of both the writer's text and the theatrical pact. And like both audience and comic performer, at the end of both *The Busie Body* and *Marplot* he remains outside the pattern of the fiction, resisting, or immune to, closure, the dance, the marriages. The writer is not helpless in this intertheatrical nexus, of course, but collaborates in it, actively creating a channel through which the work of others flows, and is enabled and developed. She participates in a process which is a manifestation of the female aesthetic discussed by Jane Marcus, 'in terms of repetition, dailiness and process':[45] the work of creation in collaboration.

It is too narrow to define intertheatricality simply as a female tradition. It is perhaps not a coincidence that group composition and devising were methods preferred by many feminist theatre groups in the 1970s and 1980s. But the point is not that only women do it, or might be argued to do it particularly well, or alternatively that they are critically assigned to consideration as parts of such groups so as to avoid giving them any higher status. I would rather regard collaborative practice as a model for understanding the creative process in the theatre that reflects, more nearly than the Aristotelian masculine metaphors of the drama do, what actually happened – 'wie es eigentlich war' – and still happens now. If that is so then it should, by classic Rankean criteria, be the basis of theatre history. That it is not bespeaks the ideological structuring of the discourse.

The rejection of the intertheatrical model of creativity has been made necessary by the aesthetic of autonomy and its insistence upon the uniqueness of the text and the creative artist. It has been achieved by dubbing intertheatrical works commercial, entertainment, professional, feminine, and in all possible ways both inferior and dangerous to true art. To fight back, that tradition must assert that real plays are not inviolable, single-authored creations. Their collaborative and multiple creation is integral to them, and includes not only borrowing from play to play, rewriting night by night, but also many more dimensions: the non-verbal systems of spectacle and sound, the other items on the bill, who is in the audience, and the presence in performances of the actors and their own personae, with their remembered other performances in this role, their known other roles, their rumoured private lives. Intertheatricality, the co-operative operation of the theatre, is a feminine aesthetic, in the same way that entertainment is a feminised tradition; neither is really confined to women, but both are excluded and down-graded by that association, in the service of 'male' models of history and of genius.

Notes

1 Judith Phillips Stanton, 'This New-Found Path Attempting: Women Dramatists in England, 1660–1800', in Mary Anne Schofield and Cecilia Macheski, eds., *Curtain Calls* (Athens, Ohio University Press, 1991), pp. 325–54, 336.

2 John Wilson Bowyer, *The Celebrated Mrs Centlivre* (Durham, NC, Duke University Press, 1952), p. v.

3 http://www.mtsu.edu/-engl100db/leighj.htm.

4 Drury Lane, 16 May 1776. See Thalia Stathas, 'A Critical Edition of Three Plays by Susanna Centlivre', Stanford University Ph.D., (Ann Arbor, University Microfilms Inc., 1966), pp. 475–8.

5 See for example the brief dismissal in Simon Trussler, *The Cambridge Illustrated History of British Theatre* (Cambridge, Cambridge University Press, 1994), p. 143, where her picture adorns a short essay on 'the female wits' safely cordoned off from the main text in a grey box; and Richard W. Bevis, *English Drama: Restoration and Eighteenth Century, 1660–1789* (London, Longman, 1988), p. 162, who discusses her work in a page under the unpromising heading 'Stagnation 1708–1720'.

6 Elizabeth Inchbald, 'Remarks on *A Bold Stroke for a Wife*', published in *The British Theatre 11* (London, Longman, Hurst, Rees & Orme, 1808), p. 4; and see Bonamy Dobree, *Restoration Comedy 1660–1720* (Oxford, Oxford University Press, 1924), in which he says (p. 140) that *The Way of the World* was 'too civilized for an age that revelled in the scribblings of Mrs Pix'. He does not mention any of Centlivre's plays except *The Gamester*, cited as an example of British dramatists' propensity to stage the obvious, where Frenchmen allow suggestion to work: p. 49.

7 Quoted in Bowyer, *The Celebrated Mrs Centlivre*, p. 97. The supposition that Congreve retreated from the stage jealous and Centlivre's success is recorded in Hazlitt, Lectures on the Comic Writers, 1819, Lecture VIII, 'On the Comic Writers of the Last Century', in *Complete Works,* ed. P. P. Howe, 21 vols (London, Dent, 1930–34), Vol. 6 (1931), pp. 149–68, p. 155.

8 For a summary of dismissive critical approaches see F. W. Bateson, *English Comic Drama, 1700–1750* (Oxford, Oxford University Press, 1929), pp. 61,

75–7; for the habit of omitting Centlivre altogether, see for example John E. Cunningham, *Restoration Drama* (London, Evans Brothers Ltd, 1966) and Oscar Brockett, *The Theatre, an Introduction* (New York, Holt, Rinehart and Winston, 1965).

9 See for example Marilyn L. Williamson, *Raising Their Voices: British Women Writers, 1650–1750* (Detroit, Wayne State University Press, 1990); Cheryl Turner, in *Living by the Pen: Women Writers in the Eighteenth Century* (London, Routledge, 1992), speaks of Centlivre only in lists; the index entry on her 'as dramatist' refers to a footnote to chapter two in which the author lists women whose achievements have remained obscure in comparison with Behn's. *An Annotated Bibliography of Twentieth-Century Studies of Women and Literature, 1600–1800* (New York and London, Garland, 1977) by Paula Backscheider, Felicity Nussbaum and Philip B. Anderson, has 75 entries under Behn and 33 under Centlivre, relying heavily on Bowyer, bibliographic notes and unpublished dissertations. Since then Centlivre has been included in general studies such as Nancy Cotton's *Women Playwrights in England, c.1363 to 1750* (Lewisburg, PA, Bucknell University Press, 1980), and Jacqueline Pearson's *The Prostituted Muse* (London, Harvester, 1988), and has been accorded a long descriptive entry by Jean Gagen in vol. 84 of the *Dictionary of Literary Biography* ed. Paula R. Backscheider (Detroit, Gale Research Inc., 1989. But all of these sources still see Centlivre as a successor to Behn, one of a group of lesser dramatists; and the only single-author study, F. P. Lock, *Susanna Centlivre* (Boston, Twayne, Publishers, 1979), is purely literary in its approach, and concludes that 'in the wider perspective of English drama as a whole, Centlivre can rank only as a minor figure' (p. 134).

10 Laura J. Rosenthal, *Playwrights and Plagiarists in Early Modern England: Gender, Authorship, Literary Property* (Ithaca and London, Cornell University Press, 1996), p. 7.

11 This formulation, and much of the following section, derive from Peter Burger, 'The Institution of Art as a Category of the Sociology of Literature' (1979), in P. and C. Burger, eds, *The Institutions of Art*, trans. Loren Kruger (Lincoln and London, University of Nebraska Press, 1992).

12 Pinero told this to his first biographer: see H. Hamilton Fyfe, *Sir Arthur Pinero's Plays and Players* (London, Greening, 1930), p. 259.

13 Quoted in Stathas, 'A Critical Edition', p. xi.

14 Review of Bowyer, *Theatre Notebook* 8, 20, cited in Rosenthal, *Playwrights and Plagiarists*, p. 133.

15 Cotton, *Women Playwrights in England*, pp. 144–5.

16 Douglas Butler, 'Plot and Politics in Susanna Centlivre's *A Bold Stroke for a Wife*', in Schofield and Macheski, *Curtain Calls*, pp. 357–70, p. 357.

17 Bateson, *English Comic Drama*, p. 64.

18 Lock, *Susanna Centlivre*, p. 134; Pearson, *The Prostituted Muse*, pp. 202–3.

19 See Terry Eagleton, *The Ideology of the Aesthetic* (Oxford, Blackwell, 1990), p. 21.

20 Jeremy Collier, *A Short View of the Immorality and Profaneness of the English Stage, 1698*; reprinted from the 3rd ed. (New York, AMS Press, Inc., 1974), pp. 163–4.

21 *Ibid.*, p. 21.

22 Bateson, *English Comic Drama*, p. 61; the quotation is from *A Comparison Between the Two Stages* (1702), attributed to Charles Gildon.

23 Cotton, *Women Playwrights in England*, p. 122.

24 Pearson, *The Prostituted Muse*, p. 228.

25 Fidelis Morgan, *The Female Wits: Women Playwrights on The London Stage 1660–1720* (London, Virago, 1981), p. 329; see also Marilyn L. Williamson, *Raising Their Voices: British Women Writers 1650–1750* (Detroit, Wayne State University Press 1990).

26 Susanna Centlivre, *The Plays of Susanna Centlivre*, edited with an introduction by Richard C. Frushell, 3 vols (New York and London, Garland Publishing Inc., 1982), Vol. 1, p. ix.

27 In her Preface to *The Platonick Lady* (1706).

28 Sybil Rosenfeld, *Strolling Players and Drama in the Provinces 1660–1765* (Cambridge, Cambridge University Press, 1939), *passim*.

29 Lock, *Susanna Centlivre*, p. 72.

30 Frushell, *Plays*, vol. 1, pp. xvii, xxviii; *The Busie Body* had 22 royal command performances, including the night, 22 October 1717, when the Prince of Wales demanded it instead of *Othello*.

31 Frushell, *Plays*, vol. 1, p. lxvii.

32 Bowyer, *The Celebrated Mrs Centlivre*, p. 103.

33 Joseph Centlivre was a cook in the royal household.

34 Stathas, 'A Critical Edition', pp. xxi, 477.

35 Quoted in Frushell, *Plays*, vol. 1, p. xxvii.

36 See examples given in *ibid.*, p. xciv, n. 68.

37 Morgan, *The Female Wits*, p. 59.

38 *The Tatler*, no. 19, 24 May 1709, quoted in Bowyer, *The Celebrated Mrs Centlivre*, p. 98.

39 Suz-Anne Kinney, 'Confinement Sharpens the Invention': Aphra Behn's The Rover and Susanna Centlivre's The Busie Body', in Gail Finney, ed., *Look Who's Laughing: Gender and Comedy* (New York, Gordon and Breach, 1994), p. 96; see also Pearson, *The Prostituted Muse*, pp. 220–1.

40 Haymarket, 1825; Coburg, 1827.

41 Jim Davis, *John Liston Comedian* (London, The Society for Theatre Research, 1985), p. 56.

42 See Frushell, *Plays*, p. xxix; he cites Arthur Murphy's story that Garrick took on the role because Woodward, confident of his drawing power in the part, refused to continue without a rise in his salary.

43 *Busie Body* is the first play in *The New English Theatre in Eight Volumes, Containing the most valuable plays which have been Acted upon the London Stage*, (London, Rivington *et al.*, 1776); it occurs in vol. 8 of *Bell's British*

Theatre, also dated 1776; most editions from 1777 onwards reflect these same alterations.

44 See Pearson, *The Prostituted Muse*, p. 210, for an interesting interpretation of Marplot as a feminised figure, parodying stereotypes of female inquisitiveness and weakness – a notion which reinforces the tension his stage activity creates.

45 'Daughters of anger/material girls', in Regina Barreca, ed., *Last Laughs*, Women's Studies Vol. 15 (New York, Gordon and Breach, 1988), pp. 281–308, 287.

2

THE INVISIBLE SPECTATRICE: GENDER, GEOGRAPHY AND THEATRICAL SPACE

Viv Gardner

The female club-lounger, the *flâneuse* of St James Street, latch-key in pocket and eyeglasses on the nose, remains a creature of the imagination. (Amy Levy, 'Women and Club Life' (1888))[1]

A restricted area like a club, a theatre or a nation state has a set of rules to determine how its boundary shall be crossed and who should occupy that space. Those who enter it share certain defining features: they will perhaps have met specific criteria of club membership, bought a ticket or passed a citizenship test. In some way they must be recognised, say by a gate-keeper, such as a hall porter, an usherette, or an immigration officer … In studying the way people pattern their perceptions, attention has been drawn to the perimeters of categories that we make in order to codify and confront the worlds we create, in which we then live, and how we cope with some of the problems that arise from the existence of these boundaries. (Shirley Ardener, 'Ground Rules and Social Maps for Women' (1992))[2]

This essay is offered in the spirit of this series in 'providing a forum for discussion on research'. Whilst doing something more than 'flying a kite', I do not see this essay as 'an answer', but more a suggestion of ways of looking and seeing in a particular area of women's theatre history. My title pays homage to Janet Wolff's essay 'The Invisible *Flâneuse*' (1985) which was one of the first essays that I encountered that dealt with the problematics of gender and movement in the modern city. Wolff, echoing Amy Levy, argues that '[t]here is no question of inventing the *flâneuse*' (the female equivalent of Baudelaire's archetypal *flâneur*, the painter Constantin Guys) as 'such a type was rendered impossible by the sexual divisions of the nineteenth century'.[3] Judith Walkowitz's book *City of Dreadful Delight: Narratives of Sexual Danger in Late-Victorian London* (1992)[4] also treats the themes of mobility, spectatorship and gender and of the 'panic' engendered by the melodramatised threat that arose from contemporary sexual scandals and murders – a panic that reinforced a notion of both dangerous and endangered womanhood.[5] In addition, Walkowitz also discusses London as a contested terrain created by 'new social actors', those groups of the disenfranchised who in the 1880s and 1890s took to the streets in their attempt to gain social and thus political space: protesting workers and political autobiographers, shopping ladies, charity workers, the 'glorified spinster' and the 'manly woman' amongst them. Tracy C. Davis, in the chapter in her book *Actresses as Working Women* entitled 'The Geography of Sex in Society and Theatre', looks at both the erotic neighbourhood outside the playhouses of London and the erotic zones within the playhouse, touching upon the problematics of female spectatorship in the West End within her larger discussion of the working life of the 'ordinary' female performer.[6]

These, and other books and articles that engage with the problematic of the *flâneuse*, were the genesis of this essay. Whilst they occasionally touch upon theatre and other cultural forms, none deals directly with the specifics of female spectatorship in the environs of the London theatres, both inside and outside – and the ways in which the one impacts upon the other.[7] The essay deals with the second half of the nineteenth and early part of the twentieth century, a fruitful period of gender instability and change, that offers a vein for feminist theatre scholars to research, well worked, but by no means exhausted. Above all, I will argue the 'invisibility of the *spectatrice*', both historically and metaphorically.

It is not easy to locate the contemporary spectator, much less the historical. From the past, our evidences are fragmentary, partial and contradictory – defensive actors, nostalgic memorialists, narratising journalists, anti-theatrical pamphleteers and social reformers. Within this frame the spectator is almost always silent, unless a theatre critic. Whilst the critics, almost always male, occasionally make passing reference to the audience – as Shaw does to women and their hats (see below) – their concern is the actor on stage not in the auditorium. In these circumstances, speculation and imagination become a necessary historiographic tool. Borrowing freely and eclectically from a range of contemporary disciplines that mesh with theatre studies, cultural geography, architectural theory and literary studies[8] – I hope to map in pencil at least the boundaries for the female spectator in the period.

All space, it has been widely argued, be it geographical or architectural, is ideological. Citing Erving Goffman – 'The division and hierarchies of social structure are depicted microecologically, that is, through the use of small scale spatial metaphors' – Ardener argues that 'space reflects social organisation' and that,

> [t]he 'theatre of action' to some extent determines action. The environ-
> ment imposes certain restraints on our mobility, and, in turn, our
> perceptions of space are shaped by our own capacity to move about,
> whether by foot or by mechanical or other transport.

She concludes that 'behaviour and space are mutually dependent'.[9] Thus by exploring the spatial metaphors offered by the changing geography of London's West End, the internal and external architecture of the theatres, maps as measures of contemporary social perception, and other examples of spatial organisation, we may arrive at some understanding of the physical and ideological environment within which nineteenth-century theatre-going women moved.

London and its theatreland is the space under review because it offers the most 'evidence', for although some commentators have argued that London, as the capital, offers a unique model in Britain for the modern city, I believe that similar if not identical geographical narratives might be found in other major cities with measurable cultural activi-ties.[10] The notional female spectator that is the subject of this study is Virginia Woolf's Pargiter girl from 'one of those typical English families whose members are to be found in the Army, the Navy, and the Church; the Bar; the Stock Exchange; the Civil Services; the House of Commons; who never rise very high or sink very low' who in the 1880s represented 'English life at its most normal, most typical, and most representative'.[11] The study's concentration on leisured middle-class women is an acknowledgement that working, and working-class, women's ability to move in geographical space is different and demands a separate study, and that Walkowitz's female 'social actors' and the New Women of the era are not necessarily representative of the majority of women. The incursions into, and appropriations, of the male domain of the spectator that the former made in the 1880s and 1890s undoubtedly affected the mobility of the 'Pargiter girl', but also, I shall argue, further circum-scribed her world. The reorganisation of central London, the creation of more 'woman-friendly' spaces, facilities and modes of transport, para-doxically, reaffirmed the exclusion of women from many male territo-ries. The theatres were no exception and, to an extent, they absorbed that appropriation by the very process of feminisation – a process that starts arguably with Eliza Vestris's domesticated box-sets at the Olympic and

Marie Bancroft's antimacassars on the seats of the refurbished Prince of Wales's Theatre.

The terrain

Spectatorship is not neutral, spectatorship in the theatre is not neutral. Access to spectatorship is restricted by class, race and – the concern of this essay – gender. When Ardener argues that a ' restricted area like a club, a theatre or a nation state has a set of rules to determine how its boundary shall be crossed and who should occupy that space ...', this is significant in considering not only the theatre itself, but the area around the theatre that gives access to the theatre. The freedom to move in and around London's West End in the nineteenth century has determined not simply 'who goes to the theatre', but 'who participates in the making of theatre'. Virginia Woolf in *A Room of One's Own*, asked 'what might have happened if Charlotte Brontë had possessed ... more knowledge of the busy world, and towns and regions of life ... if experience and inter-course and travel had been granted her ... more experience of life than could enter the house of a respectable clergyman?' Or if, like the other writers Woolf cites, her 'sensibility had not been educated for centuries by the influences of the common sitting-room' – one of the reasons, Woolf avers, that George Eliot did not write *War and Peace* and that other women in the nineteenth century did not write plays.[12] Spectatorship both of the theatrical process and 'the world' is a prerequi-site not simply for dramatic writing but engagement in other aspects of the professional theatre world.[13]

The world of the West End of London, bounded by Regent's Park to the North, Trafalgar Square and the Strand to the South, Holborn in the East and Marble Arch to the West, was the 'epicentre of 19C Britain and the focus of Empire ... It contained the central institutions of male power and pleasure, as well as the homes of the leaders of the social, political and economic establishment'.[14] In the nineteenth century women were disenfranchised in more ways than one and their lack of 'citizenship' is reflected in their access to the spaces of London's West End. As middle-class women their boundaries were further circum-scribed. The very 'remodelling' of London that took place throughout the nineteenth century – beginning with Nash's Utopian reconstruction of Mayfair – created a 'pale' beyond which middle-class women ventured with caution. The project was conceived in 1811 for the future George IV, then the Prince Regent, when Marylebone Park – later Regent's Park –

reverted to the Crown. The plan was to build a 'garden city' for the nobility. Regent Street was constructed to link Regent's Park with Carlton
House, with 250 houses and 700 shops being demolished to create a
broad, classically-influenced thoroughfare to rival the boulevards of
Napoleon's Paris.

What Regent Street also effectively did was to divide the West End
into two – the fashionable Mayfair of the nobility and gentry, characterised by broad, straight streets, squares and large houses, and Soho to
the east characterised by narrow, eccentric streets and artisan's dwellings.
It is in this area that the theatres were, and are still, to be found. Further
remodelling included the building of Trafalgar Square in 1830, for which
a further 515 houses were demolished, the area around the Aldwych, and
the building of the Embankment – all of which further encircled
'theatreland'. The new railway terminals, built in the 1850s and 1860s
with their grandiose frontages facing into central London, and accretion
of goods yards, machinery, lines, cuttings and bridges radiating out from
behind those frontages, were kept out of the West End itself, with only
Charing Cross allowed to encroach from the periphery.[15] In general the
impact of the railways was threefold; geographically they created an arc
around the West End, they made the West End more accessible to all, and
accelerated the removal of the middle classes and 'respectable' working
classes to the suburbs.[16] These, and other changes in the public transport
system, radically affected movement into and across the West End of
London.

The flâneur and the flâneuse

Lynne Walker and Mary P. Ryan both argue that women's access to the
geographical and ideological terrain of the nineteenth-century city was
less restricted than we assume, but that the nature of that access is
'fraught with contradictions and cleaved by the division between dangerous and endangered women'.[17] Women's right of access to these areas
was circumscribed firstly and most significantly by the Victorian binary
of public and private spheres in which women were accorded no place
in the former and through the latter were relegated to the domestic
sphere and the suburb, ideologically if not always physically.[18]

All public institutions were run by men, for men – as owners, industri-
alists, managers and financiers. 'The public sphere – despite the presence of
some women in certain contained areas – the theatre for example – was a
masculine domain.'[19] Evening and night-time leisure space was equally

dominated by men. Their ability to move in the public arena was compara-
tively uncircumscribed – except in some areas by class. Baudelaire, identified by many critics as the archetypal 'prophet of modernity', exemplifies
the mid-nineteenth-century man as *flâneur*, free to move around the city –
the essential locus of modernity – to observe and be observed, but never
interacting with others. Benjamin in his essay on Baudelaire felicitously
describes the *flâneur* as 'botanising on the asphalt'.[20]

Henry James, coming to London in 1876, found that he had 'complete liberty, and the prospect of profitable work; I used to take long
walks in the rain. I took possession of London; I felt it to be the right
place'.[21] James was here celebrating the traditional privileges of the
flâneur, the idle man about town, the urban spectator, to experience the
city as a whole. He had access to all parts of the metropolis. Whether
the *flâneur* was a writer, like James, Charles Dickens, George Gissing or
Robert Stevenson, or a social 'anthropologist' like Henry Mayhew or
Charles Booth, or journalist like Dickens (again), W. T. Stead, G. R.
Sims, Douglas and Blanchard Jerrold, or artist-journalist like George
Cruikshank and Gustave Doré, each used his experience of the city to
create fantasies of metropolitan experience that fed contemporary
views of the urban landscape, many of which found their way on to the
stage of the period. These men could move from West End to East End,
salon to saloon, playhouse to Church mission. There were class inhibi-
tions that sometimes had to be negotiated. Sims travelled with a
'minder' to protect him in the rougher areas of London; others used
disguise, but this did not undermine their belief in their *right* to be
there and to observe. This right was the right of the dominant culture
to observe and classify the lower classes, be they women, Jews, dockers,
milliners, derelicts, street musicians *et al.* Even where, as was often the
case, the gaze was 'sympathetic' it was not empathetic and served to
confirm the hegemonic discourse of 'the Other'.[22] The voyeuristic
nature of these traversals and incursions is perhaps best exemplified by
the salon poet, barrister and man about town, A. J. Munby and his
obsessive photographic records of working women. His fascination was
both anthropological (he wished to study and record), philanthropic
(he campaigned on behalf of the women), erotic and alienated.
Education and poetry confirmed his upper middle-class status, an
inheritance enabled him to indulge his pursuit of working women into
their own 'countries' be they geographical (Wigan pits) or cultural (the
circus). His camera – as others used their pens – afforded him distance
and ultimately disassociated him from his 'subjects'.

Richard Sennett in his influential book, *The Fall of the Public Man,* has in addition identified the interior 'lonely crowd' into which the nineteenth-century male could escape in his leisure hours, the clubs – whether the gentlemen's clubs of St James and Piccadilly, or nightclubs like the Corinthian, the Lyric, the Nell Gwynn, the Supper Club and the Gardenia where supper, dancing and gambling were the main entertainment – the West End restaurants, and of course the theatres. Richard H. Dana, an American visitor to London, recorded one typical experience of *flânerie* in July 1856 when, after listening to a debate at the House of Lords, he walked to Covent Garden.

> It being about midnight, I stroll through the purlieus of Covent Garden, all alive with Gin Shops, gas lights, flaunting women and rattling carriages, and into Evans' famous Cyder Cellar. Here is a hall, as large as the largest concert rooms in America, open to all (*sic*), with good music, vocal and instrumental, and supported solely by what the people who enter it buy to eat or drink. It was crowded almost to suffocation. Only men were admitted, and the conduct of all was decent, and the passing in and out, showed the great number of people who visit it in the course of the night.[23]

These meeting places, and more particularly the gentlemen's clubs, were, however, not only places where 'silence was a right',[24] but places of social, political and economic exchange. Often the commercial, municipal and cultural decisions by which women's public space in the nineteenth-century city were created, without their participation,[25] were made or at least initiated in these exclusively male domains. It was here that male spectator met with male man of the theatre, be he actor, actor-manager, critic or dramatist.

A swift review of memoirs and records from this era in any second-hand bookshop confirms the dominance of the male in these areas: *Fifty Years of a Londoner's Life* and *A Playgoers Memories* (H. G. Hibbert), *The Pleasure Haunts of London* (E. Beresford Chancellor), *Nights at the Play* (H. M. Walbrook), *English Night Life* (Thomas Burke), *Twice Around the Clock: Or the Hours of Day and Night in London* (George Augustus Sala) – and those are only the ones I have pulled from my own shelves. There are no similar titles by women that record what is often a lifetime's theatre-going, clubbing and eating in public. No nineteenth-century woman wrote a 'A Playgoer's Memories' because women did not go to the theatre with the same freedom as men.[26] Mary Hughes, a 'London Girl of the 1880s', educated at the North London Collegiate School for

Girls and trained as a teacher at Cambridge, had only once been to the
theatre by the age of eighteen. 'And that', as her experienced elder brother
said disparagingly, 'was to a farce … you haven't seen what a play can be
till you've been to a Shakespeare or a melodrama.' Chaperoned by her
brother she saw Wilson Barrett in the *Silver King*, but whilst her taste for
theatre is whetted, all recorded future visits were again with her brother.
Later outings in the 1890s were with her typical 'modern girl' friend,
Mary Wood – 'one of the first women to ride a bicycle, to go on the top
of a bus, and to indulge in mixed bathing' – and were to 'an occasional
lecture or an educational evening as an excuse for an evening together'.
To reach these she felt safe travelling from Gower Street to Kensington,
skirting the West End, 'as there were no real dangers on that route'.[27]
Compare, too, Dana's account of male *flânerie* with this lament by Marie
Bashkirtseff in her diary entry for 2 January 1879:

> What I long for is the freedom to go about alone, of coming and going,
> of sitting on the seats in the Tuileries … of stopping and looking at the
> artistic shops, of entering the churches and museums, of walking about
> the old streets at night; that is what I long for … Do you imagine I can
> get much good from what I see, chaperoned as I am, and when, in order
> to go to the Louvre, I must wait for my carriage, my lady companion, or
> my family. Curse it all, it is this that makes me gnash my teeth to think
> that I am a woman! – I'll get myself a *bourgeois* dress and a wig, and
> make myself so ugly that I shall be as free as a man … [but] even if I
> succeeded in making myself ugly by means of some disguise I should
> still be only half free, for a woman who rambles alone commits an
> imprudence.[28]

Some, like George Sand in Paris, found the freedom to *flâner* by dressing
as a man, as did the bonnet-maker Munby interviewed at one of the
pleasure gardens.[29] However, Munby's interviewee was working class,
and Sand was an exception, as were, it would appear from its tone, the
women referred to in the following item from *The Times* dated 17
October 1868:

> I was last Tuesday evening at the Royalty Theatre and was very much
> astonished by the entrance of a young nobleman, very well known
> among the 'upper ton' accompanied by a woman dressed up in man's
> clothes. Her entrance caused a great deal of sensation in the theatre, as
> the disguise was palpable even to the most casual observer. I have heard
> since that the same young nobleman has been to the Holborn and
> several other theatres, with sometimes two or three other women
> disguised as men. As the act renders the perpetrator liable to heavy

penalties and at the same time intensely disgusts the spectators, I trust, sir, by your kindly inserting this letter in your columns, we shall see no more of it for the future.[30]

Where middle-class women did begin to 'take to the streets' in the 1880s and 1890s, their project was different. Work and politics gave them access to the streets, but their leisure remained predominantly domestic. For example, Beatrice Potter – later Webb – worked as a rent collector near St Katherine's Docks and recorded in her diaries her 'journeys down the Thames by the ferry steamers, especially back by the evening light: the picturesque side of London lower-class life, the background of grand public buildings with their national historic associations. And then back in that perfect house [Cheyne Walk] ... I, lying on the sofa watching the river and the barges on it creeping by'.[31] Here Potter is viewing 'lower life' at a distance created either by being on the water or viewing the world through her window. She is not on foot, not 'strolling' and she is not 'out' at night. She is a spectator but one that is behind a partition, unobserved, unseen. Most importantly for this essay, Potter was a 'New Woman' rather than a 'Pargiter girl'.

Unexceptional women did not *flâner*, they did not spectate, and particularly not during the hours of darkness. And this has implications for them as theatre spectators. If one 'reads' pictures of the exteriors of the 'legitimate' London theatres from the beginning of the century, where they do show women in numbers, they are almost always with men, escorted. One can identify some lone men, but not lone women. Pictures of the auditoriums – cartoons, sketches and latterly photographs – of the 'respectable' theatres show mixed audiences, men with women and groups of men, but large groups of women are rare. Where middle-class women are recorded in any number it is at the radical theatres of the 1890s and 1900s, and at matinées, daytime performances when it was safer for a woman to negotiate the dangerous territory of Soho. The presence of women at matinées is commented on both directly and indirectly. *Punch* in the 1890s regularly featured cartoons on the subject of women's 'matinée hats' in which the 'exasperated Old Gentleman' or 'Mr Jones, who has not been able to get a glimpse of the stage all afternoon' asks the lady in front of him to remove her hat. The ultimate satirical moment for *Punch* was the invention of 'Mr Punch's Patent Matinée Hat. Fitted with binocular glasses for the benefit of those sitting behind the viewer'.[32] Shaw instigated a campaign against the matinée hat in the *Saturday Review* following a visit to a matinée at the Comedy Theatre … The stalls were filled for the most part by quite the most disagreeable collection of women I have ever seen. They all wore huge towering hats, piled up, for the more effectual obstruction of the view, with every conceivable futility, vulgarity, and brutality (in the dead bird line) that a pushing shopkeeper can force on the head of a woman … solely [out of] a dull fear of not being in the fashion. (21 March 1896).[33]

These jibes attest to a significant, fashionable, female presence at the matinée. As Dennis Kennedy observes,

the female matinée audience seems a marvellous demonstration of Thorstein Veblen's theory of vicarious leisure: wives and daughters of hard-working men of commerce sent out in daylight in flagrantly impractical dress to proclaim the freedom from drudgery for women bought by their masters' successful toil. Unable to afford the leisure of the aristocracy themselves, the merchant classes showed off women as surrogate signifiers of wealth.[34]

At the other end of the political spectrum, the audience for Madge Kendal's 1889 production of Ibsen's *An Enemy of the People* was described by one critic as composed of 'masculine women and effeminate men', who went on to tell how '[t]he fearful business made by these two dozen members of the superior sex in getting into the theatre was the most appalling thing of its kind that [he] had ever witnessed', knocking each other down, dragging and trampling each other underfoot.[35] The audience for Shaw in the 1900s at both the Court Theatre and the Savoy is also depicted, often pejoratively, as being largely female.[36] Thus the radical audience is shown to be either sexually ambiguous or unfeminine – not an identification sought by the Pargiter girl. The Pargiter girl was, if she was any sort of theatrical spectator, a matinée girl.

Consuming ladies

There were a number of other factors that contained and controlled women's spectatorship in the second half of the nineteenth century. It has been argued that women found greater freedom of movement in the West End through the rise of the department store, the quintessential female space. Here women could find 'a place to take one's friends; a fashionable resort, a lounge, an art gallery, a bazaar and a delightful promenade'.[37] The domestic interior and feminine leisure pursuits were transposed to one protected site. Many, if not most, of the major department stores are located on the edge of theatreland: Regent Street, Oxford Street and Bond Street – John Lewis opened on Oxford Street in 1864, Liberty's and D. H. Evans on Regent Street in 1876 and 1879. These shopping areas were, for middle-class women, daylight areas. The original, great colonnade of Regent Street allowed women to stroll – to 'window shop' during shop hours, for at night this same area – where Mayfair meets Soho – became the haunt of the 'working girl', the prostitute. Ironically, the advances in street lighting and shop illumination did not help the independence of the *flâneuse* nor the *spectatrice*. With the 'illuminated window as stage, the street as theatre and the passers by as audience' Regent Street and the adjacent commercial streets came to look like 'an interior out of doors' but one that was populated by 'working girls'.[38]

What separated the reputable from the disreputable woman, just as it separated the respectable female from the *flâneur*, was the ability to look. Women did not have freedom of movement and gaze, upward and outward. At the beginning of this period, the 1850s and 1860s, codes of behaviour discouraged middle-class women from walking alone in the streets of London. If they did, their 'gaze' was regulated by the fear that the respectable woman might be mistaken for 'the Other', whose bold gaze marked her out as a working girl. A series of letters to *The Times* in 1862 asserted the dangers for young women on the streets of central London and stated that 'no good-looking (*sic*) girl or woman is safe from … molestation unless she be under a man's protection'. The 'cause of this gross stain … is that the experience some London young men have of a certain class of women is applied to all; they therefore sally out upon intrigue believing the same desire is universally prevalent'.[39] The *Girl's Own Paper*, as late as 1890, advised its readers 'to avoid stroll[ing] … and always look straight before you, or on the opposite side when passing any man. Never look at them when near enough to be stared at in any impertinent and abrasive way'.[40] Jeanette Marshall recalled how she 'knew exactly which route should be avoided'. And she regularly promenaded, chaperoned, along the edge of Green Park, carefully avoiding the 'masculine' territory of clubs and bachelor chambers on the north side of the street. The 'heavenly' Burlington Arcade, one of her shopping haunts, was also the haunt of street girls and was forbidden from lunchtime on.[41]

This contested space was not limited to the street nor increasingly from the 1880s to the night-time. William Acton in his book on prostitution asked: 'Who are those fair creatures, neither chaperones nor chaperoned: those "somebodies whom nobody knows", who elbow our wives and daughters in the parks and promenades and the *rendez-vous* of fashion?'[42] The middle class Pargiter sisters in Virginia Woolf's novel-essay, *The Pargiters*, growing up in the 1880s, express the same fear of movement in the West End:

> Eleanor and Milly and Delia could not possibly go for a walk alone – save in the streets around Abercorn Terrace,[43] and then only between the hours of eight-thirty and sunset … For any of them to walk in the West End even by day was out of the question. Bond Street was as impassable, save with their mother, as any swamp alive with crocodiles. The Burlington Arcade was nothing but a fever-stricken den as far as they were concerned. To be seen in Piccadilly was equivalent to walking up Abercorn Terrace in a dressing gown carrying a bath sponge. A large radius of the West End indeed was closed to them, whether by day or night, unless they went with a brother or their mother, and even a hansom cab, in which they were forced to make their transit of the dangerous area, had to have both flaps of its door shut.[44]

Even allowing for a degree of comic exaggeration the parameters of these middle-class girls' lives are clear.

The fear bred by contiguous sites of bourgeois and artisan life in Mayfair and Soho was not limited to problems with prostitution. The area behind the Strand was notorious for the sale of pornography[45] and the National Temperance League's map of 'The Modern Plague' from 1884, shows the city centre drinking houses which were open from five in the morning to midnight. These drinking houses are shown by a mass of devilish red dots coalescing in the Soho area and diminishing as the map extends westwards and eastwards.[46] Again the accretion of these in theatreland and the concomitant threat to the respectable middle classes, and more particularly its women, is easy to see.

If the proximity of 'sin', sexual or otherwise, were not enough, then the presence of the poor themselves was, at the very least, uncomfortable. Booth's Poverty Map of London of 1889 delineates areas of gradated wealth from the 'vicious and semi-criminal' to the wealthy. The boundary formed by Regent Street is clearly readable. West of Regent Street the map is dominated by the reds and oranges of the 'well-to-do' and 'wealthy', while east of the boundary is 'stained with the mixed blues that indicate poverty and chronic want', with pockets of black to indicate the vicious and semi-criminal.[47] Virginia Woolf, this time in *The Years*, paints a clear picture of the alienation felt by the middle classes on one of their forays into the alien land of the working classes in Soho. Kitty,

Lady Lasswade, travelling to the Opera House in Covent Garden alone in the family's newly acquired motor car, is struck by the incongruity of her own, and her fellow theatre-goers', situation:

> Men and women in full evening dress were walking along the pavement. They looked uncomfortable and self-conscious as they dodged between costers' barrows, with their high-piled hair and their evening cloaks, with their button-holes and their white waistcoats, in the glare of the afternoon sun ... the gentlemen kept close beside [the ladies] as though protecting them ... Covent Garden porters, dingy little clerks in their ordinary working clothes, coarse-looking women in aprons stared in at her. The air smelt strongly of oranges and bananas ... [T]he car drew up under the archway; she pushed through the glass doors and went in. She felt at once a sense of relief. Now that the daylight was extinguished and the air glowed yellow and crimson, she no longer felt absurd. On the contrary, she felt appropriate.

Still in 1910, Kitty observes the world from her motor and is the object of the gaze of the working men and women; the women walking the streets are 'protected' by their men, and inside the theatre Kitty becomes 'invisible' amongst all 'the ladies and gentlemen who were mounting the stairs ... dressed exactly as she was'.[48]

The invisible spectatrice

Lynne Walker argues that by the 1890s the creation of women-only spaces had opened up the urban terrain of Britain's cities – women's clubs like Mrs Massingberd's Pioneer Club on Cork Street, The Women's University Club,[49] department stores and women-only restaurants like the Dorothy chain, run by women, for women, in Oxford and Mortimer Streets, separate waiting/rest rooms for women at the major stations, and women's public toilets, opened in the 1890s.[50] Whilst Griselda Pollock has declared that women were never positioned 'as the normal occupants of the public realm',[51] Walker sees the incursions made into the public space by women 'engender[ing] a dissonance between ideology and lived experience that made spaces for real change through the development of a public ideology for women – in the cracks in the pavement'.[52]

But I want now to argue that without denying the advances made by women in the public arena in the 1880s and 1890s, something else is happening – more specifically in the theatre buildings themselves – that renders the female an 'invisible *spectatrice*', that perhaps suggests that

Walker's cracks in the pavement were but another fissure into which many 'ordinary' women dropped. George Augustus Sala observed of 'woman' in London,

> [u]nobtrusive, gentle, womanly, she is just the person to slip through a crowd unobserved, like one of those grey moths in the evening which come and go on their way, unseen by men and undevoured by birds.[53]

Whilst some women in the 1890s eschewed the demure demeanour and dress required of them by the *Girls' Own Paper*, like the female Slade students who adopted the Trilby bonnet and skirt during the Trilby craze of 1895, invisibility rendered most women safe on the streets. As women began to move on to the streets in greater numbers, they imitated

> the discreet and secretive style of the business or professional man. There was often a furtive masculinity in women's street dress … since out of doors women went veiled, bonneted and cloaked in the dark colours that did not show the mud or soot, and also suggested respectability.[54]

This desired invisibility was, as we have seen, unavailable to the middle-class, theatre-going woman, as fashion dictated a more ostentatious dress for theatre visits. However, changes in theatre architecture, text and ideology over the period all afforded women a return to the unseen state within the theatre.

Paradoxically it is the very development of a more respectable, woman-friendly theatrical space that confirms the 'private sphere' as the realm of the female within the public arena, just as the department stores replicated a domestic space for women. As Kerry Powell has written:

> The cup-and-saucer comedies … at the Prince of Wales's Theatre beginning in the 1860s intensified a campaign to make theatres respectable … Macready and Madame Vestris banned prostitutes from the promenade and refreshment areas of their theatres, and the Theatres Licensing Act of 1843 reduced the annoyance of drunken playgoers by forbidding legitimate theatres from selling alcohol. As theatres became more like homes and less like houses of prostitution, the carriages of respectable families could once again be seen stopping outside.[55]

The pioneering Marie Bancroft played her part in the gentrification and feminisation of the theatre when she undertook a deliberate policy at the Prince of Wales's Theatre to exclude the lower classes by creating a middle-class milieu. Her description of the changed theatre on the opening night reads like a household article in a women's journal:

> the house looked very pretty, and, although everything was done very inexpensively, had a bright and bonny appearance, and I felt proud of it. The curtains and carpets were of a cheap kind, but in good taste. The stalls light blue, with lace antimacassars over them; this was the first time such things had been seen in a theatre. The pampered audiences of the present day, accustomed to the modern luxurious playhouses, little know how much my modest undertaking was the pioneer, and would hardly credit that a carpet in the stalls was until then unknown.[56]

The reduction of the pit area in the stalls and the replacement of the old benches with stall seats brought more women into the body of the auditorium and in closer proximity to the stage.

In the new century, the work of women managers in remodelling their theatres was often described in similar terms. Mrs Langtrey's £40,000 refit of The Imperial in 1900 was described by *The Era* as 'exquisitely beautiful [bearing] the stamp of the fair manageress's individuality'. The elaborate embroideries and 'suspended curtains of buttercup yellow silk with powderings of *Fleur de lys*' were given special attention as 'artistic in design and ... marvellous examples of modern needlework' and special praise is given to her architect, Frank Verity, for the careful study he has made of the 'comfort of the audience'.[57] Lena Ashwell in opening her redesigned Kingsway Theatre in 1907, with its cream, Louis XIV interior, emphasised the theatre's convenience and comfort, and its accessibility by all means of public transport, thus appealing to the non-car or carriage-owning middle classes. All seats were 'numbered and reserved, thus avoiding the necessity for tedious waiting' and enabling women – or their menfolk – to book in advance and avoid the scrum at the box office and the necessity of carrying money abroad.[58] The characteristic pink programmes from these early years of her management, with their advertisements for 'Models from Paris' from Maison Lewis and the Elite Ladies Dress Co., Papière Poudre and Chappell Pianos, further emphasised the 'femininity' of her enterprise.

Rather than appropriating the masculine domain, the women spectators in these gentrified and feminised theatres often merely exchanged one domestic interior for another. Henry James observed how the world on the Bancrofts' stage too replicated the world of the audience with, a great many chairs and tables, carpets and curtains, and knicknacks, and an audience placed close to the stage. They might for the most part have been written by a cleverish visitor at a country-house and acted in the drawing-room by his fellow inmates.[59]

The world of the department store found its way on to the stage and in the 1890s there is an increasingly symbiotic relationship of a different type to be found between the world of the stage and the world of the female consumer as Kaplan and Stowell have delineated in their book *Theatre and Fashion*.[60] In a large number of West End theatres – from the production of Wilde's comedies at the St James' Theatre to the fashion-plate choruses and stars at the Gaiety, modish designers produced fashionable models on stage for their female audience members to emulate. Women in the auditorium, as outside the theatre, were once again invited to identify themselves as consumers of trivia rather than art.

In other ways, too, the theatres of the late nineteenth century changed the audibility and visibility of the spectator of both sexes. In the larger theatres, architecture became more monumental and ornate – a thing to be admired for itself, according to Richard Sennett, thus reducing the visual significance of the spectator. At the same time, the introduction of dimmed auditorium lights, which began in the 1850s in London, discouraged impolite – or indeed social behaviours of any kind – during the performance. As Sennett has written:

> In the 1850s, a Parisian or London theatre goer had no compunction about talking to a neighbour in the midst of a play, if he or she had just remembered something to say. By 1870, the audience was policing itself. Talking now seemed bad taste and rude. The houselights were dimmed too, to reinforce the silence and focus attention on the stage ... Restraint of one's feelings in a dark, quiet hall was a discipline.[61]

Through the nineteenth century, the audience became more passive, more private, more feminine and more invisible. Within that process, despite the increased access of the female spectator to the world of the legitimate theatre, the identification of certain aspects of theatre specifically with the feminine, returns the female once more to the private domain and renders her invisible in the sites of worldly power.

Some conclusions

The social maps, as Ardener calls them, for men and women are different, and it is paradoxical that as women in the late nineteenth century became more visible on the streets and appropriated male territories – as explorers and adventurers, New Women and suffragettes – the roles the Pargiter girls assumed were often more narrowly and dangerously narcissistic, more concerned with fashion, image and consumption. The physical maps for women *had* changed by 1910, and the mental maps too. The freedoms that ordinary women had acquired to circulate more freely in geographical and architectural space in the centre of London were real, but this was often achieved by the creation of the domestic or private space within the public – the department store, the woman-only club or restaurant, the station waiting-room. The physical freedom brought by the improved range of public transport still did not encourage women to *flâner*, to wander the streets at night, as their male counterparts did. There was no night-time equivalent of the bicycle. Ownership of the streets as a right, remained a male prerogative.

The theatre too inevitably mirrored social practice. Access to the theatre of the West End was made easier by the changes in transport, but the sexual, class and criminal threats remained to discourage women from venturing into the terrain alone, particularly at night. There is evidence that some of the theatre practices of the 1890s and 1900s, the experiments of the independent theatre movement and the Court Theatre, the female-led Little Theatres and the growth of the matinée, attracted a specifically female audience. But this audience was often marginalised by mainstream critics and commentators as 'mannish', trivial and inconsequential. This and the gentrification, domestication and feminisation of the theatres themselves ironically may have perpetuated the invisibility of the *spectatrice*.

Notes

1 Amy Levy, 'Women and Club Life' (1888), cited in Deborah Epstein Nord, *Walking the Victorian Streets: Women Representation and the City* (Ithaca and London, Cornell University Press, 1995), p. 184.
2 Shirley Ardener, ed., *Women and Space: Ground Rules and Social Maps*, Cross-Cultural Perspectives on Women, Vol. 5 (Oxford and Providence, Berg Publications, 1992), p. 1.
3 Janet Wolff, 'The Invisible *Flâneuse*: Women and the Literature of Modernity', in Andrew Benjamin, ed., *The Problems of Modernity: Adorno and Benjamin* (London and New York, Routledge, 1989), pp. 141–55. Other essays on the *flâneur/flâneuse* include: Susan Buck-Morss, 'The Flaneur, the Sandwichman and the Whore: The Politics of Loitering', *New German*

Critique, 39 (Fall 1986), pp. 99–142; Anke Gleber, 'Female Flanerie and the *Symphony of the City*', in Katherina von Ankum, ed., *Women in the Metropolis* (Berkeley, Los Angeles and London, University of California Press, 1997), pp. 67–88; Elizabeth Wilson, 'The Sphinx in the City', in Lynne Walker, ed., *Cracks in the Pavement: Gender/Fashion/Architecture* (London, Sorella Press, 1992).

4 Judith R. Walkowitz, *City of Dreadful Delight: Narratives of Sexual Danger in Late-Victorian London* (London, Virago Press, 1992).

5 For a consideration of 'dangerous and endangered women' see Mary P. Ryan, *Women in Public: Between Banners and Ballots, 1825–1880* (Baltimore and London, Johns Hopkins Press, 1990), especially chapter 2, 'Everyday Space, Gender and the Geography of the Public', pp. 58–94.

6 Tracy C. Davis, *Actresses as Working Women* (London, Routledge, 1991), pp. 137–63.

7 One of the essays that does explore the interstices between gender, *flânerie* and art is Griselda Pollock's chapter, 'Modernity and the Spaces of Modernity', in which she examines the work of Mary Cassatt and Berthe Morisot in this context. One interesting observation Pollock makes in her redrawing of the 'Baudelairean map' of Paris is that Cassatt paints women in the auditorium of the theatre, Degas those backstage. The male artist has access to the 'privileged' areas of the theatre: Griselda Pollock, *Vision and Difference: Feminity, Feminism and Histories of Art* (London, Routledge, 1988), pp. 50–90.

8 My 'borrowings' are not entirely random and have been undeniably fruitful, even if not used directly in this essay. They include: Christine Battersby, 'Hermaphrodite of Art, and Vampires of Practice': Problems of Women in Architecture', in Walker, *Cracks in the Pavement;* Nancy Duncan, ed., *BodySpace: Destabilizing Geographies of Gender and Sexuality* (London and New York, Routledge, 1996); Peter Jackson, *Maps of Meaning* (London and New York, Routledge, 1989); Neil Leach, ed., *Rethinking Architecture: A Reader in Cultural Theory* (London and New York, Routledge, 1997), particularly for essays by Eco, Habermas, Jameson and Lefebvre; Doreen Massey's *Space, Place and Gender* (London, Polity, 1994); Stephen Pile, *The Body and the City* (London and New York, Routledge, 1996); Edward Soja, *Postmodern Geographies* (London, Verso, 1989); Lynne Walker, 'Home and Away: The Feminist Remapping of Public and Private Space in Victorian London', in Rose Anthony, ed., *New Frontiers of Space, Bodies and Gender* (London, Routledge, 1998), pp. 67–75.

9 Ardener, *Women and Space:* p. 2.

10 See for an example: study of the gender and class implications in the nineteenth-century remodelling of Birmingham, Lee Davidoff and Catherine Hall, 'The Architecture of Public and Private: English Middle-Class Society in a Provincial Town, 1780–1850', in D. Fraser and A. Sutcliffe, eds, *In Pursuit of Urban History* (London, Edward Arnold, 1983), pp. 326–46.

11 Virginia Woolf, *The Pargiters: The Novel-Essay portion of THE YEARS* (London, The Hogarth Press, 1978), p. 9.

12 Virginia Woolf, *A Room of One's Own* (Harmondsworth, Penguin Books, 1945), pp. 56–9.

13 Women did, of course, write for theatre in much larger numbers than Woolf and many others commentators have credited, but under markedly different circumstances from their male colleagues. See Tracy C. Davis and Ellen Donkin, eds, *Women and Playwriting in Nineteenth Century Britain* (Cambridge, Cambridge University Press, 1999); Viv Gardner, 'Out of the Attic: Women and Writing at the *Fin de Siècle*', in Marion Shaw, ed., *An Introduction to Women's Writing* (London, Prentice Hall, 1998), pp. 182–3.

14 Lynne Walker, 'Vistas of Pleasure: Women Consumers of Urban Space in the West End of London 1850–1900', in idem, *Cracks in the Pavement*, pp. 1–2.

15 This was due partly to the cost of land in central London and partly to the recommendations of the Royal Commission on Metropolitan Railway Termini that was fearful of the disruption the railways would bring, both physical and social, to the West End. See Charles Dickens, *Dickens Dictionary of London, 1888* (Moretonhampstead, Old House Books, 1998); Donald J. Olsen, *The Growth of Victorian London* (Harmondsworth, Penguin Books, 1976); Peter Thorold, *The London Rich: The Creation of a Great City from 1666 to the Present* (Harmondsworth, Viking, 1999).

16 For the impact of the 1883 Cheap Trains Act see *ibid.*, p. 278.

17 Ryan, *Women in Public*, p. 92.

18 The theory of 'separate spheres' is not unproblematic and has been contested in a number of recent works: see *ibid.*, pp. 3–18.

19 Wolff, 'The Invisible *Flâneuse*, p. 142.

20 Walter Benjamin, *Charles Baudelaire: Lyric Poet in the Era of High Capitalism* (London, New Left Books, 1973), p. 36.

21 Henry James, 'London', in his *Essays in London and Elsewhere,* cited in Walkowitz, *City of Dreadful Delight*, p. 15.

22 See chapter one, 'Urban Spectatorship', in *ibid.*, pp. 15–39.

23 Cited in Brian N. Morton, *Americans in London* (London, Macdonald, 1988), p. 69.

24 Richard Sennett, *The Fall of Public Man* (London, Faber and Faber, 1993), pp. 215–17. For a list of the principal London clubs and the gender distribution within them, see Dickens, *Dickens Dictionary of London, 1888*, p. 82. This list does not include the radical women-only clubs that emerged in the 1890s like Mrs Massingberd's Pioneer Club.

25 Ryan, *Women in Public*, p. 92.

26 Kate Terry Gielgud's *A Victorian Playgoer* might be mistaken for one of these memoirs, but is a record of performances seen by this non-acting member of the Terry family, written as letters to a friend and published after her death. She was 'an inveterate playgoer', but as a member of the Terry clan her relationship to the theatre was different from the Pargiter Girls and, as her

nephew John Gielgud records, once married she went either with her husband or her husband and children. Kate Terry Gielgud *A Victorian Playgoer*, ed. Muriel St Clare Byrne (London, Heinemann, 1980).

27 M. V. Hughes, *A London Girl of the 1880s* (Oxford, Oxford University Press, 1978), pp. 79, 233, 234. Mary Hughes also quotes her mother as warning her that '[many mothers will] seize on anything – say a man dances with a girl more than twice, or sits with her for a talk, or takes her to a theatre. Her mother will "ask his intensions"', p. 239.

28 Marie Bashkirtseff, *The Journal of Marie Bashkirtseff* (London, Virago Press, 1985), p. 347. Bashkirtseff is of course writing about Paris not London, but her experience would not appear untypical of both capital cities.

29 Recorded in Munby's Diaries, cited in Julie Wheelwright, *Amazons and Military Maids: Women Who Dressed as Men in Pursuit of Life, Liberty and Happiness* (London, Pandora Press, 1989), pp. 112–13.

30 *The Times*, 17 October 1868. It is interesting that both theatres mentioned in the letter had, or had just had, female managers. The Royalty, a burlesque house in 1868, had a succession of female managers. Martha 'Patty' Oliver managed the theatre from 1866–70 and Fanny Joseph managed the Holborn Theatre Royal between September 1867 and March 1868. The respected Barry Jackson was manager in October 1868, promoting 'Performances of the Highest Class of Dramatic Literature', and opening with Lytton's *Money*. See Raymond Mander and Joe Mitchenson, *The Lost Theatres of London* (London, Rupert Hart-Davis, 1967), pp. 194–5 and 414–15.

31 Cited in Nord, *Walking the Victorian Streets*, p. 187.

32 J. A. Hammerton, ed., *Punch Library of Humour: At the Play* (London, The Educational Book Co., n.d), pp. 84, 143, 148.

33 George Bernard Shaw, *Our Theatres in the Nineties, Volume II* (London, Constable and Company, 1932), p. 73.

34 Dennis Kennedy, 'The New Drama and the New Audience', in Michael R. Booth and Joel H. Kaplan, eds, *The Edwardian Theatre* (Cambridge, Cambridge University Press, 1996), p. 137.

35 Quoted in Kerry Powell, *Women and Victorian Theatre* (Cambridge, Cambridge University Press, 1997), p. 71.

36 See Kennedy, 'The New Drama and the New Audience', pp. 136–41.

37 Cited in Michael J. Winstanley, *The Shopkeeper's World, 1830–1914* (Manchester, Manchester University Press, 1983), p. 35. See also Alison Adburgham, *Shops and Shopping, 1800–1914* (London, Allen & Unwin, 1981).

38 Wolfgang Schivelbusch, *Disenchanted Night: The Industrialization of Light in the Nineteenth Century* (Berkeley, Los Angeles and London, University of California Press, 1988), pp. 148–9 and pp. 81–154 for a larger history of the impact of street lighting on the night life of the capital cities of Europe.

39 *The Times*, 18 January 1862. And 9 January 1862; 17 January 1862.

40 *Girl's Own Paper*, 6 December 1890, cited in Judith R. Walkowitz, *City of Dreadful Delight*, p. 51.

41 *Ibid.,* pp. 51–2.

42 Cited in Nord, *Walking the Victorian Streets*, p. xiv.

43 'One of [those] large old fashioned houses … to be found between Ladbroke Grove and Bayswater': Woolf, '*The Pargiters*', p. 10.

44 *Ibid.,* p. 37.

45 See Davis, *Actresses as Working Women*, p. 138.

46 'The Modern Plague of London' reproduced in Phillipa Glanville, *London in Maps* (London: The Connoiseur, 1972), p. 190.

47 Charles Booth, 'A Descriptive Map of London Poverty', Appendix to *Life and Labour of the People* (London: Charles Griffen and Company, 1889), Reproduced in F. Parker and P. Jackson, *The History of London Maps* (London: Barrie & Jenkins, 1990), pp. 144–5.

48 Virginia Woolf, *The Years* (London, Penguin Books, 1998), p. 133.

49 See 'Appendix B: Model Housing and Clubs for Women', in Martha Vicinus, *Independent Women: Work and Community for Single Women, 1850–1920*, (London, Virago Press, 1985), pp. 295–399.

50 Public lavatories for women were not introduced until the 1890s. Before that women had to find a shop or order food in a confectioners or restaurant. One testimony to the 'invisibility' of women in most nineteenth-century theatres was the paucity of toilet provision for women: see Tracy C. Davis, 'Filthy – Nay – Pestilential: Sanitation and Victorian Theaters', in Della Pollock, ed., *Exceptional Spaces: Essays in Performance and History* (Chapel Hill and London, North Carolina University Press, 1998), pp. 161–86.

51 Pollock, 'Modernity and the Spaces of Femininity', p. 50.

52 Walker, 'Vistas of Pleasure, p. 6.

53 George Augustus Sala, *Twice Around the Clock: Or the Hours of Day and Night in London* (London, Houlston and Wright, 1859), p. 148.

54 Elizabeth Wilson, *Adorned in Dreams: Fashion and Modernity* (London, Virago Press, 1985), p. 136.

55 Marie Bancroft and Squire Bancroft, *The Bancrofts: Recollections of Sixty Years* (London, Nelson, 1909), p. 80.

56 Powell, *Women and Victorian Theatre*, p. 47.

57 Cited in Mander and Mitchenson, *The Lost Theatres of London*, pp. 214–15.

58 *Ibid.,* p. 232.

59 Cited in Powell, *Women and Victorian Theatre*, p. 48.

60 As Florence Alexander, wife of actor-manager George Alexander of the St James's Theatre recalled, 'I was rather "extreme" [meticulous] with clothes on stage, for in those days people went to see St. James's plays *before* ordering a new gown': cited in Joel H. Kaplan and Sheila Stowell, *Theatre and Fashion: Oscar Wilde to the Suffragettes* (Cambridge, Cambridge University Press, 1994), p. 9.

61 Sennett, *The Fall of Public Man*, p. 206.

3

THEATRE HISTORY, HISTORIOGRAPHY AND WOMEN'S DRAMATIC WRITING

Susan Bennett

One of the most thorough and radical changes in drama studies since the early 1980s has been the reorientation and reorganisation of dramatic and, more generally, literary canons to include works by hitherto excluded 'minorities' and, especially, women. To take but one observation, Robert White comments in a discussion of the state of English studies in the 1990s, 'Renaissance Literature is no longer the bastion of patriarchy, but the study of a period when vigorous and innovative women were writing poetry, while some male writers were contesting stereotypes of femininity and masculinity'.[1] This much is true: there are differences, as White indicates, not only in the texts under examination, but in the type and nature of the scholarly criticism that is brought to bear on those materials. Moreover, women scholars (and some men) have taken on projects of dazzling originality, not to mention size and scope, to redress the omissions in the telling of history. Thus her/his stories might produce, on the one hand, more inclusive accounts of particular historical periods (say, the 'Renaissance') and genres (say, drama) and, on the other, counternarratives to those which insist, still, on the public events of male-focused wars and politics as primary indicators of cultural practice at any given moment – that is, as Katherine Kearns notes about traditional history-making, 'At the most obvious level, there is a convenient forgetfulness regarding women that is reflected in endless negotiations within a formula whereby history is up for grabs as either "biography of great men," Carlyle's position, or as "the science of men in time," Bloch's formulation'.[2] Thus feminist revisionist theatre history has endeavoured to expand the range of texts considered as well as what might be construed as important to history.

By way of illustration, we can look to an important and groundbreaking volume such as S. P. Cerasano and Marion Wynne-Davies's *Renaissance Drama by Women: Texts and Documents*.[3] What is so significant – and so useful – about *Renaissance Drama by Women* is not just that it collects six otherwise un- or under-known dramatic texts, but that it also permits a deep cultural context for our reading of these same texts through its complementary second half, sections of historically contemporary documents on women as actors, producers and spectators. This is a particularly helpful strategy of inclusion since it suggests a more diverse route to comprehension of both the period itself and women's participation in it. Generally speaking, it is all too common to see women *only* as theatregoers in this historical period and, even in this context, audiences have not, until very recently, been considered as a gendered phenomenon. Jean E. Howard's 1991 essay 'Women as Spectators, Spectacles, and Paying Customers' has led the way in this realm of study.[4]

In other words, the editors present the dramatic production of six Renaissance texts (five authored by women, including one by Elizabeth I and one authored by a man for performance by his exclusively female pupils for an audience including the Queen herself) as part of women's involvement, generally, in the affairs of the theatre. These women are, the text emphatically insists, both producers and receivers of culture; they are, by this understanding, valued players in the formation of ideas and ideologies. What I admire about the scope of the Cerasano/Wynne-Davies volume is its insistence on seeing the plays by women in this context of other public activity by women and in relation to the *business* of theatre. The collection does not concern itself with comparison (such as whether Elizabeth Cary is the equal of xyz – name your own male canonical Renaissance playwright – as more apologetic volumes might have been tempted to assert).

Yet even as it avoids this no-win approach, the editors claim as the very last sentence of their introduction to the collected plays, '[t]he range of literary activity represented here – from the 1590s to the 1640s and from formal translation, through powerful tragedy to witty comedy – shows conclusively that Renaissance theatre by women must finally assume its rightful place in the canon of English literature'.[5] What is 'rightful', in the end, for the co-editors is an expanded canon and, by implication, a more honest representation of the period's achievements in the various dramatic genres that we recognise as foremost on those stages. Similarly, in their introduction to the bibliography of *Drama by Women to 1900*, editors Gwenn Davis and Beverly A. Joyce note, 'Only the broadest definitions of form and of time frame can accommodate women's dramatic writings'.[6]

Of course, one can turn to almost any historical moment and find work written by women of equal worthiness for canon accommodation and which has had the capacity to raise new questions about those male-authored texts that we have previously thought of as constitutive of the canonical – or, indeed, all – literature of a given period. Other women's research projects, such as Virginia Blain, Patricia Clements and Isobel Grundy's *The Feminist Companion to Literature*,[7] have pursued similar objectives over a larger historical sweep. In our more contemporary moment (and one, depressingly, where women's dramatic writing seems still too vulnerable to disappearance from the historical and critical record), a number of landmark volumes have enabled at least certain women playwrights and some feminist theatre companies to become, as it were, the contemporary feminist canon. Exemplary here are Elaine Aston's *An Introduction to Feminism and Theatre*, Charlotte Canning's *Feminist Theatres in the USA: Staging Women's Experience*, Lizbeth Goodman's *Contemporary Feminist Theatres: To Each Her Own* and Peta Tait's *Converging Realities: Feminism in Australian Theatre*.[8] In short, in their various national contexts – and, occasionally, with some reference beyond their own national boundaries – these authors have confirmed and committed to our collective memory a range of feminist theatres that might otherwise be neglected by conventional theatre history or criticism.

The results of all of this work have been extraordinary and the difference this has made to the scholarly endeavour is palpable at every level of academic practice including not only what is understood as distinguished scholarship, but also what texts get taught in the classroom and how; the constituencies we teach since women students often seek out women-centred curriculum and make themselves a majority 'identity' for that class; what plays are included in the production seasons of college and university theatres as well as the methodologies for how those plays are then produced. But the work that has been done often points vividly to how much remains yet to be accomplished. Referring to Aston's monograph, Jacky Bratton comments, 'With this work feminist theatre study in Britain could be said to come of age; but Aston still has to propose, as a project urgently to be undertaken, that bringing the "lost" tradition of women's theatre history into view is an important political step if feminist theatre scholarship is to change the future history of the stage'.[9] There is a sense here of Bratton's exasperation that it is still necessary for Aston to make such a claim, yet she, too, recognises the importance of that claim: only by asserting a women's theatre history as a key narrative of the past will there be any possibility that future histories of the stage will deal with women any more thoroughly. Can it really be as far back as 1988 when Joan Scott called 'not only for a new history of women, but also a new history'?[10] And, I think, that endeavour remains at the heart of the matter. So, with that in mind, what registers are crucial in our achievement of a new theatre history?

The published canon of dramatic literature is one site where history readily finds its evidence and, of course, the ways that history has, historically speaking, distorted canon formation are now well understood. Even the most mainstream manifestation of the practices of canon definition within the 'business' of theatre studies – those anthologies targeted at first-year college and university students – show their market-driven awareness of this new historical fact: some women wrote good plays that can be included in an expanded canon of dramatic literature. So, as a consequence of this new consciousness, the very 'same' anthology that I was instructed to use as a first-time graduate assistant in 1983, *Masterpieces of the Drama*[11] (then available in its fourth edition, its contents 28 plays all written by men), includes in its sixth edition (1991) three texts by women (Lady Gregory's *The Gaol Gate*, Caryl Churchill's *Top Girls* and Lorraine Hansberry's *A Raisin in the Sun*. A more liberally-minded collection like Lee Jacobus's *The Bedford Introduction to Drama*[12] offers some eight women's plays in its roster of 49: Lady Gregory again (though represented this time by *The Rising of the Moon*), *Top Girls* again and *A Raisin in the Sun* again, along with Aphra Behn's *The Rover* (perhaps now the most oft-anthologised play by a woman writer), Susan Glaspell's *Trifles*, Marsha Norman's *Night Mother*, Maria Irene Fornes's *The Conduct of Life*, Suzan Lori-Parks's *The Death of the Last Black Man in the Whole Entire World* and Anna Deveare Smith's *Twilight: Los Angeles, 1992*. Notwithstanding, in the North American academic market at least, the huge push for a racial and cultural diversity that extends the mandate of these anthologies way beyond 'sensitivity' to gender issues, the last two choices in *The Bedford Introduction* indicate just how far we've come in the representation of dramatic 'literature' by women. The standard for anthologies has come to include playwriting in a variety of formats often far beyond the classical tragedies and comedies of Western stages that characterised earlier invocations of 'masterpieces' and, furthermore, without the usual conditions of mainstream theatrical success as a precondition of anthologisation. This in itself surely contributes to a different notion – and, indeed, a different impact – of theatre history.

I do not want to deny or diminish any of these very real achievements or to see this as other than progress – insidious word though that is. In fact, I want to acknowledge unequivocally my debt to those ground-breaking endeavours which have made it a great deal easier – though not always easy – to do scholarly work about and with women. What interests me here are the implications of these changes and shifts. I am concerned with both the structures of inclusivity which have characterised revisionist work *and* with the very theoretical framework by which scholarship has presented its findings about women's dramatic writing. In both contexts, I think, we need to address explicitly the assumptions and, importantly, the limitations, of historiography. The destination of such an endeavour is a point where we might reconceptualise what gets called theatre history. Bratton makes a related point in her discussion of the rewriting of nineteenth-century theatre history: 'There is a new history in the making and if it is an appendix or supplement, then it is so in a Derridean sense – it will eventually supplant what it was supposed to subserve.'[13] That seems to me to be exactly right; what is less clear, however, is how we, as feminist theatre historians, impel that eventuality where supplement both exceeds and revisions its own terms. Only then might we be said to have a history that delivers, in a full and functional sense, the presence of women's dramatic writing.

Before elucidating such questions of inclusivity, theory and history, I want to refer briefly to some key iterations of historiographic method and, in particular, to where those methods have been identified in the arena of feminist thinking. Historiography, as Michel De Certeau puts it, 'takes for granted that the place where it is itself produced has the capacity to provide meaning, since the current institutional demarcations of the discipline uphold the divisions of time and space in the last resort'. The problem historians must confront, as De Certeau argues, is the passing off, in the writing of history, of fiction as the 'real'. Historiography, then, 'legitimises' a place, that of its production, by 'including' others in a relation of filiation or of exteriority. It is authorised by this place which allows it to explain whatever is different as 'foreign', and whatever is inside as 'unique'.[14] It is this dynamic of filiation which most interests me in the production of new histories of women's dramatic writing. Self-evidently, it is a kind of filial relation that is evoked by canon expansion. In this setting, women's dramatic writing is almost never categorised as 'unique' – I cannot think of a single example – but it is generally categorised only inasmuch as it meets – or charmingly fails – the criteria that men's plays and male-authored dramatic theory have laid down as exemplary for a given historical moment or for a particular trajectory of dramatic genre. We might remember, for example, that Aristotle's precepts remain the *sine qua non* for tragedy.

A filiation which is produced in the organisation of discourse employed in the categorisation, characterisation and analysis of those same texts by women is perhaps somewhat less transparent. The critical endeavour might appear to be more easily committed to revisionist aims through its multiplicity of approaches to its subject texts and by the mere insistence on bringing these women's plays to our scholarly atten-tion. But the risks (captured well in this idea of filiation) are equally present. The potentials of narrative are ably demonstrated in Kearns's hopes for history's recovery from its own aporia and amnesia:

> Perhaps only a non-historian, by definition already capable of the considerable promiscuities associated with literature and literary criti-cism, could imagine a historian capable of both a commitment to the necessity and value of theory and a commitment to the necessity and value of narrative: this would be the historian who combines theory and history, psychoanalysis and history, not in the same texts but concur-rently. This will not happen as long as even the most self-aware, analyti-cally astute writers remain within a conceptual scheme that subordinates story-telling to some fantasy of attainable truth and that locates narrative only as relative to, at most in an asymptotic relation-ship with, more powerful, more 'masculine' modes of assessment.[15]

Into infinity, then, goes criticism and analysis following but never reach-ing, related but never definitive to, the curve of theatre history. Like Kearns, I see the task as one that must draw emphatically not on notions of 'truth' or 'fact', but on what history most fears: imagination. How can we imaginatively reconceive theatre history itself in order to make the new questions we should ask of women's dramatic writing not only possible but self-evident? This is, after all, a direction in which a more rigorous historiography might lead us.

To retrace my steps briefly, then, theatre history and the canon of dramatic literature have changed indelibly thanks to scholarly work on texts by women playwrights; some of this has been archival and some has been critical. In both instances, this is labour that De Certeau would characterise in terms of minority discourse – 'where historiographical discourse treats matters that put the subject-producer of history into question'[16] and which Joan Scott would describe as a 'mission'. Scott suggests that these historians 'documenting the lives of those omitted or overlooked in accounts of the past' have produced 'a wealth of new evidence previously ignored about these others and has drawn attention to dimensions of human life and activity usually deemed unworthy of mention in conventional histories'.[17] And, for many of us, there has, indeed, been a kind of missionary zeal about producing editions of plays by women, writing books on women playwrights, creating curriculum from this work and, of course, insisting on the representation of women (and other so-called minorities) in survey courses of any and all periods.

This strategy whereby we document what has been previously excluded or ignored has led, obviously, to the virtual revolution in what goes into our foundational anthologies of dramatic literature as a whole, but also of specific periods and genres. What is interesting about the particular example of comprehensive dramatic literature anthologies is a homogeneity of selection even when the necessity of expansion is admitted. It would be hard, I suspect, to find an anthology without Aphra Behn and/or Caryl Churchill (and, equally, almost always in the examples of *The Rover* and *Top Girls*) followed by a second tier of women playwrights comprising Susan Glaspell, Augusta (Lady) Gregory, Lorraine Hansberry and, perhaps of late, Maria Irene Fornes. And, it seems to me, that there is no great magic here that accounts for a new 'universal' approval rating for these particular women writers. It is not, or at least not necessarily, that these are the most accomplished playwrights or these anthologised examples their best plays, somehow commonly recognised by the computed evaluative criteria either articulated or assumed by the anthology itself. More accurately, it is, as Joan Scott suggests, that:

> [t]he challenge to normative history has been described, in terms of conventional historical understandings of evidence, as an enlargement of the picture, a corrective to oversights resulting from inaccurate or incomplete vision, and it has rested its claim to legitimacy on the authority of experience, the direct experience of others, as well as of the historian who learns to see and illuminate the lives of those others in his or her texts. [18]

In other words, it is to be expected that those plays which gain admission into the now more inclusive canon will do so because of some performance of a filial relation either by the play, the playwright, or the editor. It is virtually impossible, apparently, to avoid the drive to measure these new canonical stars against their male-authored counterparts or to resist their contextualisation by the conditions we have historically identified as relevant to an understanding of drama and theatre. So, despite *knowing* that there is other work to be done, historiographic method inevitably pulls our history – even our alternative histories – back into the trajectory of what has always already been known.

This antagonistic relation – but, nonetheless, a relation – is palpable in the instructions editors Susan L. Cocalis and Ferrel Rose gave to other essayists in their volume *Thalia's Daughters: German Women Dramatists from the Eighteenth Century to the Present*: '[W]e requested that the contributors focus on one author and examine one or more of her dramatic texts in the context of her life, other works, and times. We also recommended that, wherever possible, the subject be situated within the history of the German theater'.[19] By this kind of impetus, even the most anomalous text can be explained in relation to what Kearns calls 'more "masculine" forms of assessment'.[20] Inevitably theatre history, as it has been understood, is supplemented rather than supplanted.

Let me state again that it is not that this is inappropriate. This is precisely the procedure which has led to revisions of what we understand as the canon as well as what it might at any moment be said to contain as its subject texts. It is just that this is so partial. Partial in its preference (willing or resigned) for the categorical organisation that has preceded its endeavour (theatre history lying in wait for the discovery of women's plays) and partial in its representation of what those texts are or can be. De Certeau is again pertinent: 'The subject is constructed as a stratification of heterogeneous moments'.[21] Minority discourse, he suggests, has the potential to write the subject as multiple and to render identity, in any simple sense, impossible. This, it seems to me, is one crucial, if enormously difficult, challenge for the historian (or critic, archivist, director or teacher) of women's plays. How do we render that stratification of heterogeneity? Not by writing the plays into theatre history or even revisionist theatre history – or, in any event, not until we have reconceptualised theatre history in a way that might imaginatively recognise some of its own totalising or reductionist impulses. Jean Howard urges feminist scholars 'to remake the very categories through which the past is discursively constituted', albeit with the observation that '[w]hile this may sound like a straightforward enough project, it, of course, is not'.[22]

In part, this project demands that we perform as archaeologists, in the Foucauldian sense of that term. Such a mandate, above all else, requires an interdisciplinary agility that few scholars, as yet, have been trained to perform. But feminist scholars have seldom hesitated at the seeming impossibility of their task. So what directions must we pursue in order to detour from theatre history's well-trodden if slightly re-routed path and to recontextualise or stratify the subjects of our investigations? I am both persuaded and encouraged by an argument made by Sarah Davies Cordova in the characterisation of her own work on the lives of nineteenth-century ballet dancers. Davies Cordova looks to the process of what she calls 'autobiographing'. This action, she suggests, 'relates a cumulation of artifacts (memoirs, letters, contracts, documentation on salaries and pensions, newspaper articles, guide books, realist fiction, historical and medical texts) to register the gaps in stereotypic depictions of nineteenth-century dancers. These lacunae which emerge from the cliched evanescence of dance and the monoscopic visualisation of the dancing body register the absence of women's experience of the dance as spectatrices and professional performers'.[23] This, then, like the Cerasano/Wynne-Davies volume on women's involvement in Renaissance drama, insists on the multiple contributions of women to the cultural practice we recognise as dance. The dancer is present not just as the ballerina, object *par excellence* of the male gaze, but as, too, a looker in her own right and, further, as a powerful subject constituted by and constitutive of a particular profession whose life must be read in the economic conditions of its enactment. More important, still, is the means by which Davies Cordova achieves her depiction of the female dancer as a complex subject. The list that she has so far created could, obviously, be more or less infinitely extended but not in an asymptotic relation to dance history *per se*, but instead in its intersections and head-on confrontations with that history which take us far beyond the usual scope of evidence that the diligent (revisionist) historian might be expected to consult. Moreover, her project insists on the imagination of a life precisely made from all of the contradictions that such evidence will certainly provide; in short, it is the lack of fit in her historical context that animates the dancer. Once animated, the dancer's life might graph a history of her movements.

Thus, and more provocatively yet, Davies Cordova asserts that

> [t]he gerund in 'autobiographing' inflects an intratextual practice of interpretation which does not privilege autobiography, biography or fiction, but which takes the corporeal, the textual and the visual together in their status   as socio-cultural records to examine the double binds of the nineteenth-century dancer. The composite of corporeality viewed and written with the body-at-dance and at-work graphs a complex of a

self who danced and experienced the nineteenth century as working woman. Such a representation situates her identity as inherently fractured and multiple.[24]

This is surely exactly what De Certeau was describing as a subject and where Kearns hopes history might get made.

In theatre studies, there have been some landmark books on the profession of women actors. Tracy C. Davis's *Actresses as Working Women* remains paramount in this area while other, more recent volumes have contributed further elaboration in particular historical contexts (and I think here of Faye Dudden's excellent study, *Women in the American Theatre: Actresses and Audiences 1790–1870*).[25] From such supplemental evidence, we must begin to devise that new history which would supplant our received knowledge of the actress's contribution to theatre and which instead promotes the heterogeneity of her cultural experiences. It is the insistence on a complex rendition of corporeality that promises to extend and disturb historiographical method beyond its usual evidence. I think that the cumulative effect of feminist scholarship in this area will provide us with a framework for new questions (those that go further than asking 'what did women do?') and these may well be the fundamental ones for a new trajectory through theatre history. In this context, it is useful to refer again to Joan Scott's interrogation of 'experience'. She reminds us that:

> When experience is taken as the origin of knowledge, the vision of the individual subject (the person who had the experience or the historian who recounts it) becomes the bedrock of evidence upon which explanation is built … The evidence of experience then becomes evidence for the fact of difference rather than a way of exploring how difference is established, how it operates, how and in what ways it constitutes subjects who see and act in the world.[26]

Where a project such as Davies Cordova's takes us, then, is not only to evidence drawn from a startlingly wide range of traditional and non-traditional sources but also to the employment of that evidence to pose questions about the very system under investigation – in her case, 'the dancer' – and its historicity. How did that art form, ballet, become sedimented in Western culture? How did its differences (between male and female dancers, between ballet and other forms of dance, among others) operate and, further, enforce through its generic codes certain normative gender practices? In other words, this kind of revisionist scholarship produces not (or, not just) a series of narratives about particular figures for whom we have wide-ranging evidence that claims an historical 'real' for our fiction, but also an interrogation of the historical process itself. Instead of understanding, say, a single dancer in a filial relation to the genre 'dance' (which, needless to say, has itself a history), we rewrite or animate that woman as social agent in the very construction of her subject ('dance') and her subjectivity (as working woman). As Scott says, 'Experience is at once always already an interpretation *and* is in need of interpretation'.[27]

Historiography, then, is both a road block and a means to reinvigorating theatre history, energising the supplement that would, in the end, revolutionise the very terms and conditions under which the narratives of history are constructed and made to mean. As Mark Poster observers, '[w]hen a theorist asks a new question that opens a new field, the archives are redefined. The same materials that were used to investigate one question are now redeployed in another research context'.[28] The cumulation of work over the last twenty years has brought us an altogether richer archive; we have been less successful in redefining that archive or, at least, in redefining it in ways that challenge the customary impulses and agendas of theatre history. Instead of bringing those materials – the artefactual elements that give evidence to women's contribution to the business of theatre – under the scrutiny of the narrative we have always thought of as 'theatre history', it is now our challenge to ask those new questions which will redeploy the archive in a different history, wrought by an explicitly feminist historiography.

Davies Cordova's iteration of the nineteenth-century dancer is one model for such a project for new histories of women's cultural production. Another is to return to those very constituents of the history to which women have not belonged, even supplementally, until so recently, and to open up the taxonomy of its operations. It is certainly not beyond imagination to predict a detailed dissection of those categories which have attained particular significance in the articulation of Western theatre history, whatever its moment or specific geographic location. For example, we pay especial attention to the architecture and other contextual elements of public performance spaces. How can this be other than a gendered history when the history of women has been, for so long, one of domesticity and private space?

Similarly we can respond to Daniel Woolf's observation that ' the making of modern genres is … intimately bound up with the making of modern gender'.[29] When we apply a category to playwriting by women – be that tragedy, comedy, or performance art – by whose definitions do we understand those genres? Until now, I would like to suggest, it is almost always as male theorists defined them and as scholars we struggle to demonstrate how women's plays are deserving of those genres (the very markers of a brand of credibility) at the very same time we urge recognition of these same plays as *different* (often read, alas, as an explanation for why these women's plays are, say, not such accomplished tragedies as those of Shakespeare or whomever). Even in something as new as performance art, we have hastened to make particular claims for *feminist* performance art, once again a supplemental and filial relation to the 'real thing'. What does it mean to adopt these pre-existing organisational structures in order to attach the prefix ' feminist' to their conditions? Who gets lost in the necessary shuffle and how does this abet the relentless progression of a theatre history that insists on telling its singular story using a tenacious and apparently unmalleable plot line? Even if we agree to distinctions such as professional and amateur, how women have participated in that discursive history often flies in the face of the category's common-sense understanding. For example, Davis and Joyce observe about the *Parlor Charades* of Sarah Annie Shields that '[h]er work is for amateur players; she was not an amateur playwright'.[30] Perhaps ironically, it is by going back to history that we can find some other ways to proceed in this task. How did women in the past think of history? How did they give significance to the archive as they gained access to it? How has historical knowledge been configured in the particular circumstances of gender? Woolf states: 'The family therefore lay at the heart of the female understanding of the past; affective ties in the present provided a lens through which history could be "domesticated."' This same perspective was applied to episodes from history proper when women read about them. The commonplace book of Jacobean gentlewoman Lady Anne Southwell, for example, contains verses on Julius Caesar that highlight the private and emotive'.[31] This suggests that we need to revisit women's renditions of history (especially those conveyed in the less public venue of commonplace book, diary, memoir and the like) and tease out the very terms under which those women saw their history and themselves as part of it.

Here, then, are a number of locations where theatre history might be both deconstructed and revisioned. Without changes to the very practice of history, women's dramatic writing will ever linger in its filial relation to the received history which has, under pressure, come to accommodate it. Jean Howard concludes her article on feminism and history with a charge to take 'responsibility for making knowledge from some place, for some purpose'[32] and feminist theatre historians are well placed to do precisely this. Our scholarship over the last twenty years has not only described the wealth of materials on which we can productively work, but it has begun to make clear the broader claims of history that rely on certain unarticulated assumptions and which do not – and will not – ever stand in service of women's work.

Notes

1 Robert White, 'The State of English Studies in the 1990s', in *Knowing Ourselves and Others: The Humanities into the 21st Century*, Vol. 2, p. 6: http://www.asap.unimelb.edu.au/aah/research/review/b10_white.html

2 Katherine Kearns, *Psychoanalysis, Historiography, and Feminist Theory: The Search for Critical Method* (Cambridge, Cambridge University Press, 1997), p. 32.

3 S. P. Cerasano and Marion Wynne-Davies, eds, *Renaissance Drama by Women: Texts and Documents* (London, Routledge, 1996).

4 Jean E. Howard, 'Women as Spectators, Spectacles, and Paying Customers', in David Scott Kastan and Peter Stallybrass, eds, *Staging the Renaissance: Reinterpretations of Elizabethan and Jacobean Drama* (London, Routledge, 1991), pp. 68–74.

5 Cerasano and Wynne-Davies, *Renaissance Drama by Women*, p. 5.

6 Gwenn Davis and Beverly A. Joyce, *Drama by Women to 1900: A Bibliography of American and British Writers* (Toronto, University of Toronto Press, 1992), p. viii.

7 Virginia Blain, Patricia Clements and Isobel Grundy, *The Feminist Companion to Literature: Women Writers from the Middle Ages to the Present* (New Haven, Yale University Press, 1990).

8 Elaine Aston, *An Introduction to Feminism and Theatre* (London, Routledge, 1995); Charlotte Canning, *Feminist Theatres in the USA: Staging Women's Experience* (London, Routledge, 1996); Lizbeth Goodman, *Contemporary Feminist Theatres: To Each Her Own* (London, Routledge, 1993) and Peta Tait, *Converging Realities: Feminism in Australian Theatre* (Sydney, Currency Press, 1994).

9 J. S. Bratton, 'Women on Stage: Historiography and Feminist Revisionism', *Theatre Notebook*, Vol. L:2 (1996), pp. 62–5, p. 63.

10 Joan W. Scott, *Gender and the Politics of History* (New York, Columbia University Press, 1988), p. 29.

11 Alexander W. Allison, Arthur J. Carr and Arthur M. Eastman, eds, *Masterpieces of the Drama*, 4th ed. (New York, Macmillan, 1979); 6th ed. (New York, Prentice Hall, 1991).

12 Lee A. Jacobus, ed., *The Bedford Introduction to Drama* (Boston, Bedford Inc., 1996).

13 Bratton, 'Women on Stage, p. 65.

14 Michel De Certeau, *The Writing of History*, trans. Tom Conley (New York, Columbia University Press, 1988), p. 343.

15 Kearns, *Psychoanalysis, Historiography, and Feminist Theory*, p. 166.

16 Michel De Certeau *Heterologies: Discourse on the Other*, trans. Brian Massumi (Minneapolis, University of Minnesota Press, 1986), p. 217.

17 Scott, *Gender and the Politics of History*, p. 24.

18 *Ibid.*, p. 24.

19 Susan L. Cocalis, and Rose Ferrel, eds, *Thalia's Daughters: German Women Dramatists from the Eighteenth Century to the Present* (Tubingen, A. Francke Verlag, 1996), p. 2.

20 Kearns, *Psychoanalysis, Historiography, and Feminist Theory*, p. 166.

21 De Certeau, *Heterologies*, p. 218.

22 Jean E. Howard, 'Feminism and the Question of History: Resituating the Debate', *Women's Studies: An Interdisciplinary Journal*, 19:2 (1991), pp. 149–57, p. 151.

23 Sarah Davies Cordova, Talk at 'Foothills and Footsteps: New Writings in Dance Studies' conference, University of Calgary, January 1999. Forthcoming from the Banff Centre Press.

24 *Ibid.*

25 Tracy C. Davis, *Actresses as Working Women: Their Social Identity in Victorian Culture* (London, Routledge, 1993), and Faye Dudden, *Women in the American Theatre: Actresses and Audiences 1790–1870* (New Haven, Yale University Press, 1997).

26 Joan W. Scott, 'Experience', in Judith Butler and Joan W. Scott, eds., *Feminists Theorize the Political* (London, Routledge, 1992), pp. 22–40, p. 25.

27 *Ibid.*, p. 35.

28 Mark Poster, *Cultural History and Postmodernity: Disciplinary Readings and Challenges* (New York, Columbia University Press, 1997), p. 156.

29 D. R. Woolf, 'A Feminine Past? Gender, Genre, and Historical Knowledge in English, 1500–1800', *American Historical Review*, 102:3 (June 1997), pp. 645–79, p. 647.

30 Davis and Joyce, *Drama by Women to 1900*, p. xvii.

31 Woolf, 'A Feminine Past?' p. 655.

32 Howard, 'Feminism and the Question of History', p. 156.

4

WILHEMINE SCHRÖDER-DEVRIENT: WAGNER'S THEATRICAL MUSE

Susan A. Rutherford

To the comrades before whom I lay this string of thoughts upon their art I believe I finally can no better express my friendly feelings of esteem, than by herewith dedicating it *to the memory of the great Wilhemine Schröder-Devrient.* (Richard Wagner, *On Actors and Singers* (1872))[1]

Richard Wagner's dedication of his essay 'On Actors and Singers' to Wilhemine Schröder-Devrient was far from the only reference he made to his admiration for this German soprano. As we shall see, he credited her with inspiring his entire understanding and philosophy of the nature of theatrical art, as well as having influenced his broader personal and cultural development: 'I owe many of my life's impressions solely to her', he claimed in 1872.[2] 'Muse' therefore seems a fitting description of Schröder-Devrient's role in Wagner's life and work – although positioning the female artist in such a relationship to male endeavour may appear provocative to the feminist reader. Marcia Citron reminds us that the traditional notion of woman as muse to the male composer has been a limiting factor in the development of women's own artistic growth: 'The idealization of musical women as inspiration of male creativity and as reproducers of their music provided a means of displacing the threat of female creativity.'[3] Must we then (as Citron suggests women composers should do to free themselves from the limitations of this role) 'murder the image' of Schröder-Devrient as Wagner's muse in order to release her own creative history? Or rather (as I hope to demonstrate here) might proper investigation of the muse and her bemused acolyte shed new light on both female and male creativity?

If we are to understand Schröder-Devrient's contribution to the operatic stage of the nineteenth century as well as to the development of Wagner's concepts and compositions, we certainly need to rewrite history. Previous chroniclers of her relationship with Wagner have demonstrated the kind of bias against or misinterpretation of female artists which is all too familiar to the modern theatre historian. In works such as William Ashton Ellis's translation and reworking of C. F. Glasenapp's *Life of Richard Wagner* (1900–08), Ernest Newman's *The Life of Richard Wagner* (1933), and even Martin Gregor-Dellin's *Richard Wagner: His Life, His Work, His Century* (1983), Schröder-Devrient is presented in largely patronising and antipathetic terms: variously, she appears as a temperamental, promiscuous, foul-mouthed, shallow woman of limited talent. (Something of Newman's attitude might be gleaned from the phrase 'with the caprice of her sex and her profession', which he employs to describe one of Schröder-Devrient's decisions.)[4] More recent scholars such as John Deathridge, Barry Millington and Jean-Jacques Nattiez have adopted a different tack: by disputing the veracity of Wagner's own account of his first encounter with her performance style, the effect and importance of Schröder-Devrient's influence on the composer has become displaced – even, perhaps, dismissed – in the necessary search to dispel the 'myths' that surround Wagner.[5] Most surprising of all is that Dieter Borchmeyer's long analysis of Wagner's relationship with theatre contains only one brief reference to this soprano.[6] A few historians have dealt more fairly with Schröder-Devrient. Both Arthur Symons and Geoffrey Skelton acknowledge the impact the singer made on Wagner's theories of dramatic performance;[7] whilst Henry Pleasants offers a measured though brief summary of her career.[8] What is missing from these and other writings, however, is a thorough analysis of Schröder-Devrient's modes of performance within the historical context of theatrical practice, and the precise nature of her subsequent influence on the composer. The purpose of this essay is to identify the kind of terrain such an inquiry might cover.

First, a brief biography. Like many singers of her era, Wilhemine Schröder-Devrient (1804–60) was the child of professional artistes – Sophie Burger Schröder, one of the most famous German actresses of her generation, and Friedrich Schröder, an accomplished operatic baritone. The young Wilhemine accordingly acquired her own stage experience from an early age, as a child dancer and later as an actress at the Burgtheater in Vienna, performing such roles as Ophelia and Beatrice.[9] It was also in Vienna that she made her operatic debut in 1821, as Pamina in *Die Zäuberflöte* (Mozart) at the Kärntnertortheater. Two important performances during the following year – as Agathe in Weber's *Der Freischütz* (conducted by the composer) and Leonore in Beethoven's

Fidelio (attended by the composer) – marked the beginning of her international reputation. Across the ensuing twenty-six years Schröder-Devrient sang in the major opera houses of Germany, Italy, Paris, London, Vienna and Prague; and she became acquainted with many of the leading composers of the day, including Weber, Beethoven, Benedict, Liszt, Berlioz, Spontini, Meyerbeer, Mendelssohn, Schumann, Chopin and, of course, Wagner. Her working relationship with Wagner began in 1834 when she first sang as a guest artist under his musical direction at Magdeburg; later in Dresden she created three Wagnerian roles: Adriano in *Rienzi* (1842), Senta in *Der fliegende Holländer* (1843) and Venus in *Tannhäuser* (1845). Her final operatic performance appears to have taken place in Riga in 1847; her concert career continued for some years following. She died in 1860 at the age of fifty-six.

Accounts of her personal life vary. In the memoirs of Wagner, she appears as possessing a ready wit, fluency in several languages and being 'charitable to the point of royal lavishness' in her dealings with others.[10] She seems to have been married on at least three occasions: in 1823 to Karl Devrient, a fellow singer and actor who divorced her for adultery five years later; then in 1844 to Lieutenant von Döring, an adventurer who managed to gain control of her money and pensions; and finally to von Bock, a Livonian landowner. There were also a number of liaisons with other men.[11] She may have had one or four children by her first marriage; custody was supposedly awarded to her former husband. She 'resented' the scandal created by this divorce, arguing 'that she could produce the extraordinary on the stage only because she experienced it in real life', and that she should not be expected to abide by the rules of bourgeois conventionality, 'for in that kind of life there is no grist for my art'.[12] In 1849 she was arraigned for 'high treason on the grounds of incitement to revolt' for public speeches she made during the uprising in Dresden, following an episode when troops fired on the populace.[13] An anonymous volume of pornography entitled *A Singer's Memoirs* that was published after her death was attributed (almost certainly wrongly) to her authorship.[14]

Schröder-Devrient and Wagner

One area a full study of Schröder-Devrient might seek to clarify is that of the initial contact between Richard Wagner (1813–83) and the singer. In his autobiography, Wagner recorded the impact that his first sight of Schröder-Devrient in performance had made on him:

When I look back across my entire life I find no event to place beside this in the impression it produced on me. Whoever can remember this wonderful woman at that period of her life will certainly confirm in some fashion the almost demonic fire irresistibly kindled in them by the profoundly human and ecstatic performance of this incomparable artist. After the opera was over I dashed to the home of one of my friends to write a short letter in which I told her succinctly that if ever she should hear my name favorably mentioned in the world of art, she should remember that she had on this evening made of me that which I had now vowed to become.[15]

From this moment onwards, Wagner claimed his ambition was 'to write a work that would be worthy of Schröder-Devrient.[16]

This encounter has been much disputed in recent times. Wagner implies that the performance took place at the Stadttheater in Leipzig when Schröder-Devrient, a member of the Dresden Hoftheater, appeared as a guest artist in the role of Leonore in Beethoven's *Fidelio* in 1829. However, Deathridge argues that neither theatre records nor Wagner's own diary confirm this event, and that it was a much later performance by Schröder-Devrient as Romeo in Bellini's *I Capuleti e i Montecchi* in 1834 that sparked the composer's admiration. He reasons that Wagner's use of Schröder-Devrient's enactment of Leonore at this juncture of his autobiography was a fabrication designed 'to make his supposed inheritance of Beethoven's legacy, and with it his destiny as the creator of a specifically German music drama, seem inevitable from the outset'.[17] Deathridge's interpretation now seems to be the prevailing one, but Klaus Kropfinger challenged many aspects of it in 1991: notably, that Wagner 'did not record every major event' in his diary, that there is an eleven-day gap in the theatre records in 1829 during which a performance of *Fidelio* may have taken place, that Schröder-Devrient may have 'stepped in at short notice' to cover for another artist and may therefore simply have been omitted from the records and press notices, and that if not in Leipzig, Wagner may well have seen the soprano in this role in Dresden that year.[18] I would add that as Wagner had already made much of Beethoven's influence in the early pages of his autobiography prior to his discussion of Schröder-Devrient, the notion that he needed further to underline his German musical heritage seems exaggerated. If the account of this encounter was falsified, perhaps the real reason was that Leonore was the role in which Schröder-Devrient achieved her greatest fame and which to Wagner's mind revealed the extent of her originality.

Whatever the truth of this incident, Wagner's subsequent and constant references to Schröder-Devrient in his autobiography, his writings on music and drama, and in conversation to his wife Cosima emphasise the importance of the relationship between singer and composer. No other male composer of his era acknowledged the impact and influence of a female artist on their own creativity in similar terms. But why did Schröder-Devrient produce such an effect on Wagner? What special attributes or innovations did she bring to the operatic stage of this period? And how far did her notion of performance imbue Wagner's own work?

Schröder-Devrient as singing actress

There are fortunately a variety of descriptions from different sources that enable us to build a relatively detailed picture of Schröder-Devrient's performing style – albeit within the usual limitations set by historical distance. We know from H. F. Chorley's account of her appearances in London in 1832 that though her face was 'plain', it was nevertheless 'pleasing, from the intensity of expression which her large features and deep tender eyes conveyed'; that she had 'profuse fair hair, the value of which she thoroughly understood – delighting in moments of great emotion, to fling it loose with the wild vehemence of a Maenad'; and that her 'figure was superb, though full, and she rejoiced in its display'.[19] He is less appreciative of Schröder-Devrient's vocal abilities; indeed, he claims that in contrast with other northern European artists such as Henrietta Sontag (1806–54) and Jenny Lind (1820–87), she had never 'learned to sing': 'Her tones were delivered without any care, save to give them due force. There was an air of strain and spasm throughout her performances – of that struggle for victory which never conquers.'[20] But Chorley's ambivalence was not echoed by Wagner:

> I have again and again been asked if her *voice* was really so remarkable, since we glorified her as a singer … No! She had no 'voice' at all; but she knew how to use her breath so beautifully, and to let a true womanly soul stream forth in such wondrous sounds, that we never thought of either voice or singing![21]

For Wagner, Schröder-Devrient's vocalising was merely part of her performance as a whole, and he viewed her concentration on the total effect of her operatic representations as something towards which every singer should strive. Her status as an unusually talented singing actress is confirmed by other commentators of the era. Clara Schumann regarded Schröder-Devrient as 'my ideal among dramatic singers';[22] Goethe applauded her private performance of Schubert's *Erlkönig* as a 'magnificent piece of artistry';[23] Weber claimed she was 'the best Agathe in the world [in *Der Freischütz*], and surpassed anything that I had conceived for the role'.[24] In his diary on 6 May 1833, the British actor William Macready recorded his disappointment at the 'unnatural gesticulation and redundant holding up of hands and beating of breasts' he had witnessed at a performance of *Fidelio* at Covent Garden, yet noted: 'Madame Schröder-Devrient is a splendid exception to the commonplace of the rest: it was as tender, animated, passionate and enthusiastic as acting in an opera could be – she quite abandoned herself to her feelings: she was admirable.'[25] An account of her performances in Monaco in 1836 in the Italian journal *La Moda* praised 'l'esattissima coerenza della sua caratteristica, nella quale tutto è preparato e connesso … nell unione del rappresentare drammatico e musicale, nessun la supera, e nessuna la pareggia nella verità della caratteristica' [*the very precise coherence of her portrayal in which everything is prepared and connected … in the union of drama and music on the stage, no one surpasses her, and no one equals her in the truthfulness of her rendition'*].[26]

Such comments are to be found in numerous reviews of the day, but they rarely reveal sufficient detail about the singer's performance. In his essay 'On Actors and Singers' (1872), however, Wagner offered the 'glorious' Schröder-Devrient as the exemplar of his 'every view on noble mimicry'.[27] We might tentatively read this essay therefore as a description of both the soprano's actual mode of performance as well as a delineation of the theories of dramatic art that Wagner developed from her example.

Wagner declared that 'all my knowledge of mimetic art (*des mimischen Wesens*) I owe to this grand woman; and through that teaching can I point to *truthfulness* as that art's foundation'.[28] This notion of 'truthfulness' does not of course wholly correspond to modern notions of realism. Wagner's ideas of histrionic display were formed in the 1830s and 1840s, when both the Italian and German operatic stages were victims of what he termed 'affectation'. For the Italian singers, acting 'is all done by rule; thus after a period of billing and cooing an explosion makes an incomparable effect; none of it has anything to do with real life, but then of course it is precisely that which makes it "art"'.[29] The German stage was equally beset by 'false pathos' or 'Effect', a legacy borne out of Goethe's requirements for stylised modes of performance and his

emphasis on the 'Ideal'.[30] Thus German singers 'do not articulate prop-
erly' nor do they 'know the meaning of their speeches', their sense of
character is merely that of 'general hazy outlines', and they think 'they
have sung quite "dramatically" if they bellow out the phrase's closing
note with an emphatic bid for applause'.[31]

In contrast, Schröder-Devrient offered Wagner a quite different
paradigm for his later efforts to revolutionise operatic staging in favour
of a freer, more spontaneous representation and a total commitment to
realising the 'art of the sublime Illusion'. Her 'truthfulness' lay in her
absolute absorption in her role, or 'self-divestment' as Wagner termed it,
leading him to describe acting as this 'wondrous playing with the Self,
wherein the player clean forgets himself'.[32] We have already seen
Macready's remark that Schröder-Devrient 'quite abandoned herself to
her feelings', but what seems to have struck her commentators most was
that her performances did not revolve purely around the 'active'
moments on stage – rather, she perceived her role as unending, as the
comments of the music critic Ludwig Rellstab (1799–1860) on her interpretation of Leonore revealed:

> Her part does not begin when she first speaks or sings, or has business to
> do; it never ceases so long as elements of the poem concern the charac-
> ter. Thus, her pantomime, in particular, establishes a chain of subtle
> devices which, when closely examined, are distinguished equally by
> organic homogeneity and imaginative variety. Every reference to the fate
> of the prisoner, every innocent utterance of the adoring Marzelline,
> finds a softly awakened echo in Leonore's features.[33]

Chorley also refers to this trait when he describes Schröder-Devrient's
'passion of by-play' in the same opera:

> Her eyes, quickened by the yearnings of her heart, were everywhere; her
> quivering lip, even when her countenance was the most guarded, told
> how intensely she was listening. It was impossible to hear the 'Prisoner's
> Chorus', as given by the Germans in London during that year, and to see
> the eager woman as she unclosed cell after cell, and ushered its ghastly
> tenants into the fresh air, questioning face after face, all in vain – without
> tears.[34]

Wagner cited a similar instance of the soprano's acting in the finale of
Der Freischütz, where Agathe 'has but twice to make herself heard';
Schröder-Devrient nevertheless invested so much detail in Agathe's
mute responses to the action that she 'expressed a poetry that none of us

had suspected in the drama'.[35] The special praise accorded to this aspect of Schröder-Devrient's performances implies that such detail was regarded as unusual on the operatic stage. This is not to suggest that she was displaying a wholly original approach within the broader context of dramatic performance in Europe: the acclaimed Dutch actress Johanna Wattier (1762–1827) was also commended for her 'perfection' as a 'silent participant in the stage action' when 'the eye and the mind of the majority [of spectators] were fixed on the speaking actor only'.[36]

Schröder-Devrient's more rounded approach to operatic acting was almost certainly a product of her family connections to the legitimate stage – not only through her mother but also by her marriage into one the most influential theatrical dynasties in Germany led by the actor Ludwig Devrient (1784–1832). One of his nephews, Karl (1797–1872), was Schröder-Devrient's first husband; another, Eduard (Karl's brother), was Oberregisseur für Schauspiel und Oper at the Dresden Hoftheater during the 1840s when both Schröder-Devrient and Wagner formed part of that company. Ludwig Devrient was part of a movement opposed to the stylisation of Goethe and the Weimar school, and eschewed the 'mosaic of single, carefully prepared movements' (or 'points') that were so much a part of eighteenth- and nineteenth-century dramatic performance; his nephew Eduard recalls that his 'performance issued solely from the nature and the inherent necessity of his characters as he had created them. He *lived* his parts, he did not *act* them'.[37] Something of that approach is visible from the above descriptions of Schröder-Devrient's methodology; she herself offered the following account of the processes that lay behind her interpretation of Leonore:

> When I was studying the character of Fidelio at Vienna … I could not attain that which appeared to me to be the desired and natural expression at the moment when Leonora (*sic*), throwing herself before her husband, holds out a pistol to the Governor, with the words 'Kill first his wife!' I studied and studied in vain, though I did all I could to place myself mentally in the situation of Leonora (*sic*). I had pictured to myself that situation, but I felt that it was incomplete, without knowing why or wherefore. Well, the evening arrived; the audience knows not with what feelings an artiste, who enters seriously into a part, dresses for the representation. The nearer the moment approached, the greater was my alarm. When it did arrive, and as I ought to have sung the ominous words, and pointed the pistol at the Governor, I fell into such utter tremor at the thought of not being perfect in my character, that my whole frame trembled, and I thought I should have fallen. Now, only

fancy how I felt when the whole house broke forth into enthusiastic
shouts of applause, and what I thought when, after the curtain fell, I was
told that this moment was the most effective and powerful of my whole
representation. So that which I could not attain with every effort of
mind and imagination, was produced at this decisive moment by my
unaffected terror and anxiety. This result, and the effect it had upon the
public, taught me how to seize and comprehend the incident, so that
which at the first representation I had hit upon unconsciously, I adopted
in full consciousness ever afterwards in this part.[38]

Schröder-Devrient's remarks here are interesting not only as an insight
into her performance process, but also because they reflect debates
concerning dramatic performance on the legitimate rather than the
operatic stage. Few singers (with the possible exception of the Spanish
prima donna Maria Malibran) of the era would have articulated the
histrionic element of their performance in such terms. Schröder-
Devrient, however, is describing a usage of the fusion between 'imagination and memory, character biography and autobiography' amidst the
'emerging psychology of the unconscious' which became a hallmark of
the new Romantic attitude to acting and which, via the French actor
François-Joseph Talma's 1825 edition of Lekain's memoirs, itself later
influenced Stanislavsky and his theories of 'affective memory'.[39]
Schröder-Devrient's physical (as well as mental) slippage into uncon-
sciousness at this point in *Fidelio* became enshrined as an essential part
of the opera's *mise-en-scène*, and was copied by other singers; it was
apparent as late as 1860 in a performance at Covent Garden by Rosa
Czillag (n.d.), who was commended for her 'half swoon' during her
encounter with Pizarro.[40] Of course, it should be argued such antics were
misplaced, and that their effectiveness with the mid-nineteenth-century
audience was due to the then current notions of womanhood which
required a more vulnerable Leonore than that originally conceived by
Beethoven. But if in this opera Schröder-Devrient seems to have
overemphasised the femininity of her characterisation, elsewhere her
commitment to 'truthfulness' and to exploring every nuance of the
dramatic action had a rather different effect. During the rehearsals of
Rienzi, where she was playing the *travesti* role of Adriano, Wagner
recorded with glee that 'at the end of the opera she intends to come
galloping on to the stage on horseback, riding *cross-saddle!*'.[41] Berlioz
complained about the 'exaggeration' of Schröder-Devrient's acting as
Valentine undermined the masculinity of her supposed father (Saint-
Bris) and husband (Nevers) in the conspiracy scene in a performance of

Les Huguenots (Meyerbeer) in Berlin in 1843. Schröder-Devrient's conception of the role seems to have been far from the 'timid woman' imagined by Berlioz: 'instead of masking her agitation and remaining almost passive, like other sensible tragediennes in this scene, Madame Devrient approaches Nevers, forces him to follow her to the back of the stage, and there, striding along beside him, appears to dictate to him both his line of conduct and his reply to Saint-Bris'. The result, Berlioz argued, was that Nevers 'only looks like a submissive husband repeating the lesson his wife has taught him'.[42]

Schröder-Devrient's status as an accomplished and original singing actress might be regarded as sufficient to explain Wagner's interest in her – especially when combined with her championship of his work and her willingness to lend the ever-penurious composer money. But it does not necessarily account for the sheer depth of his admiration for her: no other singer, despite his praise for their talents, ever occasioned the kind of comments he makes about this soprano. What, then, especially drew Wagner to Schröder-Devrient?

Perhaps he found in her what Roland Barthes terms the 'the grain of the voice' – that is, the 'the materiality of the body' which eludes the 'tyranny of meaning' and instead opens the way to '*jouissance*' and '*signifiance*'. Barthes ascribes this notion to the symbolic realm of the 'geno-song', as opposed to that of the culturally determined 'pheno-song' which encompasses 'everything in the performance which is in the service of communication, representation, expression'.[43] His remarks about the nature of *signifiance* offer a useful concept for interpreting the potency of Schröder-Devrient's singing for Wagner:

> The 'grain' of the voice is not – or is not merely – its timbre; the *signifiance* it opens cannot better be defined, indeed, than by the very friction between the music and something else, which something else is the particular language (and nowise the message). The song must speak, must *write* – for what is produced at the level of the geno-song is finally writing.[44]

This 'friction between the music and something else' is very apparent in Wagner's description of Schröder-Devrient's enactment of Leonore:

> She had often previously demonstrated what overwhelming effect can be produced by tones approaching pure speech in *Fidelio*, carrying the public away whenever, at the words 'One more step and you are dead!' she brought out the word 'dead' in her speaking rather than singing voice. The tremendous effect, to which I, of all people, was particularly

sensitive, was derived from the strange shock, like the blow of an execu-
tioner's axe, which I received at being abruptly brought down from the
exalted sphere into which music lifts even the most gruesome situations
to the bedrock of harshest reality. This gave a direct sensation of the
peak of sublimity which, in recalling this feeling, I can only describe as
the instant like a flash of lightning which, at the moment when two
utterly different worlds touch and yet are completely separate, illuminates them both for us simultaneously.[45]

Clearly, Schröder-Devrient's sudden, unlooked-for use of the spoken
word transcended the literal meaning of the text ('the message') and
revealed multiple meanings: in Barthes's words, 'meaning in its potential
voluptuousness'.[46] Its effect on Wagner, the shattering of his 'cultural
identity'[47] (his expectations as a nineteenth-century opera spectator), in
a 'sensation of the peak of sublimity', equally accords with Barthes's definition of the action of *signifiance* in promoting *jouissance*.

Not everyone experienced the same response to this element in
Schröder-Devrient's performances. Berlioz, one of her chief detractors,
found her transgressions of prevailing musical style exasperating; he
declared her singing not only to be 'often wanting in exactness and taste'
but also 'most anti-musical and trivial',[48] and disliked her 'spoken inter-
jections' intensely:

> She never sings *such* words as O God; yes; no; impossible! They are
> always spoken, or rather shouted in the loudest voice. I cannot express
> my aversion for this anti-musical declamation. To my mind it is a
> hundred times worse to speak in an opera than to sing in a tragedy ...[49]

The fact that reviewers such as Berlioz and Chorley found much to
complain about in Schröder-Devrient's performances is read by some
commentators as proof that Wagner's own critical faculties were in a
sense blinded by the singer.[50] This is not the case. In his autobiography
he acknowledges the limitations of her vocal technique and the mannerisms that had grown to pervade her acting by the time they came to
rehearse *Rienzi* in 1842. Nevertheless, such 'weaknesses' still did not
obscure for him the 'grand and incomparable element' in her performances which continued to bring him 'profound delight'.[51] Barthes makes
it plain that his notion of the 'grain of the voice' is an individual one, to
be accorded where the listener deems it appropriate;[52] and it seems clear
that whatever aspects of technical assurance and stylistic congruence
('pheno-song') might have been missing from Schröder-Devrient's
singing, for Wagner the visceral, irreducible nature of the 'grain' of her

voice ('geno-song') was ever-present. The question is perhaps not so much whether Wagner was short-sighted in his evaluation of this singer, but whether Berlioz, Chorley *et al.* could see beyond the 'tissue of cultural values (the matter of acknowledged tastes, of fashions, of critical commentaries)' of their period and recognise genuine originality.[53]

Schröder-Devrient as mythic sign

Barthes's assertion that 'what is produced at the level of the geno-song is finally writing'[54] perhaps also has a particular resonance for another aspect of the relationship between Wagner and Schröder-Devrient. It may seem fanciful to try and ascribe certain practices within Wagner's composition to the influence of this singer; nevertheless, it is a claim he was happy to make himself:

> Moreover, she had the gift of teaching a composer how to compose, to be worth the pains of such a woman's 'singing': this she did through that 'example' aforesaid, which she, the mime, gave this time to the drama-tist, and which, among all to whom she gave it, has been followed by *myself* alone.[55]

Wagner leaves us few clues to the precise meaning of this statement. One hint may be found in the comments he made to Cosima in 1878 on his earlier composition of *Tristan und Isolde* (1865): 'How did I ever achieve the rapture of the 2nd act? I know, it was through seeing Schröder-D. as Romeo, and it isn't so silly to have a woman in that role, for those little runts of men, and particularly tenors, can never do those lovely wild embraces.'[56] This indication that Schröder-Devrient's ardent performing style found musical manifestation in *Tristan und Isolde* is interesting not simply in itself, but also in the notion that operatic rep-resentation of impassioned masculinity in the latter part of the nine-teenth century might have been influenced by female performance of *travesti* roles.

But there may be other dimensions to Wagner's statement about Schröder-Devrient as exemplar for the composer. From *Rienzi* onwards, Wagner's operas are dominated by a specific kind of male hero – 'a great individual to whom there attaches both charisma and a stigma'.[57] Wagner's heroines of his middle to late operas – Senta, Elisabeth/Venus, Isolde, Brünnhilde and Kundry – are similarly closely matched in vocal and dramatic terms. Each is a strong-willed, passionate and sensual woman unafraid to break with convention in pursuit of the man she loves; each employs the powerful, dark-toned voice of the *hochdramatis-cher Sopran*. Jens Malte Fischer declares that this voice 'may seem to one person to be the crowning achievement of Wagner's female roles, to another a monumental misdevelopment straying far from the bel canto ideal'.[58] Until the 1840s, this '*bel canto* ideal' had been exemplified by the *coloratura* soprano, whose high clear tones and decorative embellishments conveniently provided a kind of musical depiction of nineteenth-century notions of femininity. By the end of the century, the pre-emininent female voice was that of the dramatic soprano – either the Italianate *spinto* utilised originally by Verdi, or the *hochdramatischer Sopran* of the German repertoire – which offered a richer, more incisive and vigorous aural delineation of womanhood.[59]

Vocally, Schröder-Devrient was almost certainly one of the prime models for Wagner's development of the *hochdramatischer Sopran* in his later operas. The low tessitura of several of her roles including Romeo in Bellini's *I Capuleti e i Montecchi*, Desdemona in Rossini's *Otello* and Adriano in *Rienzi* are evidence that she possessed the strong, warm middle register Fischer identifies as a necessary quality for this voice.[60] She also scored her first major successes in roles now commonly sung by dramatic sopranos, Leonore (*Fidelio*) and Agathe (*Der Freischütz*). Both these utilise the key of E major in the soprano's most important aria in each opera (respectively 'Abscheulicher!' and 'Leise, leise'): a key which is particularly favourable for this kind of voice because its tonic, subdominant and dominant triads in the upper register provide ample scope for the display of the dramatic soprano's most arresting and urgent tones.

We can to some extent still hear Schröder-Devrient's voice in the second and most successful of the Wagnerian roles she created and the role in which the true beginnings of the *hochdramatischer Sopran* might be discerned: Senta in *Der fliegende Holländer*. Although not specifically composed for this soprano, it bears the indelible traces of her influence. Senta's Ballad ('Traft ihr das Schiff?') was transposed down a tone from its original A minor to accommodate Schröder-Devrient's voice. Even in its original key, the aria did not challenge the highest reaches of the soprano range (it spanned c` to b``), but the lower tessitura of the transposition enables the heavier voice to float the *piano* phrases around f` and g`` in the 'Piu lento' sections more easily, as well as emphasising the strength and determination of Senta's character. In the duet with the Dutchman, the key of E major predominates (with modulations into related keys of E minor, B minor and B major), and certain musical phrases of Senta's part such as the final repetition of 'Wonach mit

Sehnsucht es dich treibt' bear a marked resemblance to the heroic passages in the arias for Leonore and Agathe – again suggesting that Schröder-Devrient (who for Wagner was identified closely with both these roles) had figured either consciously or unconsciously in the mind of the composer during the creative process.

Senta was also the character in which Wagner set out to construct a new kind of female protagonist he dubbed the 'woman of the future'. This was no 'home-tending Penelope of Ulysses', but rather the 'quintessence of womankind ... the still unmanifest, the longed-for, the dreamed-of, the infinitely womanly woman'.[61] Although hardly a feminist in the modern sense, Wagner's emphasis on 'womanliness' may obscure the fact that his notion of this quality was at variance with that of most bourgeois society. His final essay was in support of female emancipation, where he argued that woman was a 'victim of power structures determined according to masculine principles and reproduction' (he died before completing it);[62] years earlier he had sympathised with the plight of his sister Klara, whose career as an opera singer had ceased after a promising beginning, 'and who now had to drag herself along through life as a wife and mother in trivial domesticity'.[63] Senta too rejects the narrow domestic life at the side of her original betrothed, Erik, in favour of a grander, more daring adventure as the redeemer of the Dutchman; and Wagner urges that she should not be played with 'a modern, sickly sentimentality' but as a 'robust Northern maid'.[64] This was presumably Schröder-Devrient's reading (Wagner described her performance at the première as 'magnificent');[65] and the composer later claimed that the period of rehearsal he spent with her on this opera was 'one of the most exciting and, in many important respects, most instructive experiences of my life'.[66]

Whilst we cannot know precisely what Wagner might have learned from the singer during this time, the conjunction of his idea of the 'woman of the future' and Schröder-Devrient as its interpreter nevertheless bears some investigation. She was not, I think, Wagner's ideal woman, as his comments to Cosima following one of his many dreams of the singer years later reveal: he claims that she 'could never have aroused love longings in me, there was no longer enough modesty in her, no mystery in which to probe'.[67] Cosima herself, young, devoted and unquestioning ('Every utterance from him is doctrine to me', she wrote of her husband in her diary in 1871)[68] now fulfilled that role admirably. But Schröder-Devrient was arguably Wagner's ideal heroine: tempestuous, passionate, unconventional, exacting.[69] He was relatively undisturbed by her distance from the 'feminine ideal'. Although dismayed by her use of strong language, he nevertheless recognised it as common backstage parlance;[70] he excused her promiscuity on the grounds that it was an understandable trait in one so gifted ('for such a person, with that formidable talent, there was only one possible compensation, and that was sensuousness; without this she would have been unable to bear it');[71] and rather than condemning her as a difficult colleague, he seems to have admired the fact that she 'could not bear slapdash work'.[72]

Yet Schröder-Devrient's unconventionality as a woman was perhaps acceptable only because of her other persona as an artist – even more specifically, for Wagner, in her identity as what might be termed 'Wilhemine/Leonore'. I suggest that the lasting impression that Schröder-Devrient made on Wagner through her performances of Leonore was not due simply to her histrionic ability or even her demonstration of the 'grain of the voice'; rather, it was these qualities as they were used to enact a particular female character, whose mission was to secure the release of her imprisoned husband. Wilhemine/Leonore is thus the coalescence of two identities (singer and role, real and fictional) into a third mythic sign of exalted, selfless but extraordinary womanhood. Barthes's discussion of myth as a 'second-order semiological system'[73] (Figure 1a) offers a way of delineating the development of this relationship and theorising about the possible framework of Wagner's perception of Schröder-Devrient, as Figure 1b demonstrates. Figure 1c extends this notion into further, more contentious speculation of the influence of Wilhemine/Leonore in the construction of Wagnerian heroines, of which there is space to offer only a fragmentary discussion here. Leonore restores life, love and sanity to Florestan when she rescues him from Pizarro's dungeon; and this vision of woman as the architect of man's salvation is evident as a central thesis in various Wagnerian operas, noticeably *Der fliegende Holländer*, *Tannhäuser*, *Tristan und Isolde*, *Der Ring* and *Parsifal*. Writing about *Der Ring* (1869–76), Wagner declared that 'man by himself' was not 'the complete human being' but 'merely the half': 'To the isolated being not all things are possible; there is need of more than one, and it is woman, suffering and willing to sacrifice herself, who becomes at last the real, conscious redeemer: for what is love itself but the "eternal feminine" (*das ewig Weibliche*)'.[74] Such ideas sit oddly with contemporary feminism; nevertheless, their embodiment as the warrior-woman Brünnhilde became the most powerful operatic heroine of the late nineteenth- and early twentieth-century stage,

1a

1. Signifier	2. Signified

Language {

3. Sign
I SIGNIFIER · II SIGNIFIED

Myth {

III SIGN

Barthes' 'second-order semiological system'

1b

artist	woman

Schröder-Devrient · Leonore

WILHEMINE/LEONORE

Rutherford after Barthes I

1c

Wilhemine/ Leonore	Nordic myth of Senta

SENTA
'woman of the future' · Brünnhilde

BRÜNNHILDE

Rutherford after Barthes II

providing a singular portrait of female determination and demanding exceptional resources of strength and stamina from her interpreters. It was perhaps no coincidence that several of the most active suffragettes among the prima donnas of the *fin de siècle* (such as Lillian Nordica, Anna Bahr-Mildenburg and Marie Brema) all wielded Brünnhilde's spear. And within Brünnhilde herself there are strangely suggestive echoes of Schröder-Devrient and the roles she once played: the chain mail she wore as Romeo becomes Brünnhilde's armour,[75] her revelation of Leonore's femininity foreshadows Brünnhilde's acceptance of her womanhood, her daring entry on horseback at the end of *Rienzi* finds new shape in Brünnhilde's ride into the funeral pyre on her horse Grane – even the ecstatic joy[76] that Wagner admired most in her is (as Carolyn Abbate has demonstrated) present in the music of Brünnhilde as laughter.[77]

Conclusion

Schröder-Devrient as woman, actress, singer, singing-actress-interpreter, mythic sign – all these are areas which need further investigation. Perhaps it is enough to say at present that she was no ordinary muse, the kind of passive sex object George Upton envisaged in 1880 as the 'impulse, support and consolation' of male composers;[78] rather, if myth is to be invoked again, we should understand her in the context of the original Muses, as a creator in her own right whose example inspired others to attain a similar level of artistry. She herself regarded that task as part of her artistic responsibilities: in 1850, a decade before her death, she wrote to Clara Schumann:

> I have loved my art, and practiced it with a hallowed enthusiasm. Whether I accomplished anything, whether I have left anything for those who came after me, that is the question! My goal was ever the highest, and I have been happy to pass on the fruit of my experience where there was a desire for it and where I thought the soil fertile. Unfortunately, I can point to no results … The poverty of heart and spirit was too great, the soil too barren, to nourish the strong roots torn from my own heart.[79]

Was she referring to Wagner? Their once productive working relationship ended badly in 1846,[80] although they remained in occasional contact in later years. Wagner only – and perhaps significantly – re-established his original concord with her after her death, via his memories. Yet she remained a potent force in his work. On 9 July 1882, a few months before he died, Cosima Wagner relates her husband's dissatisfaction with the rehearsals for his final opera, *Parsifal*:

> The big scene between Kundry and Pars[*ifal*] will almost certainly never be done in the way he created it. R. complains about how insensitive the singers are to all there is in it, and he thinks of Schröder-Devr.[*sic*], how she would have uttered the words '*So war es mein Kuss, der [welt]hellsichtig dich machte.*' Now the music has to do it all.[81]

Might we read this line – 'So it was my kiss that made you see all these things clearly' – as a metaphor for the influence of one great artist on the creativity of another? If so, it is indeed within the music that the final traces of that relationship remain.

Notes

I am grateful to Geoffrey Poole for his helpful insights on an earlier draft of this essay, and to Laura Richards for her linguistic expertise.

1 Richard Wagner, *Actors and Singers*, trans. William Ashton Ellis (Lincoln and London, University of Nebraska Press, 1995), p. 228.

2 10 April 1872: *Cosima Wagner's Diaries*, Vol. I 1869–1877, ed. Martin Gregor-Dellin and Dietrich Mack, trans. Geoffrey Skelton (London, Collins, 1978), p. 475.

3 Marcia J. Citron, *Gender and the Musical Canon* (Cambridge, Cambridge University Press, 1993), p. 71.

4 Ernest Newman, *The Life of Richard Wagner*, Vol. I (London, Cassell, 1933), p. 320.

5 See John Deathridge and Carl Dahlhaus, *The New Grove Wagner* (London, Macmillan, 1984), p. 7; Barry Millington, ed., *The Wagner Compendium: A Guide to Wagner's Life and Music* (London, Thames & Hudson, 1992), pp. 133–4; and Jean-Jacques Nattiez, *Wagner Androgyne: A Study in Interpretation*, trans. Stewart Spencer (Princeton, NJ, Princeton University Press, 1993), p. 183.

6 Dieter Borchmeyer, *Richard Wagner: Theory and Theatre*, trans. Stewart Spencer (Oxford, Clarendon Press, 1991), p. 328.

7 Arthur Symons, 'The Ideas of Richard Wagner' (1905), in Eric Bentley, ed., *The Theory of the Modern Stage: An Introduction to Modern Theatre and Drama* (Harmondsworth, Penguin Books, 1968), pp. 284 and 313; Geoffrey Skelton, *Wagner in Thought and Practice* (London, Lime Tree, 1991), pp. 132–4.

8 Henry Pleasants, *The Great Singers* (London, Victor Gollancz Ltd, 1967), pp. 152–7.

9 Schiller's *Die Braut von Messina*.

10 Wagner, *Actors and Singers*, p. 227.

11 Wagner wrote of her penchant for tall, slim young men, and cites her affairs with Hermann Müller and a Herr Munchhausen.

12 Pleasants, *The Great Singers*, p. 156.

13 Richard Wagner, *My Life*, ed. Mary Whittall, trans. Andrew Gray (Cambridge, Cambridge University Press, 1983), p. 392.

14 Rupert Christiansen, *Prima Donna: A History* (London, Penguin Books, 1986), p. 142. Other singers (including Elizabeth Billington and Lucia Vestris) were also targets of such volumes; Tracy C. Davis has described the common usage of known or fictional actresses and dancers as subjects within Victorian pornography – see her *Actresses as Working Women: Their Social Identity in Victorian Culture* (London and New York, Routledge, 1991), pp. 137–9.

15 Wagner, *My Life*, p. 37.

16 *Ibid.*

17 Deathridge and Dahlhaus, *The New Grove Wagner*, p. 7.

18 Klaus Kropfinger, *Wagner and Beethoven: Richard Wagner's Reception of Beethoven* (Cambridge, Cambridge University Press, 1991), pp. 32–3.

19 H. F. Chorley, *Thirty Years' Musical Recollections*, Vol. 1 (1862; repr. New York, Da Capo Press, 1984), p. 55.

20 *Ibid.*, p. 56.

21 Wagner, *Actors and Singers*, p. 219.

22 11 March 1841: *The Marriage Diaries of Robert and Clara Schumann*, ed. Gerd Nauhaus, trans. Peter Ostwald (London, Robson Books, 1994), p. 61.

23 David Luke and Robert Pick, eds and trans., *Goethe: Conversations and Encounters* (London, Oswald Wolff, 1966), p. 218.

24 Pleasants, *The Great Singers*, p. 155.

25 *The Diaries of William Charles Macready: 1833–1851*, Vol. 1, ed. William Toynbee (London, Chapman & Hall Ltd, 1912), p. 29.

26 *La Moda*, 14 April 1836, p. 120.

27 Wagner, *Actors and Singers*, p. 217.

28 *Ibid.*, pp. 219–20.

29 *Wagner Writes From Paris*, ed. Robert L. Jacobs and Geoffrey Skelton (London, George Allen & Unwin Ltd, 1973), p. 58.

30 Richard Wagner, 'The Destiny of Opera', in idem, *Actors and Singers*, pp. 132–3.

31 *Ibid.*, p. 203.

32 *Ibid.*, p. 219.

33 Pleasants, *The Great Singers*, pp. 152–3.

34 *Ibid.*, p. 57.

35 Wagner, *Actors and Singers*, p. 219.

36 Matthijs Siegenbeck, *J.C. Wattier Ziezenis, eerste toneelkunstenaresse van Nederland* (1827), in George Brandt, ed., *German and Dutch Theatre, 1600–1848* (Cambridge, Cambridge University Press, 1993), p. 485.

37 Eduard Devrient, *Geschichte der deutschen Schauspielkunst* (1848), cited in Brandt, *German and Dutch Theatre*, p. 305.

38 Ellen C. Clayton, *Queens of Song* (London, Smith, Elder & Co., 1863), pp. 70–1.

39 Joseph R. Roach, *The Player's Passion: Studies in the Science of Acting* (London and Toronto, Associated University Presses, 1985), pp. 170–3.

40 Henry Morley, *Journal of a London Playgoer* (1866; repr. Leicester, Leicester University Press, 1974), p. 211.

41 *Selected Letters of Richard Wagner*, ed. S. Spencer and B. Millington (London and Melbourne, J. M. Dent and Sons Ltd, 1987), p. 95.

42 Hector Berlioz, *Memoirs of Hector Berlioz: From 1803–1855 Comprising his Travels in Germany, Italy, Russia and England*, annotated Ernest Newman (New York, Dover Publications Inc., 1966), p. 316.

43 Roland Barthes, *Image Music Text*, trans. S. Heath (London, Fontana Press, 1977), p. 182.

44 *Ibid.*, p. 185.

45 Wagner, *My Life*, p. 285.

46 Barthes, *Image Music Text*, p. 184.

47 Heath, 'Translator's Note', *Ibid.*, p. 9.

48 Berlioz, *Memoirs of Hector Berlioz*, pp. 311–17.

49 *Ibid.*, p. 317.

50 Newman *The Life of Richard Wagner*, p. 74.

51 Wagner, *My Life*, p. 227.

52 Barthes, *Image Music Text*, p. 188.

53 *Ibid.*, p. 182.

54 *Ibid.*, p. 185.

55 Wagner, *Actors and Singers*, p. 219.

56 23 March 1878: cited in Borchmeyer, *Richard Wagner*, p. 328.

57 Ulrich Müller and Peter Wapnewski, eds, *Wagner Handbook*, trans. J. Deathridge (Cambridge, Mass., Harvard University Press, 1992), p. 12.

58 Jens Malte Fischer, 'Sprechgesang or Bel Canto: Toward a History of Singing Wagner', in Müller and Wapnewksi, *Wagner Handbook*, p. 539.

59 On the various factors that led to the development of the 'dramatic' singer, see John Potter, *Vocal Authority: Singing Style and Ideology* (Cambridge, Cambridge University Press, 1998), pp. 47–66.

60 Fischer 'Sprechgesang or Bel Canto', pp. 539–40.

61 Albert Goldman and Evert Sprinchorn, eds., *Wagner on Music and Drama: A Compendium of Richard Wagner's Prose Works* (New York, E. P. Dutton & Co. Inc., 1964), p. 255.

62 See Jürgen Kühnel, 'The Prose Writings', in Müller and Wapnewksi, *Wagner Handbook*, p. 618.

63 Wagner, *My Life*, p. 230.

64 Goldman and Sprinchorn, *Wagner on Music and Drama*, p. 335.

65 Wagner, *My Life*, p. 242.

66 *Ibid.*, p. 236.

67 22 July 1871: *Cosima Wagner's Diaries*, Vol. I, p. 394.

68 *Ibid.*, p. 323.

69 The *sgraffito* that adorns the exterior of Wagner's house in Bayreuth and illustrates the essential elements of his operatic vision contains the portraits of both Cosima and Schröder-Devrient: Cosima as the spirit of Music and Schröder-Devrient as the spirit of Classical Tragedy.

70 Wagner, *My Life*, p. 227.

71 9 December 1869: *ibid.*, p. 171.

72 1 March 1874: *ibid.*, p. 737.

73 Roland Barthes, 'Myth Today', *Barthes: Selected Writings*, ed. S. Sontag (London, Fontana Press, 1983), p. 99.

74 Richard Wagner, 'Letter to August Röckel, January 23, 1854', in Goldman and Sprinchorn, *Wagner on Music and Drama*, p. 291.

75 30 November 1881: *Cosima Wagner's Diaries*, Vol. II 1878–1883 (London, Collins, 1980), p. 757.

76 10 February 1881: *ibid.*, p. 618.

77 Carolyn Abbate, *Unsung Voices: Opera and Musical Narrative in the Nineteenth Century* (Princeton, NJ, Princeton University Press, 1991), pp. 206–49.

78 George Upton, *Woman in Music* (1880), in Carol Neuls-Bates, ed., *Women in Music: An Anthology of Source Readings from the Middle Ages to the Present* (Boston, Northeastern University Press, 1996), p. 210.

79 Cited in Pleasants, *The Great Singers*, p. 157.

80 The tale of this quarrel is confused. Wagner claims that she called in a loan of 1,000 thalers in a fit of jealousy at his supposed neglect of her talents in favour of his niece Johanna Wagner, and brought him to the edge of financial ruin. However, there are several indications that Wagner's account is disingenous in respect of his own culpability for the break between them.

81 *Cosima Wagner's Diaries*, Vol. II, p. 887.

5

MEMORIES OF PLESSY: HENRY JAMES RE-STAGES THE PAST

John Stokes

La voix de Célimène

In chapter 7 of Henry James's *The Tragic Muse* (1890) an aspirant English actress called Miriam Rooth is taken by an English diplomat, a keen *amateur* of the French stage called Peter Sherringham, together with Peter's friends, Nick Dormer, a would-be painter, and Gabriel Nash, a wandering English Aesthete, to meet Madame Carré, a distinguished French actress. They assemble in her drawing-room which is packed with 'votive offerings ... the presents, the portraits, the wreaths, the diadems, the letters, framed and glazed, the trophies and tributes and relics collected by Madame Carré during half a century of renown'; these are the mementos that convert it 'into a theatrical museum'.[1]

Though now retired from the Comédie-Française, Carré offers lessons and Sherringham's idea is that she will evaluate Miriam's potential. So she does, briskly apportioning judgements when Miriam displays different aspects of her still undeveloped talents. Carré's manner is autocratic as befits her status, her discriminations apparently respected, and, yet, through the responses of both Sherringham and Nash, and even of Miriam, James creates a scenario in which it is the teacher herself who is also under scrutiny, the *doyenne* who is being measured by what she was, by what her professional life means today, now that it is over.

This historical placing is immediately apparent in Nash's reply when first she greets them: '*Ah, la voix de Célimène!*', he exclaims. The voice of the youthful *grande coquette* in Molière's *Misanthrope* no doubt, but issuing from a bizarre source since 'Célimène wore a big red flower on the summit of her dense wig and had a very grand air, a toss of the head and sundry little majesties of manner; in addition to which she was strange, almost grotesque, and to some people would have been even terrifying, capable of reappearing, with her hard eyes, as a queer vision in the darkness' (p. 94).

We know, because Peter Sherringham knows, that Carré had indeed played Célimène, had been tutored in the role (though the mentor goes unnamed) by a 'great *comédienne*, the light of the French stage in the early years of the century' (p. 92). We know, too, that Carré had gone on to play many other celebrated roles, including Clorinde in Emile Augier's *L'Aventurière*. Later in this chapter Carré and Miriam will together recite the scene from Act Three of the *L'Aventurière* in which Clorinde, the adventuress, by profession an actress, is confronted by Célie, the ingenue, fiancée of the son of the ancient widower Clorinde plans to seduce into marriage. Should she succeed in her deception, Clorinde, who operates in collaboration with her drunken braggart of a brother, will gain not only money but social respectability. James gives us just one line from the play – Clorinde's '*Vous ne me fuyez pas, mon enfant, aujour-d'hui*' – and, to draw attention to the game he is playing, reverses the obvious casting so that young Miriam recites old Clorinde's speeches to old Carré's young Célie.

Though set in sixteenth-century Italy, *L'Aventurière* was thought at its première in 1848, and even much later, to be distinctly contemporary in what it had to say about female behaviour and James must surely have hoped that at least a few of his readers would have been able to recall the subsequent lines, including the powerful words in which Clorinde justi-fies her treachery:

Oui, ma vie est coupable, oui, mon coeur a failli …
Mais vous ne savez pas de quels coups assailli!
Coment le sauriez-vous, ame chaste et tranquille,
A qui la vie est douce et la vertu facile,
Enfant qui pour gardiens de votre tendre honneur
Avez une famille et surtout le bonheur! …
Comment le sauriez-vous ce qu'en de froides veilles,
Le pauvreté murmure à de jeunes oreilles?
Vous ne comprenez pas, n'ayant jamais eu faim,
Qu'on renonce à l'honneur pour un morceau de pain.[2]

Even if Miriam's tones fail to match the passion of Augier's lines – 'a long, strong, colourless voice came quavering from her young throat' (p. 102) – Sherringham nevertheless responds instinctively to her physi-cal appearance, finding in her an extraordinary resemblance not to Carré, but to another French actress of the past: 'She frowned porten-tously; her low forehead overhung her eyes; the eyes themselves, in shadow, stared, splendid and cold, and her hands clinched themselves at her sides. She looked austere and terrible …' (p. 102). That vignette evokes, quite unmistakably, one of the most potent images of Rachel Félix,[3] the great *tragédienne* of the mid-century who set the standards of hard work that Carré still respects. 'I don't care a straw for your handsome girls', Carré will say, 'but bring me the one who is ready to drudge the tenth part of the way Rachel drudged, and I'll forgive her beauty' (p. 106).

It is an essential part of James's quasi-historical scheme that he should have us believe that Carré was once the contemporary of Rachel, and that she should share the *tragédienne's* professional values. In this respect alone, Carré's fictional career matches that of one real-life French actress, and one only: Madame Arnould Plessy who lived from 1819 to 1897,[4] who had been comedy's answer to Rachel's triumph in tragedy, whose performance as Célimène had been coached by the renowned Mademoiselle Mars, the 'light of the French stage in the early years of the century'.

Starting young, Plessy made her debut at the Comédie-Française in 1834 as Emma in *La fille d'honneur* by Alexandre Duval, ascending to the roles previously the property of Mars: Elmire in *Tartuffe* as well as Célimène. Her repertoire also included Susanne in *Le Marriage de Figaro* and roles in the newer *pièces bien faites* of Scribe and in the romantic comedy of Augier, in particular his *L'Aventurière* which she had famously revived in 1860 and played into the 1870s. According to Pougin's *Dictionnaire du théâtre* of 1885 she was incomparable in these parts; she made them her own.[5]

Throughout her career Plessy paid many visits to London and took a regular part in the French seasons at the St James's that had begun in 1842. Three years later, in 1845, immediately following the visit of Macready and his company to Paris, she reciprocated by appearing at the St James's as part of John Mitchell's 'French Play' season. It was then that she caused something of a stir by marrying the writer Auguste Arnould and, instead of returning to Paris, departing for a long and remunerative engagement in St Petersburg, despite an attempt made by Mitchell to keep her in London by matching roubles with pounds. From the point of view of the Comédie-Française the move to Russia was intolerably disrespectful (she was actually taken to court for breach of contract in 1846), but Plessy was still a sufficiently valuable property in 1855 to be accepted back as a *pensionnaire* and she stayed with the company until her retirement when she took up teaching. At the *maison de Molière*, she specialised not only in the house dramatist but later (an advance upon

Mars), in eighteenth-century comedy, in particular Araminte in *Les fausses confidences*, a predilection that James's *Tragic Muse* acknowledges obliquely by having old Carré interrupt a conversation with 'charming overdone stage-horror and the young hands of the heroines of Marivaux' (p. 271).[6]

It may well have been Plessy in *L'Aventurière* that James saw on his very first visit to the Comédie-Française in 1870.[7] In any case, she soon assumed symbolic status in his personal gallery of performers, living embodiment of history, of French theatre and all that came to stand for in his enthralled perception of a European lineage in which ancient performers counted for as much as the dramatic characters they impersonated through the influence 'of a personal set of idiosyncrasies, the voice, the look, the step, the very physique of a performer'.[8] Even so, running alongside James's 'veneration' for what he said the French called Plessy's 'authority', her 'spirit and style and grace', was his allowance that 'there is something always rather hard and metallic in her style ...' (p. 50), and his awareness of what others had long seen as the limitations of tradition, the widespread accusation that Plessy, in particular, was 'too mincing and too artificial' (p. 89).

Indeed, in some quarters, Plessy who was short in stature with a small mouth that she accentuated by much pursing of her lips or '*minauderie*' (smirking) was controversial. Some found her respectability unattractive, disliked her air of antiquity, and considered her theatrical inheritance to be flawed.[9] Though aware of these charges, James could not, at first, bring himself to concede their justice since, to him, 'Madame Plessy's *minauderies*, her grand airs and her arch-refinements, have never been anything but the odorous swayings and queenly tossings of some splendid garden. Never had an actress grander manners. When Madame Plessy represents a duchess you have no allowances to make'. Even if her 'limitations are on the side of the pathetic', even if 'she is brilliant, she is cold; and I cannot imagine her touching the source of tears',[10] James still preferred to maintain that the broader cultural significance of his favourite actress outweighed any expressive deficiencies she might also possess.

In *The Tragic Muse*, then, James has Carré listen for a repeat of herself in Miriam, much as her real life model, Mlle Plessy, had echoed, though imperfectly, Mlle Mars. Yet the lesson of the novel overall will be that even if the past can occasionally be ventriloquised, usually inadequately, it can never be fully re-embodied. An initial description of Carré's drawing-room has already warned us of:

the confession of something missed, something hushed, which seemed to rise from it all and make it melancholy, like a reference to clappings which, in the nature of things, could now only be present as a silence: so that if the place was full of history, it was the form without the fact, or at the most a redundancy of the one to a pinch of the other – the history of a mask, of a squeak, a record of movements on the air. (p. 91)

And, much later, Sherringham will find himself meditating that 'Miriam Rooth's face seemed to him to-day a finer instrument than old Madame Carré's', and will conclude that 'It was doubtless that the girl's was fresh and strong, with a future in it, while poor Madame Carré's was worn and weary, with only a past' (p. 135). The passing of time, James insinuates, is measured cruelly by the pastness of performance, by ageing bodies and, equally cruelly, by changing tastes, new demands. At the same time James allows for new possibilities. The career of Miriam Rooth lies in the future; she will have to make her own way, as she is beginning to do when the novel ends, with plays far removed from those of Carré's world. Miriam will never reincarnate Carré, let alone Plessy, let alone Rachel; she may, though, become herself, whatever we (or James) may think of that.

In 1876, at the time of Plessy's retirement, James insisted that the 'conditions of artistic production are directly hostile to the formation of actresses as consummate and as complete'. 'One may not expect to see her like, any more than one may expect to see a new manufacture of old lace and old brocade', he admitted. 'She carried off with her something that the younger generation of actresses will consistently lack – a certain largeness of style and robustness of art.'[11] What James did not care to say, or perhaps in 1876 had yet to realise, was that, while they might lack 'a certain largeness of style and robustness of art', a younger generation of actresses would actively strive to leave Plessy's *coquetterie* behind. More than a decade later, in *The Tragic Muse*, he was obliged to concede the point.

A roman à clef only in the sense that its characters are composites, hypothetical lives made up from available material and from personal encounters, *The Tragic Muse* records an extended period of change,[12] showing how such processes came about, and how they felt at the time. That is why its surface is carefully scattered with verbal and visual memorabilia (many of them relating to Plessy) which hark back to moments that might be personal, shared, or even institutional. Readers must bring what they know, and what they can remember. As its author was very much aware, most theatre survives not only as a kind of mental residue, but in objects which act like mnemonics, whose very fragility speaks the ephemeral truth of the art they commemorate: 'the form without the fact'.

Social gestures

Henry James's memories of Plessy, so deeply embedded in his consciousness that she came to stand for the passing of time itself, were his personal take on a career that, more than most, had flourished and suffered with the emergence of new ideas, and on a style of acting that was revived, eroded and finally displaced in the course of the nineteenth century as a whole. We can think of it as the slow demise of *la grande coquette*, as well as a chapter in the endless sequence of transformations of the 'natural' that make up theatrical history.

Plessy's audiences certainly changed their minds. In 1855 Charles Dickens in Paris with Wilkie Collins at the time of Louis Napoleon's first Paris exhibition saw, and admired, her in *La Joconde*, a play by his friend François Joseph Regnier, and he wrote enthusiastically to the author, 'If I could see an English actress with but one hundredth part of the nature and art of Madame Plessy, I should believe our English theatre to be a fair way toward its regeneration'.[13] He ended, coupling politeness with genuine resignation: 'I have no hope ever of beholding such a phenomenon'. Twenty-five years later, in 1870, he was sighing, 'the Lord deliver us from Plessy's mechanical ingenuousness'.[14]

This prolonged turnaround is not to be attributed solely to personal preferences. Dickens undoubtedly had mixed feelings about some aspects of French theatre, but he delighted in others: in French melodrama, for instance, holding that Frédérick Lemaître was the supreme actor of the age. He had admiring friendships with Regnier and with Charles Fechter, the French actor who was credited with bringing a new kind of relaxed naturalism to the English stage. Whenever Dickens visited Paris, and he did so constantly throughout the 1850s and 1860s, playgoing was always part of the anticipated pleasure.[15] In London he knew John Mitchell and paid appropriate attention to the many French actresses who came to the St James's.[16]

But, as his jokes at the expense of the unities in *Nicholas Nickleby*, and his antipathy to Rachel – 'odious'[17] – make very clear, Dickens did have profound difficulties with neoclassicism. This instinctive dislike of the stuffier French styles was at one with his conviction that acting, at its best, was always a mode of authenticity. 'But is it not always true, in comedy and in tragedy, that the more real the man the more genuine the actor?',[18] he wrote when he witnessed the intensity of grief displayed by Regnier at the funeral of the Frenchman's own fourteen-year-old daughter. For Dickens an inbuilt capacity to feel and to express were inseparable from moral integrity. The best acting always brings out truths about the actor so that, even when impersonating a villain, the 'genuine' performer will seize the opportunity to show just what wickedness can do, providing evidence of his moral imagination through the clarity and discretion of his rendering. Dickens, the great scourge of moral hypocrisy in life, would not have been greatly impressed by Diderot's theatrical 'paradox' which argues for a necessarily critical space between actors and their roles: for Dickens, dramatic modes that were conventional and unyielding made the essential sincerity, the 'naturalness', of acting almost impossible to achieve.

Whereas Dickens's position on the emotional importance of acting was at least unambiguous, and unlikely to respect either the force of staid tradition or the value of personal subtlety alone, for some of his mid-Victorian contemporaries there was the possibility of a more measured approach. G. H. Lewes borrowed Talma's term, '*optique de théâtre*' to describe the appropriateness of style to character which creates an effect of the 'natural' through the application of symbolic devices.[19] In Lewes's eyes, both Rachel and Plessy benefited from this aesthetic. Just as he allowed Rachel to be the supreme tragic actress because she represented her roles with an intensely physical literalness, so he recognised that Plessy, because she was 'the most musical, the most measured, the most incisive speaker (whether of verse or prose) now on stage', was equally natural in her comic roles.[20] According to the '*optique de théâtre*', naturalness in acting is a matter of proportion of measure, of balance; and Lewes took matters of diction very seriously, to the extent that he could write that, although she was capable of expressing 'the quintessence of feminine wile' (p. 190) and was 'as a woman, without much charm', Plessy remained always 'well worth studying, not only because of the refined naturalness of her manner, but also on account of the exquisite skill of her elocution' (p. 194). For Lewes, reliably perfect delivery was enough to counter any suspicions of the 'mechanical ingenuousness' that Dickens eventually came to loathe.

English interest in French acting has invariably to be related to current battles within the English theatre where foreigners were often brought in as counters for debate. This was certainly the case in the 1840s when English perceptions of Plessy were heavily coloured by the comparison between different schools of acting. The French might be stuck with a rigidly formalised theatrical tradition, but at least that was serious, and, in any case, they did seem anxious to develop in directions that owed much to the ways of the English, above all to Shakespeare.

Plessy became caught up in this cross-channel exchange early on. When William Charles Macready and his company, which included Helen Faucit, visited Paris in late 1844 and early 1845 Plessy was on hand to help with the hospitality, perhaps because of her previous experience in England. If, in comparison with the theatrical events of 1828/29, when Macready and Harriet Smithson had inflamed the Romantic aspirations of Berlioz and Delacroix, the Paris season 1844/45 seems anti-climactic, we should bear in mind that the primary aim of the later trip was consolidation of what was by then an established cultural phenomenon. Ever the impresario, Mitchell actually hoped to set up an English theatre in the French capital on the basis of native interest; there were still palpable contrasts between the two theatrical traditions that were ripe for continuing exploitation.

Where Smithson had been revolutionary and explosive, Faucit offered a graceful, 'feminine' softness and, by French standards, an unusual ability to transform herself to suit a variety of different roles. Later she remembered 'how strange they seemed to think it, that the same actress should play Juliet, Ophelia, Desdemona, and Lady Macbeth – impressing each, as they were indulgent enough to say, with characteristics so distinct and so marked, as to make them forget the actress in the women she represented'.[21] Macready may, in respect for local custom, have closed the curtain at the very moment when Othello murdered Desdemona,[22] but still the French who, according to some reports, considered it indecorous even to applaud, were enraptured, or at any rate intrigued, by the artistic difference of English acting. And this reaction meant that English members of the Paris audience were fascinated in turn to discover their inscrutable neighbours engaged with an alien style: 'So near, and yet so far – united, yet severed by an impassable gulf, we sat. Nations, like individuals, know each other but in part; they cannot penetrate the labyrinth of each other's thoughts.'[23]

All too true. On 16 January 1845 there was a gala evening held at the Tuileries in front of the French Royal family, the diplomatic corps and an audience of five or six hundred. The entertainment was made up of *Hamlet* performed by Macready and his company, and *The Day after the Wedding*, a farcical variation on *The Taming of the Shrew* by

Marie-Thérèse De Camp, in which Plessy played Lady Elizabeth Freelove in English 'with accustomed grace'.[24] The following evening Plessy repeated the same performance while Macready gave the death scene from *Henry IV* and Helen Faucit portions of Juliet. Yet, both on and off the stage, the seasons were shrouded in diplomacy, of several kinds. Away from the theatre there was considerable tension in political circles as a result of clashes between English and French agents in the distant protectorate of Tahiti.[25] On stage Faucit, who was allowed by Macready to play Ophelia to his Hamlet for the very first time, appears to have been infatuated with her leading man, which may have brought a special intensity to her performances, but caused personal irritation and embarrassment. A few French observers, including Théophile Gautier, believed, for some reason, that Plessy's gestures were a cheeky parody of Macready's mannerisms, while Macready in turn found her 'sometimes graceful, but not quite concentrated enough in the passion'.[26] At the final grand gala the French Emperor presented Macready, a stalwart Republican, with an encrusted dagger in an exquisitely chiselled gold case, its hilt apparently 'enriched with diamonds, and other precious stones'.[27] The actor subsequently discovered the whole thing to be paste.

When, later that spring, Plessy reciprocated by playing in London she again performed Lady Elizabeth Freelove and, again, there was curiosity about the piquant effect of French delivery on English words. Plessy's pointed emphases, every syllable in place, made a 'pretty mincing of our northern consonants'.[28] To speak in English was only to reveal yourself as ineradicably French. And, despite a generally polite response, the London papers (who had had similar difficulties with her mentor, Mlle Mars, some twenty years earlier)[29] sometimes found it hard to be wholeheartedly enthusiastic about the actress even in her more familiar native roles. Still bothered by her mannerisms, they note that sometimes her very quietness seemed to rule out the passion that they valued most in a performance.[30] Crabb Robinson, who actually found Plessy 'pleasing' and liked the way in which she enunciated verse, told his diary that, as for acting, he 'saw nothing but ladylike talk – genteel comedy when good excited no enthusiasms'.[31] The same pattern was to be repeated when Plessy visited London at other times in the mid-century: the appreciation, even when warm, remained qualified. Her Suzanne in *Le Marriage de Figaro* may have been 'spirituelle',[32] but more often she was simply 'redolent of the *parfum de bonne Société*;[33] sometimes there was express relief at 'an entire absence of her usual mannerisms'[34] or, not much better, the kind of double-edged tribute which noted that 'there is charm and piquancy in her utterance that would make the dullest nonsense sound like bewitching eloquence'.[35] Plessy's obvious belief in her own power to deflect moral opprobrium, while entertaining her audience with the studied deployment of verbal subtleties and physical signals, was often felt to be unattractive and undramatic. There were growing complaints about her mannerisms, the way in which she ignored the dynamics of a situation in favour of 'pursing up her lips and elegantly posing her drapery'. No wonder that 'the continual puckering up of the lips in order to round a sentence nicely, and the everlasting smile, make the art rather an elocutionary than a dramatic effort'.[36]

When a role depended almost entirely on stylish dissembling, then English distaste became much more intense. This was above all true of Célimène, the role for which Plessy had been coached by Mars, the role which set her apart from all her rivals.[37] Though Rachel had, it is true, performed Célimène in London in 1847, even she had never dared to follow the venture through in Paris where memories of Mars and the present rivalry of Plessy were more serious threats. The antipathetic response to her London experiment must have also contributed to Rachel's decision not to repeat it in her native city.

> In a certain sense the performance was perfect – there was not a single fault to find – but we doubt that sympathy between the artist and the person represented which can give a joyous naturalness to a part. With the agony and passion of Phèdre still in our minds, we find our imagination unsatisfied by the neat and polished Célimène.

So Lewes pronounced about Rachel in *The Atlas*.[38] Other critics were equally grudging about the play itself. 'The comedy has not a plot which is calculated to interest an English audience; it terminates most unsatisfactorily, and there is a heartlessness about the character of Célimène which produces a very disagreeable impression'. In the early days, though, Plessy's comic delicacy saw her through so that even for this critic from *The Morning Chronicle* she 'threw a gloss over the less pleasant portion of the character, and was throughout warmly applauded'.[39] Later, as her poise became more confident so it became less welcome: the *grande coquette* was now under scrutiny on all sides.

If Célimène is the great instance of the *coquette* who may (or may not) redeem herself though her expressive self-control and her evident superiority to her courtly surroundings, Elmire, Plessy's role in *Tartuffe*, by merely mimicking *coquetterie*, raises rather different questions. When she issues her challenge to the lecherous *dévot* who has invaded her home – '*Faites-le moi descendre*' – does Elmire risk exposing her own sensual nature to temptation? Alternatively, is she entirely confident in her inherent virtue? In which case, might she not then be said to behave with a dishonest streak comparable to that of the hypocrite himself? Plessy herself claimed that if there was no risk then there was no scene, but still insisted that the point of her performance was to show how Elmire's virtue would always protect her.[40] But the actress's proven ability as *une grande coquette* meant that for some, not all, she would never be quite as effective as Elmire, the housewife who risks her honour for her husband, than as Célimène, the court beauty who cruelly mocks her male suitors with her evident sensuality.[41]

With all nineteenth-century versions of *la grande coquette* the issues remained much the same. Does flirtation imply a deep female trait that permeates the whole being or is it rather a means of preserving autonomy, exerting control, possibly for moral ends? Can sexual attractiveness be used safely as a trap, as a deceitful weapon against harassment? Or is *coquetterie* in a young woman simply a sign of a misguided upbringing?

English and French views on these matters could be very different. George Eliot was happy simply to describe Hetty Sorrel plotting to seduce Adam Bede 'as if she had been an elegantly clad coquette alone in her boudoir', because it was her intention as narrator simply to expose social pretension and suggest common ground: 'it is noteworthy how closely her mental processes may resemble those of a lady in society and crinoline, who applies her refined intellect to the problem of committing indiscretions without compromising herself'.[42] And when T. W. Robertson's adapted *L'Aventurière* for English audiences as *Home* in 1869,[43] he provided no real equivalent for the lines of self-justification that Clorinde, the sexual adventuress, speaks in Augier's original, the lines that Henry James had Miriam recite in *The Tragic Muse*. Instead, there is a final confessional which the adventuress (no longer a professional actress as in Augier's original, but a harmless musician) calls her 'punishment' and in which she lays most blame upon her sinister male accomplice:

> I am not all to blame. I never knew a mother's love or guidance … I am but a woman, and I had been schooled into the belief that all the world was bad. This home, your father's kindness, your sister's gentleness, and this young lady's goodness, have taught me better. I have one talent, music! And that will enable me to live away from this bad, silly man, whom I have now renounced for ever. Forgive me for the evil I might

have worked you. If ever you should hear of me, you will know that my repentance is sincere.[44]

Robertson opts for domestic pathos where, in the original, Augier had rescued Clorinde with self-justification as well as contrition, allowing her a moral condition was that was problematic and complex. Correspondingly, in contrast with the popular English stress on hearth and home, Plessy's stylish courtly ways made her seem not only insensitive, heartless, but increasingly irrelevant. First, Molière, then Marivaux and then a string of other parts in *la grande coquette* mode: all connected her with the past. This is surely why her mannerisms, which had always been suspect, eventually became for some English observers, Dickens among them, quite intolerable.

But even the French had problems with the latter-day Plessy:

Aujourd'hui, elle s'écoute parler, et parle tantot comme une femme qui rêve, tantot comme une femme qui se pame. Il est impossible, en l'écoutant, de comprendre qu'elle ait réuni autour d'elle une cour si nombreuse, car ce n'est vraiment pas une personne vivante. Tous ses gestes sont mesurés, tous les clignements d'yeux sont comptés.[45]

That appeared in *La Revue des Deux Mondes* as early as 1856. When Francisque Sarcey tried to sum up her career twenty years later he found himself reviewing his own past responses. Here was an actress, still in the shadow of Mars, whose strengths lay not so much in the representation of great passion (certainly not tragic passion as she had demonstrated with a disastrous Agrippina in Racine's *Britannicus*) so much as *nuance*. Sarcey had seen her for the first time when he was still a student and had been greatly disappointed: 'Elle me parut minaudière d'une coqueterrie trop raffinée et trop mièvre.'[46] Later, he had come to appreciate her more, though he was unenthusiastic about her Clorinde, for all that it marked a break with her established roles. When it came to Molière, Sarcey maintained, rather against the grain, that she made a better Elmire than she did a Célimène. But this was largely because her performances in Marivaux coloured his view of her in plays by the earlier playwright. For Sarcey, Plessy's unique skill lay in representing characters from the milieu of the eighteenth-century *haut bourgeoisie* where it was mandatory to imitate aristocratic manners. It followed that her representation of Elmire, a wife, a mother and a householder, who Sarcey saw as a kind of prototype bourgeois woman, would necessarily be more engaging than her attempt to become Célimène, the heartless creature produced by the even more distant life style of a seventeenth-century court.

Sarcey writes as a man of his own generation for whom Plessy's *grande coquettes* became more explicable, if not always more interesting, when they could be referred back, in a reverse relay taking in Mlle Mars, to the *ancien régime*. As with some other French performers,[47] the self-consciously aristocratic style, though it might attract some elements in a post-Revolutionary audience, would always alienate others. Theatre being an art of the present, as well as an object of antiquarian study, the appeal of her old-fashioned *minauderie* had to be disowned before it could be appreciated – and that, at least, was true on both sides of the Channel.

Bernhardt breaks out

At first Henry James tried to stay faithful to his earlier vision. Plessy's retirement in May 1876, the 'brilliant solemnity' of her benefit, showed her once again to be, 'the last depository of certain traditions which can never, in the nature of things, be renewed. She was the perfect great lady of high comedy, as high comedy was possible before the invention of slang.' When, at the end of the evening, 'she took Mesdemoiselles Sarah Bernhardt and Croizette by the hands, and, with admirable grace, presented them to the public as her substitutes', James thought it 'more than likely that she had measured the irony of her gesture; for from the moment it takes two actresses to make up a Madame Plessy, the cause is obviously lost. Clever as these young ladies are they will not fill the void. Their art is small art; Madame Plessy's was great art.'[48]

But faith in the enduring charm of lost causes was hardly enough to withstand the calculated force for change that came about when an individual will and talent combined with a brilliantly astute recognition of a new constituency. In the summer of 1879, having as a member of the Comédie-Française troupe conquered London, having routed her rival, Sophie Croizette, Sarah Bernhardt saw her chance. She left the company and embarked on the independent career that was to last some forty years and to take her around the world in a repertoire of plays each one selected to show her talents to their greatest advantage and to hold the attention of a modern audience. Ironically this meant reviving plays associated with past performers – but in a new guise.

Bernhardt had made her name in the plays of Victor Hugo, including *Hernani* in the rehearsals for which Mlle Mars, the first Doña Sol, had famously quarrelled with the poet over the supposedly indecorous line, '*Vous êtes mon lion! superbe et généreux!*'.[49] In contrast with Mars, Hugo's erotic *frisson* now suited Bernhardt very well indeed. In addition, she revived Desclée's *Frou-frou*, Doche's *La dame aux camélias* and brandished her modernised Phèdre, a role that, forty years on, was still replete with memories of Rachel. But, just as she co-opted some aspects of the past, so Bernhardt implicitly disavowed others: first and foremost among them, the roles of Plessy.

The precise occasion, many said it was a pretext, for Bernhardt's final break from the Comédie was a bad review of her performance as Clorinde in *L'Aventurière* by the critic Auguste Vitu[50] in which he wrote that she made use of 'impetuosities, excessive in all ways'. These were not only vocal but involved 'certain movements of the body accompanied by the fists on the hips' which would have been more appropriate to Zola. In other words, they were blatantly sexual. Bernhardt blamed the whole fiasco on a lack of rehearsal and walked out.[51] She was replaced by Sophie Croizette who had been trained in the part by Plessy herself, and who played it in a sober brown velvet dress quite different from the bright yellow satin creation favoured by Bernhardt and thought by some to be quite unsuitable for a fallen woman on the brink of repentance.[52]

> Never was the antithesis between two actresses more marked than that between Madame Plessy and Sarah Bernhardt. The former, grande dame to her finger-tips, incomparable as an elocutionist, the embodiment of careful, painstaking study of every most minute effect, and exquisite in the refinement of her manner; the latter, impulse, instinct and imagination personified … But Mdlle Bernhardt was, it is now evident, under the influence of her nerves; she played excitedly – shall I say recklessly?[53]

Bernhardt never played Clorinde again. She renounced Plessy's *grande coquette* for good. Or rather, she shifted the motivational emphasis from the *coquette* to the *nerveuse* while retaining the sexual flamboyance of the established type. To act the flattering *coquette* had been to play with false faces and, in order to maintain the essential gap between what is suggested, physically and verbally, and what is actually on offer, it was essential that both actress and character had absolute physical control. This devious inauthenticity – a slippage between the bodily sign and emotional or intellectual initiative behind it – protected the *coquette*, made her morally interesting, but at a certain dramatic cost. Unlike the tragic heroine, the *coquette* was never 'abandoned', never lost consciousness, was never at one with herself, whereas the *nerveuse* (or the 'hysteric' as she was coming to be known and would soon be described by Freud)[54] was at the mercy of an inner compulsion that pushed to the surface. The hysteric may have had a body that was out of control, but it could not help but be expressive; it manifested what has been called 'a condition of bodily writing'.[55]

To put that another way: *nerveuses*, unlike *coquettes*, don't act roles, they perform themselves, a distinction that was becoming increasingly important in the developing naturalism of late nineteenth-century theatre. An inability to sustain the part of a *coquette* is what kills the heroine in Meilhac and Halévy's seminal *Frou-frou*, and yet in *A Doll's House* her perception of the falseness of coquetry provides Nora Helmer with the precondition of her liberation. That Sarah Bernhardt could triumph in the one, but never even attempt the other, had much to do with her adherence to the lingering Romantic cult that linked sex with death. That there was also, at the same time, a universal readiness to renounce or redefine the *coquette* and to welcome the new type is shown by Bernhardt's ability to make the *nerveuse* commercial, popular and international, and to make theatrical erotics democratic, available to all audiences, including those made up in an unusually large part by women.[56]

Perhaps, though, some members of her audience recalled that Bernhardt's breakthrough, her subversion of Plessy, had been foreshadowed by another remarkable actress, now dead, but still mourned. Aimée Desclée's performances had reflected, even more accurately than those of Bernhardt were to do, the mood surrounding the Franco-Prussian war and the Commune, when the sexual relationships represented in the plays of Dumas fils, the arch misogynist, were taken to be symptomatic of national trauma.[57]

By an apt coincidence, Desclée's London debut in 1873 overlapped Plessy's last season in the capital. In theatrical terms alone this was an auspicious spring in that, before the young actress could perform her repertoire, her management had to fight the long-standing ruling of the Lord Chamberlain which banned the more *risqué* works of Augier, Hugo and Dumas *fils*.[58] And, even if it was reported in London that Plessy had recommended to the Comédie-Française that it should engage Desclée,[59] and some thought that she might attempt Célimène, it was generally agreed that Desclée's innovative presence was of a very different order from that of the *grande coquette*. Desclée 'était une femme de 1871',[60] her mode was strangely realistic, and yet she was no simple flirt, but something more complex. As the critic of *The Spectator* put it: 'Madame

Arnould Plessy and Mademoiselle Aimée Desclée are the leading representatives of their respective wholly distinct orders of dramatic art.'
On the one hand, Plessy:

> There is no vehement gesture, not a word is spoken above the natural
> tone of a highly-bred woman's voice; but what subtle expression there is
> in the slight shiftings of the hands, in the action of the wrist and fore-
> arm, quite peculiar to Madame Plessy, in the perfectly enunciated
> sentences, wherein no point is ever omitted, or ever forced, in the deli-
> cate intonation which marks her relation to each person in the scene, in
> every motion where movement is necessary; in the easy, dignified atti-
> tude when she sits still and listens, as none but she, even among French
> actors, can listen, without the slightest indication that she knows what is
> coming next, or ever so faint recognition of the presence of 'the House'.

On the other hand, Desclée:

> intense passion, the noiseless entrance, the gentle approach, the hopeless
> questioning, the quick inspiration of relief, hope, faith, joy, resolve; the
> wild clinging embrace of perfect reconciliation, the 'at last!' that is in
> every line of the face, in every quivering nerve ...[61]

Significantly enough, although Plessy won dry respect for her performances in her long-established roles, she was applauded most wholeheartedly for her unusual appearance in a play by Dumas fils, *Les Idées du
Madame Aubray*, in which she played a mother who is obliged to consent
to her only son's marriage to a fallen woman:

> Suppressed anguish, heart-broken despair, and a distorted nervous
> system has seldom been displayed with more truth, less exaggeration,
> and more consummate force. She is crying inwardly. The eyes are red
> and wet but there are no tears; the whole frame is agitated with
> suppressed convulsion; the fingers twist and wring the lace pocket-
> handkerchief, which assists the exhibition of a strong woman with a
> great sorrow hardly under control.[62]

'A distorted nervous system', the very phrase heralds the future. Even
Plessy benefited briefly, and perhaps inadvertently, from the criteria that
were to surpass her. 'You can't be a great actress without quivering
nerves', Henry James would have Gabriel Nash proclaim, ironically but
accurately, about Miriam Rooth in *The Tragic Muse* (p. 439). Dedicated
to the old, always alert to the new, James would soon go on to describe
Ibsen's fictional character, Hedda Gabler, as 'furiously nervous'.[63]

All of which left Plessy's reputation suspended in the past, like one of Madame Carré's 'votive objects'. Frederick Wedmore's precise summing up of Plessy's career at the time of her retirement in 1876 suggests that, in the hierarchy of actors, her position, while indubitably her own, was second rank, eventually leading nowhere: 'the concentrated but subdued passions of Desclée was as far from her as the poetical reverie of Sarah Bernhardt'.[64] Which may be just, though it lacks James's philosophical anguish in the face of his lost cause. *Quelle connaissance de la scène … et de la vie*', the novelist had once heard one of 'old gentlemen' who haunted the orchestra of the Théâtre Français murmur about Plessy. That was in 1872 when James was still under thirty; the 'old gentlemen' were 'classic play-goers' who looked 'as if they took snuff from boxes adorned with portraits of the fashionable beauty of 1820'.[65] Four years later, in a specific comparison with Plessy, James was to describe Bernhardt and Croizette as 'children of a later and eminently contemporary type, according to which the actress undertakes not to interest but to fascinate': 'They are charming – "awfully" charming; strange, eccentric, imaginative'.[66] Learning how to appreciate Plessy was part of the *rites de passage* of James's youth; the ability to recognise Bernhardt's novelty provided uncomfortable evidence that his maturity would take place in the context of the world's modernity, which would necessarily have to include the fascinating spectacle of the strange, eccentric, imaginative *nerveuse* who had replaced the classic *coquette*. It became Plessy's fate to demonstrate that not only is theatrical nostalgia always compensation for loss, but that private memories, however protected, are little match for the forces of historical change. Even in her lifetime the actress had become evidence of the past, no more, no less: her face, a 'mask'; her voice, 'a squeak'; her body, 'a record of movements on the air'.

Notes

1 Henry James, *The Tragic Muse*, (London, Hart-Davis, 1948), p. 91. This edition reprints the 1890 text. The Penguin edition of 1995, which is based on the revised 1908 New York edition, has excellent notes and introduction by Philip Horne.

2 Emile Augier, *L'Aventurière*, Nouvelle Edition (Paris, Michel Lévy, 1870), p. 70.
　　[Yes, I have things in my life to feel guilty about, yes,
　　my heart has failed me
　　But you do not know what blows I have suffered!
　　How could you know, you with your chaste, tranquil soul
　　To whom life is sweet and goodness comes easily,

You, child, who as guardians of your tender honour
Have a family and above all happiness!
How could you know how on cold evenings
Poverty murmurs in young ears?
You do not understand, never having been hungry,
That people renounce honour for a bit of bread.]

3 See 'Rachel Félix', in Michael Booth, John Stokes and Susan Bassnett, *Three Tragic Actresses* (Cambridge, Cambridge University Press, 1996), esp. pp. 73–7.

4 Georges d'Heylli, *Madame Arnould-Plessy. 1834–1876*, (Paris, Tresse, 1876); Charles Hervey, 'Madame Arnould Plessy', *The Theatre*, 1 April 1887, pp. 194–200; Eugène de Mirecourt, *Plessy-Arnould* (Paris, chez l'auteur), in *Les Contemporains* series 1858; idem, *Mme Arnould-Plessy* (Paris, Chez Achille Faure, 1867); Georges d'Heylli, *Journal Intime de la Comédie Française* (Paris, E. Dentu, 1879).

5 Arthur Pongin, *Dictionnaire du theatre* (Paris, Librairie de Firmin-Didot, 1885), p. 243.

6 See Maurice Descotes, *Les grands roles du théatre de Marivaux* (Paris, Presses Universitaires de France, 1972).

7 *The Complete Plays of Henry James*, ed. Leon Edel (London, Rupert Hart-Davis, 1949), p. 37.

8 Henry James, *The Scenic Art: Notes on Acting and the Drama, 1872–1901* (New York, Hill and Wang, 1957; 1st pub. 1948), p. 317.

9 A quoi George Sand repond aussitot: 'Je n'accepterai Mlle Plessy qu'après l'savoir vue jouer au theatre et faire preuve du talent que vous lui accordez. J'aime mieux retirer ma pièce que de la voir minaudee. Mlle Plessy a la reputation de la premiere grimacière du monde': Micheline Boutet, *Mademoiselle Mars l'inimitable* (Paris, Librairie Académique Perrin, 1987), p. 352.

10 James, *The Scenic Art*, p. 89.

11 James, *The Scenic Art*, pp. 89–90.

12 D. J. Gordon and John Stokes, 'The Reference of The Tragic Muse', in John Goode, ed., *The Air of Reality: New Essays on Henry James*, (London, Methuen, 1972), pp. 61–168. This essay says that a reference to Mlle Bartet made in James's *Notebooks* makes it possible that the novel is set in 1879. However, deliberate historical imprecision elsewhere suggests that it may be better to think of the time scheme as more generalised: the '1870s'. It has often been said that James's friend Fanny Kemble made her own a contribution to Madame Carré. For more recent discussion of the novel's theatricality see Rachel M. Brownstein, *Tragic Muse: Rachel of the Comédie-Française* (Durham and London, Duke University Press, 1995); Joseph Litvak, *Caught in the Act: Theatricality in the Nineteenth-Century Novel* (Berkeley, Los Angeles and Oxford, University of California Press, 1992); Gail Marshall, *Actresses on the Victorian Stage* (Cambridge, Cambridge University Press, 1998).

13 *The Letters of Charles Dickens, Vol. Seven 1853–1855* (Oxford, Clarendon Press, 1993), p. 750.

14 *The Letters of Charles Dickens*, ed. by his sister-in-law and his eldest daughter (London, Macmillan, 1893), p. 740.

15 See T. Edgar Pemberton, *Charles Dickens and the Stage* (London, George Rodway, 1888); Dutton Cook, 'Charles Dickens as a Dramatic Critic', *Longman's Magazine*, II, May 1883, pp. 29–42; Sylvère Monod, 'Une Amitié Francaise de Charles Dickens: letters inédites à Philodès Régnier', *Etudes Anglaises*, II, 1958, pp. 119–35 and III, 1958, pp. 210–25.

16 A short essay called 'A Flight' has Dickens sharing a train carriage from London to Paris with a 'Compact Enchantress', a 'French actress, to whom I yielded up my heart under the auspices of that brave child, "MEAT-CHELL," at the St. James's Theatre the night before last: *Reprinted Pieces* (London, Chapman and Hall, 1911), p. 128.

17 *The Letters of Charles Dickens, Vol. Six, 1850–1852* (Oxford, Clarendon Press, 1988), p. 120.

18 *The Letters of Charles Dickens, Vol. Five, 1847–1849* (Oxford, Clarendon Press, 1981), p. 588.

19 See George Taylor, *Players and Performances in the Victorian Theatre* (Manchester, Manchester University Press, 1989), p. 95, for a discussion of Lewes.

20 G. H. Lewes, *On Actors and the Art of Acting* (London, Smith, Elder and Co., 1875), pp. 123–4.

21 Helena Faucit, Lady Martin, *On Some of Shakespeare's Female Characters*, new and enlarged edition (Edinburgh and London, William Blackwood and Sons, 1891), p. 234.

22 *The Morning Post*, 4 January 1845, p. 3.

23 Anon [Sarah Austin], 'Shakespeare in Paris', *Edinburgh Review*, Vol. LXXXIII, No. CLXVII, January 1846, pp. 47–63, p. 48.

24 *The Morning Post*, 21 January 1845, p. 2.

25 See B. Juden and J. Richer, 'Macready et *Hamlet* a Paris en 1844', *La revue des Lettres Modernes*, Nos 74–5, 1962/63.

26 *Macready's Reminiscences*, ed. Sir Frederick Pollock (London, Macmillan, 1875), Vol. II, p. 251. When, in the course of his Paris season, Macready visited the Conservatoire, he observed, 'I … saw the inefficiency of the system clearly; it was teaching conventionalism – it was perpetuating the mannerism of the French stage, which is all mannerism': Alan S. Downer, *The Eminent Tragedian: William Charles Macready* (Cambridge Mass., Harvard University Press, 1966), p. 272. My account of the French visit is made up from these two books together with William Archer, *William Charles Macready* (London, Kegan Paul, 1890); Victor Leathers, *British Entertainers in France* (Toronto, University of Toronto Press, 1959); and various newspaper reports.

27 *The Times*, 22 January 1845, p. 50.

28 *The Morning Post*, 29 May 1845, p. 5.

29 Boutet, *Mademoiselle Mars*, p. 273.

30 For example, *Illustrated London News*, 12 April 1845.

31 25 April [1845]: *The London Theatre 1811–1866, selections from the diary of Henry Crabb Robinson*, ed. by Eluned Brown (London, The Society for Theatre Research, 1966), p. 176.

32 *Morning Post*, 24 May 1845, p. 5.

33 *The Era*, 13 April 1845, p. 5.

34 *The Morning Post*, 10 May 1845, p. 6.

35 *The Times*, 2 April 1845, p. 6.

36 *The Daily Telegraph*, 8 May 1873, p. 2.

37 Maurice Descotes, *Les grands roles du théâtre de Molière* (Paris, Presses Universitaires de France, 1960).

38 Lewes's contributions to this paper, although unsigned, can usually be identified by the presence of words and phrases he used elsewhere.

39 *The Morning Chronicle*, 28 April 1845, p. 6.

40 See Frédéric Febvre, *Journal d'un comédien, Tome premier 1850–1870* (Paris, Paul Ollendorf, 1896), pp. 107–9.

41 See D'Heylli, *Madame Arnould-Plessy 1834–1876*, pp. 114–16).

42 George Eliot, *Adam Bede* (Harmondsworth, Penguin, 1980), p. 321.

43 Haymarket Theatre, 14 January 1869 – with E. A. Sothern.

44 *The Principal Dramatic Works of Thomas William Robertson*, Vol. 1 (London, Sampson Low, 1889), p. 272.

45 'These days she listens to herself speaking, and sometimes she speaks like a woman in a dream, sometimes like a woman in an ecstacy. Listening to her it is impossible to understand how she has collected such a large following, she really isn't a living person. Every gesture, every blink of the eye is counted' Gustave Planche, 'Molière à la Comédie-Français', *Revue des Deux Mondes*, Vol. II, 15 April 1856, p. 903.

46 Francisque Sarcey, *Comédiens et Comédiennes* (Paris, Librairie de Bibliophiles, 1876), p. 16.

47 See my 'Déjazet/Déja vu', in Maggie B. Gale and Susan Bassnett, eds, *Women and Theatre, Occasional Papers 3* (Birmingham, University of Birmingham, 1996), pp. 30–52.

48 James, *The Scenic Art*, pp. 63.

49 Boutet, Mademoiselle, *Mars*, circa p. 295.

50 *Le Figaro,* 20 April 1880.

51 See 'The Comédie-Française and Sarah Bernhardt', *The Era*, 25 April 1880, p. 3.

52 *The Era*, 25 April 1880, p. 4 and 9 May 1880, pp. 4 and 6. Shortly after, Genevieve Ward gave an admired performance of the role in London which, it was said, 'inclines to that given by Mdlle. Sarah Bernhardt, who to obtain her ends, uses the seductions and wheedling graces of the courtesan, and not the commanding airs of 'La Grande Dame' which Madame Arnould Plessy assigned to the character': *ibid.*, p. 11.

53 *Ibid.*, 25 April 1880, p. 4.

54 The figure of the hysteric has, of course, been much discussed by literary historians in recent years. See, for example, Janet Beizer, *Ventriloquized*

Bodies: Narratives of Hysteria in Nineteenth-Century France (Ithaca and London, Cornell University Press, 1994).

55 Peter Brooks, *The Melodramatic Imagination* (New Haven and London, Yale University Press, 1995), p. XI.

56 See Elaine Aston, *Sarah Bernhardt: A French Actress on the English Stage,* (Oxford, Berg Publishers, 1989), p. 31.

57 See my 'The Modernity of Aimée Desclée', *New Theatre Quarterly,* Vol. VI, No. 24, November 1990, pp. 365–78.

58 See *The Times*, 5 April and 6 May 1873.

59 *The Era*, 11 May 1873, p. 10.

60 This is from Emile de Molènes, *Desclée. Biographie et Souvenirs* (Paris, Tresse, 1874), p. 101.

61 *The Spectator*, 7 June 1873, p. 726.

62 *The Era*, 25 May 1873, p. 11.

63 James, *The Scenic Art*, p. 247, also see p. 250.

64 *The Academy,* 20 May 1876, p. 497.

65 James, *The Scenic Art,* p. 7.

66 *Ibid.*, p. 90.

6

ELIZABETH ROBINS: HYSTERIA, POLITICS AND PERFORMANCE

Joanna Townsend

Now, I ask you to listen, as quietly as you can, to a lady who is not accustomed to speaking – a – in Trafalgar Square – or a ... as a matter of fact, at all. (*Votes for Women*, p. 69)

With these words – greeted scornfully by a jeering Trafalgar Square crowd with cries of 'A dumb lady ... Three cheers for the dumb lady' – the American actress and writer Elizabeth Robins introduces her character Vida Levering to a hostile audience in her 1907 pro-suffrage play, *Votes for Women*.[1] What is at stake here, made explicit in Robins's choice of language, is a move for Vida from silent suffering towards speech. By this point in the play the off-stage audience is aware that Vida has suffered at the hands of men in the past, suffering which includes an abortion carried out by a 'shady-looking doctor' in 'a lonely Welsh farmhouse' after being abandoned by the 'family friend' who had seduced her.[2] But the circumlocutory and euphemistic dialogues through which Vida's history has emerged tell their own tale of repression, of social circumstances which, to steal from Freud and Breuer's analysis of their hysterical patients, make speaking the truth impossible.[3] Indeed, in the first act of the play one of the other female characters describes Vida in terms that relate specifically to the repression of language and knowledge:

MRS HERIOT For all her Shelter schemes she's a hard woman. ...
        BEE She doesn't look –
LADY JOHN (*glancing at* BEE *and taking alarm*) I'm not sure but what she does. Her mouth – always like this – as if she were holding back something by main force.[4]

Given her chance to speak at the pro-suffrage meeting in the second act, then, Vida is enabled to make the transition from silence to speech, in the process making connections between her own suffering and the experiences of those around her. In this chapter, I trace Robins's own journey along that trajectory towards the ability to articulate her own desire, and the desires of the women in the society in which she lived, through her work as an actress, playwright and suffragist in London at the turn of the last century. Three plays and performances trace the route for this journey: the 1891 production of *Hedda Gabler* in which Robins played Hedda, the 1893 short play *Alan's Wife* written anonymously by Elizabeth Robins and Florence Bell in which Robins again took the title role, and *Votes for Women* (1907), which was written by Robins on behalf of the Women's Social and Political Union.

In my examination of these plays and of Robins's journey towards politicisation I focus on two ideas as key to her progress: first, on Robins's awareness of the ways in which her work touches on the relationships between speech and silence, knowledge and the repression of knowledge, which she and the women around her must negotiate; and second, on the way in which her work as an actress and playwright enables her to transcend those damaging divisions through performance. Drawing a parallel between Robins's performance strategies and what I term the rhetoric of hysteria, based on the figure of the Freudian hysteric who quite literally 'embodies' the split between the language of the written or 'spoken' text and that of the speaking body, I want to argue that the rhetoric of this 'performative disease', which involves the public staging of a private trauma, is employed by Robins as a means to articulate the desires of the feminine subject on the stage.

By adopting and developing the multi-layered rhetoric that is the process of conversion and cure for the hysteric, by staging the discourse of the body as well as that of speech, Robins can be seen to have negotiated a more complex, and more powerful, position from which woman can speak. Working in the 'in-between' of speech and body, text and action, she revealed different possibilities and potentials to her audiences.

In so far as it is possible to discuss performances that were created over one hundred years ago, my primary focus is thus on the practical performance of hysterical rhetoric by Robins, bringing the body back centre stage. In 1891, Robins played Hedda Gabler in the first London production of Ibsen's play; in the second section of this chapter, 'Performing Hysteria', I argue that Robins's experience in working with *Hedda Gabler* led her to develop a new style of acting based in the contradiction within the female split subject. In 1893, Robins played Jean

Creyke in *Alan's Wife*, which she had written with Florence Bell; in the third section, 'Writing Hysteria', I argue that in this play, which echoes certain themes of *Hedda Gabler*, she sought to reproduce as a playwright the double discourse of speech and action which she had developed as a performer of Ibsen. In 1907, long after her retirement as an actress, Robins wrote the Suffrage play *Votes for Women*. In the last section of this chapter, 'Politicising Hysteria', which looks more briefly at this last, more conventional drama, I draw a parallel between Robins's work in constructing a new way of representing the female subject on the stage, and her work towards constructing a new female political subject in her campaigning on behalf of the Suffrage movement: it is through performance that Robins is politicised.

Acting hysteria: *Hedda Gabler* (1891)

It was Henrik Ibsen's play about Hedda Gabler, whose 'hysteria' was said to 'motivate ... everything she does',[5] that provided Elizabeth Robins with a text in which she could begin to develop a dual performance strategy of vocal speech and silent expressive gesture, and which set her upon a path towards political awareness, although she was hardly conscious of it at the time. 'The general bearing of Hedda's story ... so little concerned us when we were producing Ibsen that we never so much as spoke about it', she told the Royal Society of Arts in her 1928 lecture, Ibsen and the Actress, yet her performance does seem to mark a new sense of self-awareness: 'I despair of giving an idea of what that little part meant, not only of vivid pleasure in working at and playing, but of – what I cannot find any other word for than – *self-respect*.'[6] *Hedda Gabler*'s ability to provide a site for Robins's development of this new kind of performance was founded in what Gay Gibson Cima has described as Ibsen's innovation in writing 'a double line of action' for his characters: 'The actor could no longer speak of the dual consciousness of self and character but rather had to discuss the treble strata of self, character, and *the role the character plays*, a phenomenon which produced a radical change in the actor's art.'[7]

Playing the part of Hedda, Robins had to find a way to communicate to her audience an awareness of her character that operated at many different levels: the past Hedda, daughter of General Gabler and 'secret' friend of Eilert Lovborg, who is hidden to Tesman but is revealed through her present actions which shape the outcome of the play; the present Hedda who participates not only in the 'realistic' world of her

marriage and social relations but also in her own melodramatic narrative through which, as Cima argues, she 'creat[es] ... a role for herself
different from the role she has been assigned';[8] the Hedda who participates in two narratives at once, one open, one hidden, as in the photo-
graph album scene with Lovborg or the final scene where, in Cima's
words,

> Hedda must follow a tiered or imbricated line of action: she must not
> only try to follow and gradually understand Brack's line of action, but
> also direct her effort toward overhearing Thea and Tesman, and deter-
> mining her own future.[9]

At a still deeper level, Robins had to portray the split between the Hedda
who must live in a restricted society governed by Brack's final dictum
that 'People don't do such things!', and the Hedda whom she describes as
'a bundle of unused possibilities, educated to fear life; too much opportunity to develop her weaknesses; no opportunity at all to develop her
best powers'.[10]

Just as the hysteric's speaking body communicates via symptom
what cannot be expressed in verbal language, so Robins, approaching
the part of Hedda, utilised the language of the body to explore and hint
at the existence of another, deeper, contradictory truth which might
explain Hedda's doubly-split self. In doing so, she staged the 'return of
the repressed', not only in relation to Hedda's hysteria, but also through
a technique of acting which allowed moments of what can only be
termed 'melodramatic' gesture to force through the 'realist' veil of
Ibsen's text: the evidence of Robins's performance practice in the 1891
Hedda Gabler reveals that Robins supplemented the techniques of realism with the 'speaking body' inherited from melodrama to enable her
to fully represent the contradictory, hysterical Hedda. Robins's comments about her development of that technique suggest that in working
to understand this new, psychological complexity of character, *and to
stage the discourse of the body as well as that of speech* – drawing on
techniques of realism and the mute discourse of melodrama – she was
herself able to experience, and begin to represent, her own subjectivity.
'No dramatist has ever meant so much to the women of the stage as
Henrik Ibsen', she argues;[11] for Robins, Ibsen's text of *Hedda Gabler*
prompted her to begin the journey towards truly representing the
self.

The background to the play's production is complex, and is the
subject of discussion elsewhere.[12] While the relative contributions of

Robins and William Archer are still debated, what is clear is that the approach taken to the production placed unusual emphasis on the quality of the acting, with lengthy rehearsals and carefully plotted stage management working together to bring out the complexity of Ibsen's character portrayal.

In seeking a way to represent Hedda, Robins made use of what she described in her lecture to the Royal Society of Arts in 1928 as 'Ibsen's supreme faculty for giving his actors the clue – the master-key – if they are not too lofty or too helplessly sophisticated to take it'.[13] Robins does not describe the operation of this faculty, but in the discussion that follows it becomes clear that she is referring to Ibsen's use of psychology to give meaning to his character's actions: an understanding of the 'interior depth' of the character provided the actor with a means of representing them on stage. Listening to Ibsen's prompting (rather than to the 'stage directions of all the Sydney Grundys of the last fifty years')[14] Robins describes the process as one of collaboration between playwright and actor:

> Ibsen was by training so intensely *un homme du théâtre* that, to an extent I know in no other dramatist, he saw where he could leave some of his greatest effects to be made by the actor, and so left them. It was as if he knew that only so could he get his effects – that is, by standing aside and watching his spell work not only through the actor, but by the actor as fellow-creator.[15]

Robins's account of her work on *Hedda Gabler* in *Ibsen and the Actress* shows that she, like Freud himself in his discussion of *Rosmersholm*'s Rebecca West in 'Some Character-Types Met With in Psycho-Analytic Work', went back into Hedda's history, seeking to fill in the gaps, feints and evasions which make up the hysterical text. In doing so, however, she seemed to come dangerously close to identifying with Hedda Gabler herself. Writing to her friend and collaborator Florence Bell, she said: 'Do you know I think it's some kind of nervous disease that descends upon one with the grasp of such a part … I'm possessed – some mocking, half-pathetic demon gets into me and whirls me along without help or hindrance from me.'[16] However, it is from this unstable and shifting position that Robins seemed best able to draw out the political implications of her analysis, drawing herself and Hedda into identification not only with each other but with other women who share their restricted place in society: 'Hedda was not all of us, but she was a good many of us'.[17]

Having discovered the 'truth' of Hedda's character, Robins's next task was to set about trying to represent that truth on the stage. More recent productions have done so by staging a wordless prologue which reveals Hedda's hysteria directly to the audience, but on the nineteenth-century realist stage Robins had to communicate these complexities within the frame of Ibsen's text. Her prompt book demonstrates the ways in which she combined word and action, setting the movements of her body alongside and against the spoken text in order to represent the conflicts within the character of Hedda, just as the hysterical symptoms of Dora and Anna O. seemed to Freud to 'join ... in the conversation'.[18] Angela V. John describes this process, writing that Robins:

> used facial expressions and her hands, and modulated her voice to help the audience interpret a complex character like Hedda who might say one thing and mean another. Hedda was herself a consummate actress and the audience had to be helped to appreciate this.[19]

But like Gay Gibson Cima, John seems to situate this split, and the process of concealment and revelation to which it gives rise, at a conscious level of character: between 'character, and *the role the character plays*'.[20] The character concerned is aware of guilt or is herself a 'consummate actress': Cima says that 'the actor's creation of Hedda's awareness of the absurdity of the role she plays, is what constituted, for female actors and audience members, a new subversive level in the theatre'.[21] I want to argue here that the process is in fact a more complex one than Cima's argument implies: that the subversiveness offered by Robins's portrayal of Hedda's hysteria operates at the dangerous level of the unconscious as well as that of the conscious mind. Hedda's hysteria, her 'repression' in Ibsen's words, means that she is not always conscious of her guilt, of what has been repressed.

Robins thus sought to display to her audience not only the *conscious* duality of the character whom she played, but also the hysterical symptom, that which could not be said in language as it had been repressed, or 'forgotten' by the conscious mind. Cima has described an 'introspective, autistic gesture' which she argues that Robins employed in order to show the audience Hedda's awareness of her double self; here I want to extend and review this category, developing an analysis of Robins's gestures at key moments of tension as a rhetorical symptom of hysteria, a 'symptomatic act'. Re-examining and reworking the autistic gesture as a specifically hysterical gesture, a speaking symptom, we can locate a still deeper layer of meaning within Robins's gestures as Hedda.

Cima's main example of Robins's use of the 'autistic gesture' in *Hedda Gabler* is taken from the first meeting between Hedda and Mrs Elvsted, after Tesman has left them alone, when Hedda hears Thea admit that she left Sheriff Elvsted to follow Lovborg 'straight to town'. Robins's annotation of the prompt book shows that she planned to deliver her line, 'My dear good Thea, how did you find the courage?', while 'still sitting on arm of chair and looking off into space'.[22] For Cima, this gesture of looking into space allowed Robins, as Hedda, an introspective facial sign; indeed, this 'gesture' recurs repeatedly throughout the text at 'important' moments, such as when she gives Bertha the instruction to 'shew him [Eilert] in' at Lovborg's first entrance in Act II.[23]

Cima's other example from the prompt book, which she offers as an example of Robins working past action and memory into the present, relates to the scene in which Brack informs Hedda of the true nature of Lovborg's death. William Archer described Robins's playing of this scene thus:

> Instead of starting, where Brack says he must dispel her pleasant illusion, Miss R[obins] used to speak three speeches: 'Illusion?' 'What do you mean?' and 'Not voluntarily?' – quite absently, looking straight in front of her, and evidently not taking in what Brack was saying. She used to draw deep breaths of relief ..., quite intent on her vision of Eilert lying 'i skonhed', and only waken up at her fourth speech: 'Have you concealed anything?' ...
>
> I shall never forget her saying of 'Not voluntarily?' with a sort of dreamy surprise, not in the least realizing what Brack's words implied, yet beginning to wake up, as when a persistent external sound forces itself into a dream, and you are just awake enough to wonder vaguely what it can be.[24]

In her prompt book, Robins has noted 'grave and absent' next to the line 'Illusion?', while next to 'Not voluntarily?' she writes, 'sad far looking eyes and a smile that says softly how much better I know Eilert than you'.[25] In her article, 'Discovering Signs', Cima appropriates this gesture as an indication that Robins revealed Hedda's 'melodramatic, self-dramatizing, past-oriented action as well as her actual present struggle to keep Brack at bay'.[26]

However, Elin Diamond reads the scene differently, rejecting the consciousness implied by Cima and replacing it with a specifically hysterical emphasis which is close to that which I want to place on Robins's performance in this chapter:

> Marking moments when her body translates the secrets of 'emotion memory', Robins consciously represents hysteria's signifier, not for her interlocutor Brack, but for the Other, the spectator who will complete the circuit of signification and read her truth.[27]

Whether the spectators in the audience of the 1891 production were able to read Robins's truth is a question for a consideration of the critical reception which I cannot attempt here; for the moment, I want to pursue a reading of Robins's performance strategies which develops Elin Diamond's. In doing so, examination of additional passages from the prompt book strengthens the argument considerably, enabling us more firmly to locate this kind of staging of hysteria within Robins's work. For rather than relying solely on facial expressions which are notoriously difficult to 'read', Robins also provided her Hedda with nervous tics and gestures which seem to speak for her at moments of agitation, using 'the body itself, its actions, gestures ... to represent meanings that might otherwise be unavailable to representation'.[28]

In her first meeting with Mrs Elvsted, when Tesman has left to write his letter to Lovborg and Hedda is interrogating Thea about her relationships with her husband and with Eilert, Robins annotates the dialogue with descriptions of a gesture which, to return to Freud's terminology in discussing his hysterical patients, seems almost to 'join ... in the conversation'.[29] Using the prompt book and the copy of the full performance script held in the Lord Chamberlain's Plays Collection at the British Library, it is possible to reconstruct this scene. Robins's annotations to the text are set out within square brackets:

> HEDDA   (*Casually*) And [examines an invisible spot on her dress] Eilert
>   Lovborg has been in your neighbourhood about three years,
>   hasn't he?
> MRS ELVSTED (*Looking embarrassed at her*) Eilert Lovborg? Yes, he has.
> HEDDA   Had you known him before – here in town? [still brushing at
>   the 'spot']
> MRS ELVSTED Scarcely at all. I mean I knew him by name, of course.
> HEDDA   But you saw a good deal of him in the country? [quick sharp low][30]

The gesture is a descendant of Lady Macbeth's guilt-ridden 'Out, damned spot!', but what Robins does with it is subtly different. In contrast to Lady Macbeth's known and acknowledged guilt, Hedda's feelings for Lovborg are multiply repressed, both (at this point in the play) from the knowledge of the audience and, in their true depth, from her own consciousness. Robins thus draws on what might otherwise be seen as a melodramatic gesture to stage what is repressed by the spoken text at this moment of performance.

This kind of hysterical gesture is repeated in the next scene when Eilert is mentioned. As Tesman returns and asks whether there has been any message from Lovborg, Hedda's answer 'No' is accompanied by the hand-written direction, 'leans against curtain clicking nail on lower teeth'.[31] Elsewhere Hedda's body as represented by Robins is in constant motion, moving from sofa to window to chair, leaning on the back of furniture at one moment and moving away again in the next, full of restless agitation which belies the words with which she maintains her relations with society. In these moments Robins creates a double-layered dialogue of voice and body, adopting hysterical rhetoric to communicate a truth to the audience which cannot be seen by the society within the play. In Peter Brooks's words, 'Language as socially defined is inadequate to "cover" an area of the signifiable. … [The gesture marks] a kind of fault or gap in the code, the space that marks its inadequacies to convey a full freight of emotional meaning.'[32] Thus Robins planned carefully the ways in which she would communicate to the audience the multiply-doubled nature of Hedda's character. While some of these doublings relate to her awareness of guilt, or her desire to 'act' to reveal her true thoughts, it seems to me that the specifically 'gestural' moments which I have identified can be interpreted as the speaking unconscious – the hysterical gesture 'joining in the conversation', so that the analyst in the audience can be sure that he or she is approaching, in Freud's own somewhat complex words, the 'region of the pathogenic organization which contains the symptom's aetiology' – Hedda's fantasy life of freedom and power over Eilert Lovborg.[33]

Robins was soon to make further use of this split, making bearing 'speak' in place of dialogue in an attempt to replicate, as playwright, the lessons that she had learned about representing female subjectivity from Ibsen. It is to this work, *Alan's Wife*, which Robins wrote in collaboration with Florence Bell, that I now turn.

Writing hysteria: *Alan's Wife* (1893)

While very different from *Hedda Gabler*, this 'Study in Three Scenes', written by Bell and Robins and based on a short story entitled *Befriad*

('The Release', or 'Set Free'), can be seen as in part a 'reworking' of the concerns of Ibsen's text. The playwrights, with their understanding of women's predicament in society reinforced by their involvement with the story of Ibsen's heroine, here offer us an alternative picture of a woman who exceeds, or tries to escape from, the bounds of patriarchal society. Jean Creyke, the north country girl married to a virile worker, and Hedda Gabler, the daughter of a General and wife of the weak Tesman, may seem to be very different individuals at first sight, but their situations and desires bear striking similarities: similarities which lead both women towards a final choice between death or submission. *Alan's Wife* thus shares a similarity of focus with *Hedda Gabler*, but my main concern in this chapter is to show how, both in writing the text with Bell and in her own performance as the eponymous heroine of the play, Robins utilised and extended her previous performance practice in *Hedda Gabler*. By reproducing and radically rewriting the 'double discourse' of speech and action which she had developed as a performer of Ibsen, in the final scene of the play Robins attempted to stage the discourse of the mute but 'speaking' body of woman to shocking effect.

The title of *Alan's Wife*, like that of *Hedda Gabler*, situates the lead female character firmly within patriarchal society, allowing her identity only as she is owned or possessed by husband or father. General Gabler is dead, but his influence lives on in his repressed, hysterical daughter, now Hedda Tesman; Alan Creyke neither speaks nor is seen by the audience in the Robins-Bell play, but Jean's fate is shaped by her relationship to him, as the following brief plot summary makes clear. In the first scene she is happily married and pregnant, looking forward to a future which will in fact never happen, because by the end of this scene Alan has been killed in an accident. His dead body, on a covered stretcher, is brought on to the stage in the closing moments. In the second scene, Jean's child has been born crippled, almost as though the pregnant Jean has hysterically reproduced the mutilation of its father's body on the frame of her male child. Jean, driven to despair by the thought that her baby might outlive her ability to protect it, decides to end its life, first baptising the boy in order to save its soul. In the third scene, Jean is brought before the judicial authorities and is asked to try to explain her actions in order to avoid being hanged for the cold-blooded murder of her own child. But she remains silent until the final moments of the play as she is led away to her death, instead letting her mute body speak for her in a gestural dialogue carefully described by Robins and Bell.

Unlike Hedda Gabler in Ibsen's earlier play, Robins's character of Jean is allowed to marry a man, rather than a scholar like Tesman: the dialogue between Jean and her mother in the first scene emphasises Alan's physicality, 'a husband who is brave and strong,' … who loves the hills and the heather, and loves to feel the strong wind blowing in his face and the blood rushing through his veins!'[34] Where Hedda lacked the courage, or freedom, to marry a 'man', and was quite literally bored to death by her marriage to Tesman, Jean Creyke has been able to do so. But as the play progresses she too will be punished for her valuing of physicality over the Word – represented by the schoolmaster's book-learning, and personified in the minister, Jamie Warren, who has been rejected as a suitor by Jean – a punishment which ultimately results in her death sentence. Jean acts through her marriage to Alan, but her body is finally acted upon by the forces of law. Her resistance to these forces, knowing the outcome of such resistance, is at the heart of her refusal to speak in the third scene: a refusal and a choice that seems more positive than Hedda's hidden retreat to death in her closed, inner room. In this scene, Robins substitutes the language of the body for that of compliant speech, building on the split performance discourse which she had developed in portraying Hedda Gabler, but in contrast to that hysterical woman the character Jean is shown to be in control, making a conscious choice: here the rhetoric of hysteria, rather than the damaging illness which underlies it, is our focus.

Throughout the play, Jean is situated as rejecting the Word and those who use it in favour of a life that is centred on the physical, on the lived body. In this final scene, despite the mutilated and crippled bodies that have multiplied around her, she attempts to assert control over her situation through the language of the body. Unable and unwilling to argue her case in words, knowing that by doing so she brings herself within the discourses of authority and punishment, Jean seeks instead a different kind of communication. Her resistance is recognised as such: discussing her with Mrs Holroyd at the beginning of the third scene, Colonel Stewart says that she 'seems strangely hardened', needing to be brought to 'a better frame of mind' *Alan's Wife* (*AW*, p. 25). This language of 'hardness', which we have seen that Robins returned to in her 1907 suffrage play as a descriptor of Vida Levering, identifies both women as nonconformers to society's expectations of compliant femininity. But where Vida succeeds in employing that hardness to strengthen her will to speak on behalf of herself and other women by the end of *Votes for Women*, Jean is as yet unable to make the transition to voiced rather than gestural protest. She refuses the 'talking cure' offered by Colonel Stewart and Warren, but is unable to stage her own within the confines of their authority. Yet in resisting this 'treatment' Jean refuses to enable the men that surround her to construct their own narrative out of the words she offers them.

When Jean is first brought before the Colonel and her mother, she acknowledges her mother with a cry, and then falls silent. Mrs Holroyd, working on the Colonel's behalf, entreats her to, 'Tell his worship how you came to do it. Tell him you hadn't your wits right; that you didn't know what you were doing to the little bairn!' (AW, p. 25). Jean remains silent, refusing to offer up a narrative as exculpation. But on the stage this silence of the voice is set against the movements of Jean's speaking body: the play text makes it clear that the actor's body is to bear the meaning that cannot be expressed in words on the stage. The text records Jean's response to her mother's urging in the following way:

> JEAN   (is silent) I knew well enough.
> MRS HOLROYD   Oh, my dear, if you could tell him something that would make
> them let you off – now think, Jean, think, honey! it may be you
> could tell them something that would save you.
> JEAN   (stares vacantly into space) I can tell him nothing. (AW, p. 25)

Any ambiguity about the way in which this scene should be performed is removed by the published text, in which the stage directions state explicitly that, 'Jean's sentences are given as a stage direction of what she is silently to convey, but she does not speak until nearly the end of the Act' (AW, p. 41). Thus Jean remains silent for the majority of this scene, but her body, making use of the lessons learned by Robins in her portrayal of the hysteric Hedda Gabler, speaks for her, reaching beyond the confines of the on-stage audience of authority to the theatre audience who, as knowing and active spectators, can work to interpret these symptomatic acts. It is interesting that the direction given to Jean at the end of this extract – 'stares vacantly into space' – is the direction which we have seen Robins previously employ for Hedda Gabler during moments of tension, such as Eilert's first entrance. Here it is connected, explicitly, with the withholding of information, with the repression of knowledge. And the withholding is total, even between women: for when Jean is left alone with her mother, watched only by two warders who 'stand at the back, apparently not listening', Jean refuses the medium, or cure, of words. Mrs Holroyd makes it clear that she 'hasn't opened her lips from the beginning' (AW, p. 25). Instead she continues, silently, to communicate by gesture alone.

In his discussion of melodrama, Peter Brooks distinguishes between mute tableau and gesture – in which the actors provide fixed and visual representations of reactions in attitudes that correspond to the situation of their souls – and the mute role, in which the character has to express increasingly complex ideas through gesture, and fails to do so. Brooks writes that in such cases: 'Gesture seems to be receiving a charge of meaning that we might suspect to be in excess of what it can literally support.' [35] In conventional melodrama, however, there is always an interpreter figure or figures, who are able to translate these mute gestures into long and complicated descriptions. Robins and Bell allow their actor, and their audience, no such respite, no easy translation back into words: Mrs Holroyd, who admits that Jean 'always knew I hadn't the wits to be up to her, or find the words to say to her', is unable to translate (*AW*, p. 25). The gestures of Jean Creyke, like those of the mute role of melodrama, here seem to be being asked to bear a meaning in excess of what they can support, without the comforting safety net of translation back into words. And while some of Jean's 'utterances' draw on the gestural codes of the mid-nineteenth-century stage, such as when the actress expresses the sentiment of sympathy, 'Poor mother!', by 'put[ting] out her hand to her mother' (*AW*, p. 26), other sentences given in the play text are more difficult to represent in gesture, as the following examples demonstrate:

MRS HOLROYD   How could you do it, my lass? Can't you remember? If you could have told them all about it and asked for mercy you could have got it.
JEAN   (*smiles strangely*) I don't want mercy.
(*silent*)
[…]
WARREN   Jean, your only hope is in Him who alone can pardon your sin; turn to Him before it is too late. Do not die unforgiven.
JEAN   (*is silent*) I shall not die unforgiven. (*AW*, pp. 26–7)

Gesture cannot bear the weight of such language; or rather, the words given in the text are inadequate approximations of what is to be communicated by gesture. Language as socially defined is once again inadequate to cover an area of the signifiable. But what does seem to be clear here is that Jean no longer wants to speak in the language of words, that she resists the talking cure urged so insistently by those around her: 'It may be you could tell them something that would save you', 'Jean, Jean, if only I could get you to speak', 'Speak, speak, before it is too late. Tell them why you did it. Put away your rebellious heart!' (*AW*, pp. 25–28). Although she is explicitly stated within the play text *not* to be hysterical, or 'mad' in any way – 'I knew well enough' is one of the 'silent' phrases given to her (*AW*, p. 25) – Jean here adopts the language of hysteria, of the speaking body, as the only language which allows her to speak true, to resist reinscription within the discourse of the Word.[36] Jean Creyke knows that it is only by resisting the talking cure that she can remain in possession of her own story. And although her chosen ending – death – might seem to be a very bad one indeed, it enables her to retain her vision of bodily strength and vigour triumphing over the restrictions of the Word and the Law. In rewriting the ending of the play for publication, Robins and Bell drive this point home: 'Maybe I shall find him up yonder made straight and fair and happy – find him in Alan's arms. Good-bye – mother – goodbye!' (*AW*, p. 28). Like Hedda, Jean's only escape is that of death, for she, like her child, is unable to live free in society. But unlike Hedda, who is cornered by despair and by her inability to influence others, Jean seems to actively choose death as a means to set herself, like her child, free. This difference in their positions is reflected by their relationship to the speaking body: Hedda's body speaks for her at moments of tension, hysterically, involuntarily, while in the final scene of *Alan's Wife* Jean consciously uses her body and its gestures as a means of communication, resisting submission to the Word and the Law and communicating that resistance to the nineteenth-century audience without the medium of the spoken word. By refusing the spoken word the character of Jean Creyke refuses to be reincorporated within the systems of justice and power represented by Colonel Stewart or Jamie Warren; by writing and performing such refusal Robins resists the closure of her text, beginning to politicise the speaking body of hysteria. It is to the completion of this final stage of the journey that I now turn, ending this chapter with a brief consideration of Robins's last play, written on behalf of the Suffrage movement.

Politicising hysteria: *Votes for Women* (1907)

You've seen the accounts of the girl who's been tried in Manchester lately for the murder of her child. ... A little working girl – an orphan of eighteen – who crawled with the dead body of her new-born child to her master's back door and left the baby there. ... A few days later she found herself in court being tried for the murder of her child. Her master, a married man, had of course reported the 'find' at his back door to the police and he had been summoned to give evidence. The girl cried out

to him in the open court: 'You are the father!' He couldn't deny it. The
Coroner at the jury's request censured the man and regretted that the
law didn't make him responsible. But he went scot free. And that girl is
now serving her sentence in Strangeways Gaol.[37]

Robins's character Vida Levering recounts this story of infanticide to her
Trafalgar Square audience, and to the audience of the Court Theatre
where Robins's play was first performed in 1907, in the second act of
Votes for Women. Making the last of a series of speeches at a pro-suffrage
rally, Levering, who has of course herself been forced into an abortion at
the hands of a 'shady-looking doctor' some years previously, uses this
story to highlight the different experiences of men and women within
the English justice system: 'A woman is arrested by a man, brought
before a man judge, tried by a jury of men, condemned by men, taken to
prison by a man, and by a man she's hanged! Where in all this were her
"peers"'? In *Alan's Wife*, Robins had told the story of Jean Creyke,
another woman who kills her child in desperate circumstances, and had
shown Jean to be caught up within this male system of justice which
Vida Levering now reveals to be so biased against her, her only option
the resort to silence as a means of resistant non-co-operation. Jean,
knowing that her voice would only be appropriated for others' purposes,
remains silent. In contrast, in *Votes for Women* Robins (like Vida herself)
is able to take the step from silent or coded resistance towards vocal criticism and protest, using 'the methods proper to writers – the use of the
pen',[38] and translating this into the on-stage language of protesting
bodies and voices.

    At the beginning of this chapter, I argued that in making this
speech at the suffrage rally, Vida is able to connect her experiences of
seduction and the maternal body with the more general experiences of
women. Unlike Jean Creyke, who explicitly refuses to identify with the
suffering of other women when reminded that others suffer as she
does, angrily asking, 'And does it make it any better for me to think of
those other wretched women?',[39] Vida Levering is able to make that
connection between her own past experiences and those affecting all
women in her society: her own 'peers' who are so seldom allowed to be
heard. Making this connection gives her the strength to speak both in
and against the dominant male discourse, doing so with the aim of co-
operation by women with women and for women, rather than the old
kind of co-operation with the patriarchal order which was urged upon
Jean Creyke by her mother, Colonel Stewart and the minister Jamie
Warren:

> We women must organise. We must learn to work together. We have all –
> rich and poor, happy and unhappy – worked so long and so exclusively
> for men, we hardly know how to work for one another. But we must
> learn.[40]

In stressing the value of 'working together', and doing so in a scene
which relies for its staging on a kind of ensemble theatre far removed
from the isolated figures of Hedda Gabler and Jean Creyke, Robins
reached the end of the journey towards political awareness and articulation of desire which I have traced in this chapter. *Votes for Women* is still
marked by moments of hysterical bodily revelation – such as when the
play's romantic heroine, Beatrice, listening to Vida's speech at the
suffrage rally, realises the connection between Vida's description of
childbirth, every woman's 'hour of darkness', and her own fiancé
Geoffrey Stonor, a prominent Conservative politician, whom she
suddenly identifies as the 'family friend' who had seduced Vida years
before: 'Her hands go up to her throat as though she suffered a choking
sensation. It is in her face that she knows.' [41] But what is different here is
that the play's narrative does not end with this silent, hysterical realisation and the inability to communicate the knowledge gained which lead
to death for both Hedda and Jean Creyke: instead the power of the body,
and its numerous betrayals, is put to political use in the last Act, where
Beatrice and Vida work together to force Stonor to repay the debt he
owes to women, and enlist his support for the suffrage cause. 'The man
who served one woman – God knows how many more – very ill – shall
serve hundreds of thousands well' (p. 141). Thus, while Robins has not
forgotten the dramatic lessons learned from *Hedda Gabler* and *Alan's
Wife*, she now uses the combination of body and word to achieve political action on women's behalf.

While the experience of acting in Ibsen aided Robins towards a new
construction and representation of the female subject, the step towards
political subjectivity was one that Robins eventually recognised needed
to be taken together with other women; what she saw as Ibsen's belief in
the 'power of the single great personality' limited the power of his work
at a time in which, she argued, 'progressive ideas are barren and without
effect except in so far as they are diffused and held in common'.[42] In Vida
Levering's final long speech of *Votes for Women* Robins thus widens the
focus from the secret pain of the individual, experienced by Hedda
Gabler and Jean Creyke, to draw a lesson of the need for communal
political action, the need to speak out and to speak out together to avoid
the possibility that all could be 'made smooth and soothed again by

some form of that phrase, 'An exceptional woman', with the prompt rider, 'sexless'.[43] Levering tells Stonor, as Robins tells her audience:

> The time has come when a woman may look about her, and say: What significance has my secret pain? Does it 'join on' to anything? And I find it does. I'm no longer a woman who has stumbled on the way. ... I'm one who has got up bruised and bleeding, ... and said to herself not merely: Here's one luckless woman! but – here is a stone of stumbling to many. Let's see if it can't be moved out of other women's way. And she calls people to come and help.[44]

The dramatic journey of Elizabeth Robins which I have traced in this chapter thus brings her to a political understanding of the way in which she and other women must work together to achieve both individual and collective aims. The stories of Hedda Gabler and Jean Creyke must no longer be seen in isolation, but rather as joined to the stories of other suffering and silent women through history.

Notes

1 Elizabeth Robins, *Votes for Women*, in Katherine E. Kelly, ed., *Modern Drama by Women 1880s–1930s, An International Anthology*, (London and New York, Routledge, 1996), pp. 108–46.

2 Robins, *Votes for Women*, p. 120.

3 Sigmund Freud and Joseph Breuer, *Studies on Hysteria* (Harmondsworth, Penguin, 1974), p. 61.

4 Robins, *Votes for Women*, p. 120.

5 Henrik Ibsen, notes on *Hedda Gabler* (1890), taken from Toby Cole, ed., *Playwrights on Playwrighting*, (New York, Hill, 1964), p. 166.

6 Robins, *Ibsen and the Actress* (London, Hogarth Press, 1928), pp. 14–15 (my emphasis).

7 Gay Gibson Cima, 'Discovering Signs, The Emergence of the Critical Actor in Ibsen', *Theatre Journal*, 35, 1983, pp. 5–22, pp. 18–19.

8 *Ibid.*, p. 19.

9 *Ibid.*, p. 21.

10 Robins, *Ibsen and the Actress*, pp. 18–19.

11 *Ibid.*, p. 55.

12 See for example, Thomas Postlewait, 'Prophet of the New Drama, William Archer and the Ibsen Campaign', *Contributions in Drama and Theatre Studies*, 20 (Westport and London, Greenwood Press, 1986), pp. 64–81; Joanne E. Gates, 'Elizabeth Robins and the 1891 *Production of Hedda Gabler*', *Modern Drama*, 28: 1985, pp. 611–19.

13 Robins, *Ibsen and the Actress*, p. 26.

14 *Ibid.*, p. 52.

15 *Ibid.*, p. 53.

16 Letter to Florence Bell, 1892, quoted in Angela V. John, *Elizabeth Robins, Staging a Life* (London, Routledge, 1985), p. 60.

17 Robins, *Ibsen and the Actress*, p. 18.

18 Freud and Breuer, *Studies on Hysteria*, p. 383. Robins's 1891 prompt book is held by the Fales Library, New York University.

19 John, *Elizabeth Robins, Staging a Life*, pp. 58–9.

20 Cima, 'Discovering Signs', p. 19. Original emphasis.

21 Gay Gibson Cima, *Performing Women, Female Characters, Male Playwrights, and the Modern Stage* (Ithaca and London, Cornell University Press, 1993), p. 48.

22 Robins's 1891 prompt book, Act I, p. 6. This prompt book, bearing Elizabeth Robins's signature, consists of a typescript of Hedda's lines and cues, annotated by Robins, sometimes on both sides of the pages. Act I contains 13 pages (pp. 2–14), Act II contains 18 pages (pp. 15–32), Act III contains 16 pages (pp. 33–48) and Act IV contains 11 pages (pp. 1–11): Fales Library, New York University. A recent play by Maria Irene Fornes, *Summer in Gossenssas*, deals with Elizabeth Robins's production of *Hedda Gabler*, staging the hysteric in a number of interesting and complex ways. See Maria Delgado and Caridad Svich, eds, *Conducting a Life: Reflections on the Life of Maria Irene Fornes* (Lyme, Smith and Kraus, 1999), and Marc Robinson, ed., *The Theater of Maria Irene Fornes* (New York, PAJ Publications, 1999).

23 Prompt book, Act II, p. 24.

24 Letter to Charles Archer, 8 July 1891, reproduced in C[harles] Archer, *William Archer, Life, Work and Friendship* (London, Allen & Unwin, 1931), pp. 186–8.

25 Prompt book, Act IV, p. 6.

26 Cima, 'Discovering Signs', pp. 20–1.

27 Elin Diamond, 'Realism and Hysteria, Towards a Feminist Mimesis', *Discourse*, 13, 1990/91), pp. 59–92, p. 79.

28 Peter Brooks, 'Melodrama, Body, Revolution', in Jacky Bratton, Jim Cook and Christine Gledhill eds, *Melodrama, Stage Picture Screen* (London, British Film Institute, 1994), pp. 11–24 (p. 19).

29 Freud and Breuer, *Studies on Hysteria*, p. 383.

30 Prompt book, Act I, p. 9.

31 *Ibid.*, Act II, p. 23.

32 Peter Brooks, *The Melodramatic Imagination, Balzac, Henry James, Melodrama, and the Mode of Excess* (New Haven and London, Yale University Press, 1976), p. 67.

33 Freud and Breuer, *Studies on Hysteria*, p. 383.

34 *Alan's Wife, A Dramatic Study in Three Scenes*, First acted at the Independent Theatre in London, introduced by William Archer (London, Henry, 1893), p. 7. Subsequent references to this edition are given after quotations in the text, abbreviated *AW*.

35 Brooks, *The Melodramatic Imagination*, pp. 59–61.
36 Archer makes it clear that Jean Creyke is not to be regarded as insane: 'She is neither lunatic nor heroine. She is a terribly afflicted woman, that is all, who acts as, somewhere or other in the world, some similarly tortured creature is doubtless acting at the very moment I write these words' (Introduction, *Alan's Wife*, pp. xlv-xlvi, repr. from *Westminster Gazette*, 6 May 1893).
37 Robins, *Votes for Women*, p. 135.
38 Elizabeth Robins, *Way Stations* (London, New York and Toronto, Hodder and Stoughton, 1913), p. 106.
39 Robins and Bell, *Alan's Wife*, p. 21.
40 Robins, *Votes for Women*, p. 135.
41 *Ibid.*
42 *Some Aspects of Henrik Ibsen*, Fales Library, New York University. Transcript of a lecture given at the Philosophic Institute, Edinburgh, 27 October 1908.
43 Elizabeth Robins, 'Woman's Secret', in idem, *Way Stations*, p. 13.
44 Robins, *Votes for Women*, p. 145.

7

FROM FAME TO OBSCURITY: IN SEARCH OF CLEMENCE DANE

Maggie B. Gale

Clemence Dane, actress, novelist, journalist, film writer, sculptor and friend and confidante to the theatrical *glitterati* of the inter-war years and beyond, had a prolific career, writing some twenty-two stage plays and numerous novels and film scripts; there are no major biographies of her life. Any overtly autobiographical elements of her 'reminiscences', *London Has A Garden* (1964), and praised as 'enchanting' by her close friend Noël Coward, are limited especially with regard to references to her own work. A number of recent dictionaries of theatrical biography refer to Dane as one of the few 'canonical' women playwrights of her era – and here this should be taken to signify women whom the editors/publishers deem to be worth a mention. Yet the authors of such entries have remained unwilling to assess her work in the light of either her theatrical career, which spanned over half a century, or in the light of the changing theatre world in which she found herself. In a sense, this refusal is a symptom of the academy's failure to reorient itself with a generalised period of theatre history, traditionally seen as trite, middle class and conventional, a period of British theatre which one recent historian has suggested was full of inconsequential entertainment,[1] and one which did not produce overtly feminist women playwrights easily slotted into ready-made contemporary categories for analysis. Equally though, the lack of interest in Dane's work or career seems also to stem from an uncanny non-problematising of selected opinions of the theatre critics of her day; critics who seemed anxious about what they saw as an influx of women, both as audience and practitioner, into theatre after the 1914–18 war.

Clemence Dane, née Winifred Ashton, raised in south London, was one of two children born into a middle-class family in 1888 (although a couple of recent biographical entries date her birth as 1887). She was well educated for a woman of her generation and had taught French to English girls in Geneva before training at the Slade School of Art in her

late teens. She also studied art in Dresden and taught at a girls' school
in Ireland before embarking on a short career as an actress under the
name of Diana Cortis, before the First World War.[2] All her biographers
claim that illness during the war caused Dane to give up teaching,
although I would suggest that her dissatisfaction with the structure of
the education system may have been a contributing factor to her decision to change career; she proposed in her 1926 social tract *The
Women's Side* that an education system which was co-educational and
similar in ethos to that proposed by William Morris would be more
appropriate to the requirements of a modern society. Her first novel
Regiment of Women (1917) caused a sensation because of its lesbian
theme, and her first play *A Bill of Divorcement* (1921), produced under
the ReandeaN banner at the Shaftesbury theatre in 1921, with a run of
402 performances, was one of the big hits of the season, causing much
discussion in the national press because of the way in which she dealt
with the then contentious issue of divorce. From this point on Dane
was identified as a successful playwright and novelist. Many of her
novels centre their narrative around the theatre (*Wandering Stars and
The Lover* (1924), *Broome Stages* (1931) and *The Flower Girls* (1954)
among them). One of the few playwrights to have their work produced
through the 1920s and 1930s and beyond, Dane often wrote for, or was
commissioned by, particular 'star' actresses of the day, such as Sybil
Thorndike and Gertrude Lawrence, and Katherine Cornell – who
brought her early plays to an eager American audience.[3] Engaged by
Radio Pictures Ltd, as a film scenarist, she worked on many films
including *Anna Karenina* (for Greta Garbo – 1935) and *St. Martin's Lane*
(for Charles Laughton – 1938) and won an Oscar for *Perfect Strangers*,
directed by Alexander Korda in 1947. Dane also had a number of collaborative professional relationships, one with Helen Simpson, with
whom she wrote a play and a number of popular detective novels, and
another with Richard Addinsell creating amongst others, *Adam's Opera*
(produced by Lilian Baylis at the Old Vic in 1928) and the experimental
Come of Age. A Life President of The Society of Women Writers and
Journalists, Dane wrote regularly for the popular press, Radio and BBC
television and published works of criticism and adaptation as well as
her work for the stage; she was created a CBE in 1953. Thus Clemence
Dane, given the seemingly affectionate but rather awful name of
'Clemmie-the-Dane' by Lewis Casson, and called Winnie by others of
her friends, was very mainstream and very successful. All this makes her
virtual disappearance from theatre history and analysis rather bizarre;

she is, after all, mentioned in numerous biographies such as those of Noël Coward, the Thorndike-Cassons, and the infamous Binkie Beaumont and her work has been published and reprinted from the early decades of the twentieth century through to the 1980s. Dane genuinely experimented with style and form in her work – so it is not that easy to relegate her to the ranks of a 'domestic or romantic comedy playwright', as has happened with so many of her female contemporaries. Clemence Dane was an important figure in British theatre history and this chapter is an attempt to relocate and (re)construct a picture of her in relation to the current relative invisibility of her life and career and in the context of the theatre of her day.

The influx of women

For theatre historian and critic Ernest Short, there was an influx of women into the theatre industry during the inter-war years, an influx which he claimed one could not pretend was an 'unmixed benefit' .[4] He suggests 'Gentlewomen, who would not have attempted to shoulder their way into theatrical careers in competition with men in Victorian times, began to do so with full assurance and success'.[5] However, recent research into women's theatre negates the generality of such a statement; both the Victorian and Edwardian periods saw numbers of women working in the theatre industry, the middle-class section of which was expanding. The revelation of a continuum of women playwrights and theatre workers also suffers through the all-pervading desire to periodise theatre; we think of careers in terms of periods of history or movements in theatre rather than in terms of a professional lifetime which may transverse such categories. Thus pre-First World War women playwrights like Elizabeth Baker, Cicely Hamilton and Gertrude Jennings continued to have their work produced after the First World War and the demise of organisations which had championed women's work, such as the Actresses' Franchise League and The Pioneer Players. Janice Oliver's assertion that, 'few women attempted at this time to write for an English stage that was not receptive to their efforts',[6] contextualises Dane's work in a framework which places her in isolation from the numerous other women playwrights of her day. Concern amongst critics that the theatre was in danger of becoming feminised after the First World War can be seen as a chauvinist response to a new generation of young women with more economic independence than their foremothers, as well as a means of using one section of the 'new' audiences as a scapegoat for fears about the class make-up of London audiences. Certainly such fears of women somehow taking over the theatres make J. C. Trewin's statement in 1953 that 'woman's hour' upon the stage had been 'sparsely filled' seem rather strangely misplaced.[7] As London theatres generally moved out of the hands of actor-managers towards private ownership and ownership by investor and cartel, critics became more and more concerned with who should control what was being produced, and for whom. The number of references to 'flapper audiences' and 'feminised theatre' would suggest that much of what was being put on had to appeal to such audiences, condemned by Louis MacNeice for using theatre 'as an uncritical escape from their everyday lives'.[8] Although this is an area into which little research has thus far been carried out, the implication that the theatre was being overrun by women had a significant impact on the way in which Clemence Dane and other women playwrights were received.[9]

J. P. Wearing's charting of London productions and production runs during the period show that not only were there a very large number of new plays being produced in the West End, but that many of them were by women or female/male teams. It is reasonable to say that the theatre was largely dominated by men in most areas of production,[10] but Clemence Dane was amongst a number of women, including Gertrude Jennings, Dodie Smith, Joan Temple, Fryn Tennyson-Jesse and Margaret Kennedy who had three or more plays run for over 51 performances in the West End between the wars – Dane's plays continued to be produced into the 1960s. A one-and-a-half to two-month run is fairly successful in a theatre economy which is being overwhelmed by new productions of new plays. Productions of plays by women or female/male teams during the 1920s and 1930s ran at an average of 16 per cent of the total: this does not include such productions as were located in the independent subscription or club theatres, many of which, despite their 'fringe' and ideological ethos, provided a 'try-out' space for large monopoly managements. An average of 16 per cent of the market is high compared to commensurate figures for the London theatre after the introduction of subsidy in the 1940s up until the 1990s. Thus Clemence Dane was not alone as a woman playwright nor was she alone in having worked as an actress before moving into writing; Dodie Smith and Gertrude Jennings are just two amongst many others, just as actresses such as Irene Hentschel and Auriol Lee moved from acting into production and directing.

Critical reception

the achievement of Miss Dane is comparable with that of any living playwright except Shaw, with the added interest, as she has said, that the men in her plays are men as women see them.[11]

When she created a part for an actress she had true insight, and the actress – Meggie Albanesi, Lilian Braithwaite, Haidée Wright, Sybil Thorndike – acted with magnificence. She had no such power with men. No stage actor was even *eager* to play for her.[12]

I have heard it said that Miss Dane cannot 'draw men'. Whenever I hear this said of a woman novelist, I always begin to suspect that she draws them too well, but as women see them rather than as they see themselves.[13]

David Waldron Smithers, in his meagre study of Dane's work falls into line with W. A. Darlington, critic for the *Daily Telegraph* when he suggests that 'her most memorable creations were women'.[14] This line of criticism seems to have been one by which Dane suffered, for example critics of both *Will Shakespeare* (62 London performances in 1921), and *The Way Things Happen* (65 London performances in 1925) admonished Dane for the fact that she wrote male roles which lacked 'male vigour' or 'real backbone'. The criticisms of her male characterisations are ones which she takes up in *Gooseberry Fool*, written with Helen Simpson, where 'artistic' novelist Larch is told by her husband, a popular novelist, that she 'will never go beyond fifteen hundred' because she 'can't draw men'.[15] Larch comments that she models all her male characters on her husband, a conceited, egotistical bully. For her, critical commentary that her males are 'incredible … nincompoops: so weak: so undignified … no man could be so greedy … so vain', has more to with a lack of acceptance by men in general and her husband in particular, that a woman could draw male characters with such precision.[16] This is not one of Dane's best-known plays, but it has a certain similarity with plays like Noël Coward's *Private Lives* in that it deals with fairly nonchalant extra-marital affairs amongst the upper-middle classes and is full of witty banter and repartee. My point here, is that Dane was well aware of the perception of her work promoted by critics like W. A. Darlington, but continued to write texts which were essentially woman-centred and this may be one of the reasons for the ambiguities in critical reception and assessment of her career. Darlington, who appears to have had a particular problem with Dane's male characterisations, praises her craftsmanship but refuses to acknowledge her achievements or her contributions to the history of British theatre. At one point later in his own career he claimed that *A Bill of Divorcement* was an immediate hit, Dane's biggest success, which was subsequently forgotten.[17] This is rather an odd way of depicting the cultural significance of a play which was successful in the West End, on Broadway, was revived successfully in 1929, was twice adapted for film and was produced on British radio and television over a forty-year period. Darlington's undermining of Dane's achievements as a playwright link in with St John Ervine, who although he calls Clemence Dane the 'most distinguished woman dramatist in the history of the theatre' also labels her a 'oncer'. St John Ervine was amongst the many who during the 1920s proposed that theatre was in danger of becoming 'womanised', but felt that theatre could stay the 'recreation of a community' (*sic*) as long as the 'production of drama largely remains a man's job'. For St John Ervine, 'the pessimist has ample ground for his gloomy belief that they (women playwrights) are oncers at best and unlikely ever to offer serious rivalry to men'.[18] The label of 'oncer', unjustified in terms of the numbers of productions of and production runs of her plays, has stayed with Dane to this day, with recent biographical entries suggesting that she was indeed a 'oncer' who although devoted to the theatre was somehow rejected by audiences and producers alike.[19] Clemence Dane's career is often framed by the implication that her diversity weakened the strength and impact of her theatre work – she genuinely played with form and style. This reading of her body of work denies the validity of the variety of her work, her aptitude for adaptation and experimentation and the simple fact that she was a prolific and sought-after writer.

Re-constructing Clemence Dane: the salon in Tavistock Street

According to Smithers, Olwen Bowen-Davies, Dane's lifelong secretary and literary executor, implied that Dane 'did not much want her biography to be written'.[20] Indeed we are left with very little information about her life over which Dane had authorial sanction – a recently bequested archive holds mainly scripts[21] – and *London Has A Garden* contains only scant mention of her own work – despite the fact that it is a book about the history of Covent Garden and her long-standing relationship as a woman and a playwright/writer with this history. Thus, although autobiography is expectedly selective and we should presume a certain amount of fictionality, Dane's *lack* of autobiography in some ways has been one of the causes of the mythologising of the cultural (in)significance of her work by critics and the mythologising of her life by a whole host of key theatre personalities and figures of her day. Clemence Dane did not actively problematise her 'self' and effectively refused to construct herself in her own terms although she occasionally offers an insight into her own daily life.[22]

Dane reminisces about her Edwardian journey on foot from Kensington to Covent Garden, seeing the journey as providing a record of 'change and loss'.[23] This is the perspective which she takes on Covent Garden, a place which by means of a small flat in Tavistock Street provided her London base, and which a number of professional friends later describe as having been a kind of theatrical and literary salon for several decades. She arrived in Covent Garden at a point when a number of writers, publishers and theatrical agents were just beginning their careers, people such as Curtis Brown, Laurence Pollinger, Michael Joseph and Olwen Bowen-Davies, an author in her own right as well as someone who was to become a lifelong companion to both Dane and her work. Thus Dane's early career was drenched in theatrical figures, those of the Covent Garden of the past, as inhabitants or frequenters, Hannah More, Kitty Clive, Fanny Kelly and David Garrick and those of her present, May Whitty and Ben Webster, Edith Craig and so on. With the exceptions of biannual family outings to the centre of London's theatrical world, Dane's early years were spent in what was then outer London, Blackheath and later Kensington. The profits from *A Bill of Divorcement* enabled her to buy a smallholding in Devon but most of her professional life was centred around Tavistock Street.

> The eighteenth century rooms were in a desolate state, with soot and a long-dead fire spilling out over the dirty oaken floorboards. These polished well later on … the rooms had a charm for me, and I took them at once … in two months I was settled in with clean paint, a bathroom, bookshelves, desk, a big bunch of carnations and anything else that could keep a writer happy … I enjoyed the easiest possible access to Drury Lane, Covent Garden, the Aldwych, the Strand, the Stoll, the Gaiety, the Tivoli, the Adelphi …[24]

This geographical placement is significant to her friendships and critical relationships with theatre people, Noël Coward in particular, which she was to develop through the inter-war period and beyond. By the 1950s, Dane's country home had moved to Sussex, to three converted Romany caravans in a field.[25] Nancy Price, actress, director and founder with J. T. Grein of The People's National Theatre who praised Dane for the achievement of plays like *Granite* and *Wild Decembers*, but with greater gusto for her depiction of Elizabeth I in *Will Shakespeare*, describes this later residence as integral to the 'other' side of Dane, a place in which to write for a woman who loved the countryside.

> I go to a place where cities are for a time forgotten … in the heart of Sussex, at the end of a lane there is a wood round the corner … there are three caravans – real Romany caravans communicating by an ingenious device and, in each, large windows have been inserted. There is everything within them for comfort, interest and delight.[26]

Price also describes Dane as having an 'outward serenity, she is unhurried, she accomplishes without hustle. She wears long skirts even in the country and this gives her an isolated look, something different from her fellows … : yet she is kindly, of infinite understanding and with a great sense of humour'. These descriptions of someone who is grounded and organised, with the 'face of a Madonna', someone whose work should be taken seriously, contrast with many of the depictions of Dane in the various theatrical autobiographies in which she appears; here she is often portrayed as eccentric, over-enthusiastic and almost overbearing – lovable but somehow a bit of an oddity, not to be taken too seriously. These caricatures may of course have more to do with the nuance of theatrical auto/biographies of the period. Thomas Postlewaite's point that theatrical autobiographies often have the characteristic of 'playing to the audience' and being full of 'well-rehearsed anecdotes' is especially germane to the case of Clemence Dane.[27] Thus we are forced to rely on the hidden and sometimes not-so-hidden agendas of other theatrical figures of her day.

Emlyn Williams and Lewis Casson both imply an overbearing and maternal quality about Dane's interactions with them. *Granite*, produced at the Ambassadors theatre in 1926 was one of Casson's favourites: it marked the beginnings of a long friendship with the Thorndike-Cassons; but this is an *actress's* play. Judith, the heroine of the play condemned to live an unsatisfactory life on the hard granite of Lundy Island, is based loosely on Emma Hamilton and was amongst Sybil Thorndike's best loved roles. Although Dane and Casson 'used to have endless vehement arguments on all manner of subjects to the great satisfaction of them both',[28] there is a sense of professional egos clashing – Casson had problems with Dane's refusal to let her scripts be altered. This was particularly the case with Dane's play *Call Home the Heart* (1947), where she mixed expressionistic styles with realism and played with concepts of time and memory in an exploration of the complexities of marital and familial relationships in the aftermath of war.[29] The play is stylistically challenging and in many ways would have been perhaps better suited to film than the stage. Sybil Thorndike, although finding similarities between this text and that of an earlier favourite of hers, Glaspell's *The Verge,* found faults with the play as did Casson, and the changes he made in production nearly caused their friendship with Dane permanent damage.[30] Again, this may have been a simple clash between playwright and producer/director; a number of other autobiographies also mention that Dane did not like having her plays tampered with. However, Casson was also known as rather despotic and demanding of his actors and as being unwilling to shift his own artistic position. The troublesome production of *Moonlight is Silver* (1934), with Gertrude Lawrence and Douglas Fairbanks Jr suggests that Dane, having written the play as a quick replacement for one which Casson was directing for Binkie Beaumont, was not only willing to adapt her scripts, but was also capable of working as a director. One of Casson's biographers makes no mention of the fact that Casson was actually pulled off the production and replaced by Dane although there is a note to the fact that Beaumont never employed him as a director again.[31] Beaumont's biographer suggests that she had only originally employed Casson to oblige Sybil Thorndike, and that as he had assisted Basil Dean on three productions of her earlier plays, Beaumont had more faith in Dane whom he likened to early twentieth-century American playwright Rachel Crothers.[32] My suggestion here is that Casson's autobiographical reminiscences are, to some extent tinged with professional jealousy.

Emlyn Williams on the other hand, although impressed by Dane as a 'gifted' and yet 'outsize' woman, felt her to be like a 'mother at a prize-giving where all her children have ended up First' when working on a radio production of seemingly her most problematic play, *Will Shakespeare.*[33] There are echoes of Williams's perception of Dane in other autobiographies also, but interestingly mostly in those constructed by men. Cole Lesley weaves an affectionate narrative about Clemence Dane into his *Remember Laughter: The Life of Noël Coward* with frequent mentions of Coward's affection and respect for her. However, he also gains much authorial pleasure from reminiscing about her social gaffes and failure to recognise sexual innuendo – implying a sexual naiveté which does not entirely match the depth of her own literary explorations of sexuality in *Regiment of Women* and *The Women's Side* or in plays like *Granite*. This is a point I take further later in this chapter. Although Lesley notes the way in which Coward

had great respect for her intellectual prowess and knowledge of literature, he also describes occasions when Coward outwitted her or derived
great satisfaction out of tricking her. So, for example, when Dane questioned Coward as to why he had rearranged his books at such an
unreachable height, he commented that the top shelf was only filled
with 'trash' – Lesley then tells us that Coward 'spoke too quickly and
could only pray that she could not recognise some of her own novels at
that height'.[34] Lesley places himself very much as an observer and com-
mentator of what *he thinks* Coward thought, and his depiction of Dane
seems to have the agenda of a schoolboy eager to undermine a mother's
opinions or a child sending up an eccentric maiden aunt. More
recently, Philip Hoare picks up on this characterisation but also credits
Dane as having valid opinions about and criticisms of Coward's work.[35]
Indeed, Coward's own words imply a far more complex and dependent
relationship with Clemence Dane.

Coward's Madame Arcati

> My first evening in London was almost always spent in Clemence Dane's
> rickety little house in Tavistock Street, Covent Garden. There we all fore-
> gathered … Olwen (Winifred's secretary), Winifred herself … her
> capacity for friendship is without limits; apart from her recognised fame
> as a writer she is a brilliant sculptress and painter, and her vitality is
> inexhaustible. From 1930 onwards, whenever I have returned from
> abroad, or even from the wilds of Manchester, I have always winged my
> way, like a homing pigeon, to that cosy, friendly, long-suffering room on
> the first floor overlooking the market … its pictures are changed
> constantly; it is often flecked with paint and spattered with clay; it has
> been deafened for years by discussions, play-readings, piano playing and
> film conferences: it has been barked in, sung in, shouted in, eaten in and
> occasionally slept in … [36]

Clemence Dane's friendship with Coward lasted from the late
1920s/early 1930s – from peak times in both their careers through the war
years and the enormous changes in the structure and output of British
theatre enhanced by the introduction of subsidy, through to the growth
of television and so on, until her death in 1965.[37] He appears to have
depended on her opinions of his work at times and to have socialised
with a similar circle of friends. Whereas Binkie Beaumont's initial
emotional perception of her was in part as a maternal figure, for Coward
she was an adviser and someone whose approval he, to some extent,

needed.[38] Told that she was the 'Lady Blessington and Madame Sevigné of Covent Garden' by Beaumont,[39] Dane had an open door policy for Coward and others in her theatrical circle. Cole Lesley notes that she would give guidance to Coward on his reading – she had been more formally educated than Coward – and that she had a well-developed and active knowledge of English literature and history which would sometimes annoy him, persuading him to read Dickens and amongst other things, the King James Bible.[40] Dane and Coward had various disagreements about professional allegiance and practice; one particularly bad phase was in late 1945 and early 1946 where Coward noticed a 'change in atmosphere' after falling out with Dane's sometime collaborator Richard Addinsell over the score for the film of *Blithe Spirit* and Coward's removal of some of Addinsell's work from one of his reviews.[41] Dane was fiercely loyal to Addinsell, and as 1946 progressed Coward commented on Dane's 'female prejudice' and what he perceived as a 'deep and genuine hostility'.[42] Things came to a head when during a 'heart to heart' she told him that he had become 'unbearably arrogant … surrounded by yes-men', that he was no longer in touch with what was going on in the world, and that he was 'disloyal'. Things calmed down after this but Coward found space for retort in his diaries, stating that he thought Dane's work as a writer was deteriorating, that she was stubborn to a degree of 'mania', and that she simply wanted to kick him 'good and proud' when he was down. Two days later everything was fine although some of his later opinions of Dane's work continued to imply that her best days as a writer were over. Dane's theatrical work during the 1940s and 1950s is, I would suggest, heavily influenced by her work in film. In plays like *Call Home The Heart* (1947) and even in her comedy *Cousin Muriel* (1940), which Bernard Shaw kindly offered Edith Evans rewrites for,[43] Dane asks audiences to follow either very complex and twisted narratives or demands of them an acceptance of characters who may, at the time, have been far less 'threatening' on film. The ending of *Cousin Muriel* was changed in order to accommodate what was perceived as an uncomfortable reaction to Muriel's thieving: a film audience, with the distance of – and perhaps more obvious self-referentiality of – film may have found crime committed by an elderly lady more acceptable. Beaumont felt the play to be just missing the mark, but despite Huggett's insistence that the play was produced as a favour, Beaumont did not have the reputation of letting personal favours get in the way of his professional prowess – he would not have produced the play if he didn't think it had a chance of success.[44]

Coward's *Blithe Spirit*, despite some damning original reviews, ran in the West End for some four and half years, and the film version, made in 1945, was as successful. *Blithe Spirit* is a play in which the paranormal intercedes in discussions of love, marital arrangements and infidelities, via the conjurings of Madame Arcati, an eccentric mixture of schoolmistress and spiritualist. Arcati was a role which had grown and 'refused to leave the stage'; Clemence Dane had, according to Hoare, 'declined the part created for her'; Madame Arcati was consequently made famous by Margaret Rutherford.[45] Cole Lesley proposes that not only was the role written for Dane but that it was in fact modelled on her with her eccentric style of dress, and her 'schoolmarmish' enthusiasm. For Terry Castle, Madame Arcati is both instrumental to everything essential which occurs in the play, and to the play's 'allegory of homosexualisation'. She sees that Coward's investment of all his own 'zany energy and comic ebullience' into the character is in part his tribute to Dane's role as a 'Lesbian Muse' in his own life.[46] Whether one agrees with this reading or not, Arcati's femininity in the play is certainly juxtaposed with that of Ruth and Elvira – she has an interest outside of heterosexual and marital game-playing, and she has a distinctive and unusual field of professional knowledge which she is able to put into practice.[47] The role, according to Lesley, was based on Dane's 'Junoesque' qualities, qualities which Coward and his circle clearly saw as going beyond the traditionally 'feminine' qualities of the era; it is also interesting to note that Dane's uncle, Teddy Bentley, was a Victorian spiritualist healer. Her flowing dresses and long tresses of black hair, her large physique and the intellectual demands which she made of herself and those around her, appear indicative of the way in which many found it difficult to place her femininity in a world full of more obviously glamorous women.

When Coward was informed of Clemence Dane's death he wrote that he found it hard to believe that he would never see his 'gallant old girl' again and of how much he was in her debt.[48] He had 'never published a book or produced a play … without first indulging … in the warming radiance of her enthusiasm and the kindly but nonetheless perceptive shrewdness of her criticism'.[49]

Femininity, sexuality and sexual politics

Amongst the women playwrights whose work was being produced in the mainstream during the inter-war period, Clemence Dane was the most public, if not the most outspoken in her opinions. Despite her ideas on divorce and 'sex and the business woman' and despite the numerous articles written for the popular press about women's rights to equal pay for equal work, the 'modern girl' and so on, it would be difficult to place Dane alongside her more activist contemporaries like, for example, Rebecca West. Dane, although she lived with a female companion for many years, was not 'out' as a lesbian, and it has recently been suggested that her early novel, *A Regiment of Women* does not present positive images of lesbianism.[50] Lillian Faderman calls it one of the 'most noxious of lesbian Vampire novels, with a predictable school setting', and goes on to propose that it was a prototype of the 'lesbian as sickie' novel. She also states that Dane's friendship in the early 1920s with Violet Trefusis, Vita Sackville-West's lover, was primarily a means for Trefusis to make Sackville-West jealous.[51] Trefusis makes no mention of Dane in her memoirs, but wrote to Sackville-West that both she and Dane were bad judges of their own work, that Sheila Kaye-Smith's work was better than Dane's and that she thought that Dane was jealous of Sackville-West's work. Despite this a number of her letters castigate Sackville-West for spending time with Dane rather than her, and she seems also to have found Dane to be 'kind and comforting'. Trefusis also sought Dane's advice about her writing, at a time when both were in the early years of their careers.

> She is wonderful in making one see that everything must have a *function* and that it is not permissible to introduce any episode, however picturesque, that has no influence, direct or indirect, on the main theme. She made me look for the 'function' … [52]

I only explore their short friendship on the grounds of establishing Dane not just as lover's bait but as someone whose professional advice was sought and appreciated, much as in her later relationship with Coward. The 'bad press' given to Dane about her depiction of lesbianism is to some extent justifiable, for example, when asked by Radcliffe Hall to adapt her controversial novel *The Well of Loneliness*, for the stage, Dane refused on the grounds that it was not 'suitable for theatrical adaptation'.[53] But whatever Dane's reaction to lesbianism or the controversy surrounding the novel, her refusal may simply have been based on the Lord Chamberlain's known attitude to licencing plays which implied 'other' or 'forbidden' sexual practices. She would not have been alone in wanting to avoid clashes with the Lord Chamberlain's office; very few other plays of the era make overt reference to lesbianism.[54]

Thus Clemence Dane, from the standpoint of the late twentieth century, leaned towards the conservative; however, so much of her journalism and popular writing promoted a quest for equal citizenship between the sexes that it would be crude to dismiss her variety of feminism. Arguments set forth in *The Women's Side*, her popular social tract written in 1926, took the starting point of woman as emancipated and independent; Dane was concerned that women should not 'evade the responsibilities of citizenship'.[55] She did not, however, take a radical position in terms of the battle between the sexes, admonishing women who thought that the fight for equality was a fight for supremacy. Rather, Dane proposed that between the 'struggle for power' and the feeling of disability there must be a 'third' way, a middle path which led to equal companionship between the sexes. This was not, as I have already said, a radical position, but it brings Dane in line with other modes of liberal thinking of the 1920s and 1930s. She was against what she saw as the 'petty tyrannies' of old-fashioned social values and outdated legislation; that women should only dress in a certain way, that women should give up work once married, that women should not be allowed divorce on grounds of adultery or insanity and so on. During the run of *A Bill of Divorcement*, Dane wrote numerous articles on divorce for the popular press; of the play one critic and theatre historian stated, 'Her play, extremely contentious in its time, can scorch a theatre years after the reform it called for'.[56] Her attitude to women's rights is sustained through and extends beyond the war. She was as adamant about women not being pushed back into the home after the Second World War, as had happened after the 1914–18 war, and was equally adamant that they should be paid the same wages for the same work. Dane also questioned, in the national press, whether women were really expected to accept without question the withdrawal of crèche facilities at work after the war was over: she pointed out that daytime child-care, always considered a right within upper middle-class households, had become a necessity for women from less privileged classes who worked to keep their families financially afloat during the war, and would want to continue work during the post-war years.[57] Dane was fully aware of the social and cultural constraints under which women were working. From this we can read her ideas on 'sex and the business woman' or her ideas about single sex education from the position of knowing that Dane really was on the 'women's side'.

Statements about Dane's sexual naiveté, her 'Winnisms', her inability to understand double entendre and so on, abound in the male-authored auto/biographies in which she features as an eccentric 'maiden aunt', enthusiastic 'amateur' or never quite successful playwright. Yet, plays like *Granite*, *Wild Decembers* and *Call Home the Heart* in particular suggest that not only was Dane knowledgeable about female sexuality, but that she understood the workings of marriage even though she herself had never been in one. Virtually all of her plays feature strong female leads whose behaviour has been shaped by the clash between their own desires and the requirements made of them by the world in which they live. Her suggestion in *The Women's Side* that, in a society where single men are in short supply, single women with 'brains and health and the pioneer spirit' should emigrate to find romance, is based on a belief that women have the right to sexual fulfilment with a man if that is what they desire, even if it means leaving their homeland.[58] That Dane chose to live with a woman all her adult life is not something which is open to investigation through analysis of her own auto/biographical construction of self. The point about Dane's work here is that recent theatre historians, who propose that 'feminist drama' disappeared after the First World War but that some plays by women engaged with 'contemporary debate', seem to be missing the point; this contemporary debate was a *form* of feminism, more liberal, less separatist and less legislatively focused but nevertheless dealing with similar issues around women's lives.[59] After all, by the mid-1920s Dane felt that she was writing for a generation who had, 'not so much forgotten as never known the significance of the modest green and purple knot twisted into the button-hole of a woman's coat'.[60]

Politics and the practice of writing

Lord Salisbury was the great father figure, and Mr Balfour and Joseph Chamberlain were our Gary Coopers and Marlon Brandos.[61]

Clemence Dane was a political creature, and her politics reached far into her writing. Although she found television to be an art form which limited the ability or necessity of an audience to be active participants in the creation of meaning of a text, she felt that for writers it provided an 'enlargement of opportunity' which was 'life giving'. She was aware that television and film invited the audience to 'invent and select at pleasure', but felt that theatre offered more of a challenge.[62] The audience features largely in her thoughts about writing, aware of the writer's dilemma, caught between scorn and respect for the audience, she also felt that plays should not be 'high-brow' for the sake of being so, nor should writers forget that both the audience and the era of writing sets a great deal of the agenda for what a writer should say.[63] In terms of her playwriting, Dane was systematic and worked using a diagrammatic plotting system, 'a complex of squiggles, angles, squares and Morse code'.[64] This was the approach of a jobbing writer, not a 'oncer' , but a serious writer who did her research and was able to move from theatre to the novel to journalism to film scripting with ease. Like Coward and many of her circle, she had patriotic impulses. These were the impulses behind her historical characters and plays and those which led her to participate in productions such as the wartime pageant, *Cathedral Steps*, produced in September 1942 by Basil Dean for ENSA, on the steps of St Paul's Cathedral, and later at the cathedral in Coventry. Set up as an 'Anthology in Praise of Britain', Dane turned the script around in a short time, with very little need for changes, 'save to restrain a certain predilection for Queen Boadicea that might have involved Sybil Thorndike in a chariot race around St Paul's churchyard'.[65] The performance held up the central London traffic and caused a great stir; it was an exhausting but patriotic success. Dane's patriotism combined with her love of theatre also caused her to work on celebratory projects of historical significance such as her *Ellen Terry in The Theatre* – a celebration of the actress's life and work produced as the annual performance at the Barn Theatre in Tenterden, Kent, in 1956. Although one recent historian finds Dane's attitude to Ellen Terry's relationship with Edy Craig and Edward Gordon Craig 'reductive' in her play, *Eighty in The Shade*,[66] the piece, written as a celebration of the Casson-Thorndike's golden wedding in 1958 and as a further celebration of Ellen Terry, gives a very amusing reading of the way in which Edy Craig's career was overshadowed by her mother and of Edward Gordon Craig's inability to live up to his mother's expectations.

Dane continued to write until her death in 1965. Although perhaps no longer working with her finger on the pulse of a theatre which had changed greatly since her work as an actress before the First World War and her introduction to the theatre as a successful playwright in 1921, Dane could still claim positive attention from the critics in the early 1960s. In reviewing one of her many television plays, *Marriage Lives*, produced in 1961 by the BBC, one critic praised her sustained ability to 'dissect the complicated anatomy of marriage with skill and insight'.[67] Dane felt that the theatre of the inter-war years had reflected a 'feeling of revolt against the waste of war and the tearing up of a way of life' and that this analysis even stretched to those drawing-room comedies, so damned by critics of our own age, which she felt reflected a desperate need to relax and forget that a 'worse tomorrow was probably on the way'.[68] For Dane the approach to drama was, by the early 1960s, 'too grievance-ridden, too class-conscious and too fond of a "private language"', yet she praises plays like Behan's *The Hostage* and Wesker's *The Kitchen* for the way in which they accepted 'the challenge of the old approach'. Equally her praise of Pinter's skilful crafting of dialogue in *The Caretaker* indicates the depth of her appreciation and understanding of the trend of changes which had occurred in theatre over her long career.[69]

In an attempt to evaluate Dane's career one easily gets caught up in misconceptions of the relationship between the old world in which her career began, and the new in which it finished. Depicting Dane as someone who 'relished the opportunity to sparkle in a well-turned curtain speech',[70] contributes very little towards the re-evaluation of the contribution to British theatre made by this rather extraordinary woman. Equally, Laura Marcus's assertion of the 'fictionality' of much discourse in the literary construction of a life and of the instability of auto/biography problematises many of the auto/biographical sources which mention Clemence Dane, although I suggest one can read these in a number of ways.[71] Liz Stanley points to the fact that the importance of relationships between the subject and her colleagues cannot be underestimated, noting that we should recognise that the significance of those relationships is hard to measure; this argument has been central to this attempt to (re)construct Clemence Dane.[72]

Dane was not a marginal figure, she was part of a circle of theatre people who had real practical, critical and managerial power – star actresses like Katherine Cornell and Sybil Thorndike promoted her work and powerful managers and producers like Basil Dean and Binkie Beaumont knew that they could rely on her to produce the goods when required. Although I question the authority of many of the depictions of her in theatrical auto/biographies, they become a vital tool in a search for Clemence Dane. Many such memoirs contain thinly disguised hidden agendas and tend to play down the quality and popularity of Dane's prolific output. This is not particularly unusual where women's work is concerned, but this chapter ends as a plea for a re-evaluation of Dane which goes beyond the limitations of a contemporary feminist framework and beyond those of outdated theatre criticism and history. Clemence Dane falls foul of many failings in theatre historiography: the unwillingness to view women's work in the mainstream; the fear of the 'conservative'; and the general lack of interest in mid-twentieth-century theatre. It remains quite extraordinary that there is so little critical, biographical and historical material on a playwright so recently working in theatre, a playwright, once a household name, who has been somehow removed from fame to obscurity.

Notes

1 Jean Chothia, *English Drama of the Early Modern Period: 1890–1940* (London, Longman, 1996), p. 88.

2 See Erica Beth Weintraub, 'Clemence Dane', in Stanley Weintraub, *Modern British Dramatists: 1900–1945* (Michigan, Gale Research Corp., 1982), pp. 133–8; and Janice Oliver, 'Clemence Dane (Winifred Ashton)', in William Damastes and Katherine Kelly, eds, *British Playwrights 1880–1956, A Research and Production Sourcebook* (Westport, Conn., and London, Greenwood Press, 1996), pp. 97–104. Both claim that her acting name was Portis which doesn't tally with programmes for two productions in which she played Baronne des Herbettes in Maurice Farokoa's *This Way Madame* and Vera Lawrence in H. V. Esmond's *Eliza Comes to Stay*.

3 J. C. Trewin, *The Turbulent Thirties* (London, Macdonald, 1960), Trewin lists Shaw, Maugham and Coward alongside Dane as amongst the few playwrights whose work was produced over the two-decade span. See Katharine Cornell, *I Wanted to Be An Actress* (New York, Random House (1938), 1941), for references to and reviews of, in particular, the American productions of *A Bill of Divorcement*, *Will Shakespeare*, and *The Way Things Happen*. *Wild Decembers* (produced in 1933) was dedicated to Cornell.

4 Ernest Short, *Sixty Years in The Theatre* (London, Eyre and Spottiswoode, 1951), p. 204.

5 *Ibid.*, p. 26.

6 Oliver, 'Clemence Dane (Winifred Ashton)', p. 97.

7 J. C. Trewin, *Dramatists of Today* (London, Staples Press, 1953), p. 132.

8 Cited in John Carey, *The Intellectuals and The Masses* (London, Faber and Faber, 1992), p. 87.

9 For more on the 'feminisation' of the inter-war London stage see Maggie B. Gale, *West End Women, Women Playwrights on the London Stage 1918–1962* (London, Routledge, 1996) and idem, 'Women Playwrights of the 1920s and 1930s, A Lost Generation' and 'The "Woman Question"', in Elaine Aston and Janelle Reinelt, *The Cambridge Companion to Modern British Women Playwrights* (Cambridge, Cambridge University Press, 2000), pp. 23–37.

10 Marie Stopes, in *A Banned Play (Vectia) and A Preface on Censorship* (London, Bale Sons and Daniellson, 1926), condemns the male domination of the means of production and criticism in theatre in a vitriolic attack upon those who banned her play.

11 Ernest Short, *Thearical Cavalcade* (London, Eyre and Spottiswoode, 1942), p. 199.

12 W. A. Darlington, 'Among My Souvenirs', undated cutting, Theatre Museum, London.

13 Beatrice Kean Seymour, 'He That Ruleth His Own Spirit', review of Dane's Babyons, 11 February 1928, unmarked clipping in, File on Clemence Dane, Mander and Mitcheson Collection.

14 David Waldron Smithers, '*Therefore Imagine*', *The Works of Clemence Dane* (England, The Dragonfly Press, 1988), p. 17.

15 Helen Simpson and Clemence Dane, *Gooseberry Fool* (1929), unpublished manuscript, Theatre Museum, London, p. 19.

16 *Ibid.*, p. 49.

17 Undated obituary clipping in File on Clemence Dane in the Theatre Museum, London.

18 St John Ervine, *The Theatre in My Time* (London, Rich and Cowan, 1933), pp. 137–9.

19 Weintraub, 'Clemence Dane', p. 134. Weintraub also states that *Eighty in The Shade* is set in and deals with 'an old people's home'; anybody who has read the play, which is loosely based on the relationship between Ellen Terry, Edy Craig and E. G. Craig will find her statement hard to digest. The play ran for 179 performances at the Globe theatre in 1959.

20 Smithers, '*Therefore Imagine*', p. 20.

21 At the time of writing the Theatre Museum, London, had just been given this archive.

22 See Liz Stanley, *The Auto/Biographical I* (Manchester, Manchester University Press, 1992).

23 Clemence Dane, *London Has A Garden* (London, Michael Joseph, 1964), p. 36.

24 *Ibid.*, p. 43.

25 Dane's home, bought for £80, was situated in a 'corral of caravans' eight miles outside Midhurst, far from any telephone: *Daily Mail,* 10 March 1960.

26 Nancy Price, *Into an Hour Glass* (London, Museum Press Ltd, 1953), pp. 192–3. For an interesting account of Nancy Price's work with the People's National Theatre, see J. P. Wearing, 'Nancy Price and the People's National Theatre', *Theatre History Studies,* 16, June 1996, pp. 71–89.

27 Thomas Postlewaite, 'Autobiography and Theatre History', in Thomas Postlewaite and Bruce McConachie, eds, *Interpreting the Theatrical Past* (Iowa City, University of Iowa Press, 1989), pp. 248–72.

28 Elizabeth Sprigge, *Sybil Thorndike Casson* (London, Victor Gollancz, 1971), p. 176.

29 Clemence Dane, *Call Home The Heart* (London, Heinemann, 1947). The play ran at St James's theatre for 44 performances in 1947.

30 Sprigge, *Sybil Thorndike Casson*, p. 259.

31 Diana Devlin, *A Speaking Part, Lewis Casson and The Theatre of His Time* (London, Hodder and Stoughton, 1982), p. 179.

32 Richard Huggett, *Binkie Beaumont, Eminence Grise of the West End Theatre* (London, Hodder and Stoughton, 1989), p. 140. The production was not a great success which Beaumont put down to the fact of Dane's inexperience as a director and the star cast having taken advantage of his own apparent youth. Lawrence liked working with Dane because she felt that she 'understood an actress's problems', although she also cited one of these problems as line learning: *ibid.*, p. 141.

33 Emlyn Williams, *Emlyn, An Early Autobiography, 1927–1935* (London, The Bodley Head, 1973), p. 344. The original production was under constant threat of closure because audiences were slow to respond to the play, written in verse. Darlington suggested that such an 'imaginative stage biography' would have proved more popular with a suburban audience: W. A. Darlington, *Six Thousand and One Nights* (London, George G. Harrap & Co., 1960).

34 Cole Lesley, *Remembered Laughter, The Life of Noël Coward* (New York, Alfred A. Knopf, 1977), p. 237.

35 Phillip Hoare, *Noël Coward, A Biography* (London, Sinclair Stevenson, 1995), p. 372.

36 Noël Coward, *The Autobiography of Noël Coward, Future Indefinite* (London, Methuen, 1986), p. 349.

37 Terry Castle suggests that by the mid-1920s Coward had many friends in common with Radcliffe Hall, one of whom was Clemence Dane; thus although Coward dates his regular visits to Dane from the early 1930s, it is likely that they were aquainted before this point: Terry Castle, *Noël Coward and Radcliffe Hall* (New York, Columbia University Press, 1996).

38 Huggett, *Binkie Beaumont*. Huggett proposes of the relationship between Dane and Beaumont that she was the 'mother he had never had', introducing him to key theatrical people, and nurturing him professionally during his early years in management: p. 139.

39 *Ibid.*, also cited in Castle, *Noël Coward and Radcliffe Hall*, p. 104.

40 Lesley, *Remembered Laughter*, pp. 305–8.

41 Graham Payn and Sheridan Morley, eds, *The Noël Coward Diaries* (London, Weidenfeld and Nicholson, 1982), pp. 33–52.

42 *Ibid.*, p. 71.

43 Brian Forbes, *Ned's Girl, The Life of Edith Evans* (London, Hamish Hamilton, 1977), pp. 199–201.

44 Huggett, *Binkie Beaumont*, p. 252.

45 Hoare, *Noël Coward*, p. 320.

46 Castle, *Noël Coward and Radcliffe Hall*, pp. 99–101.

47 Noël Coward, *Coward, Plays One* (London, Methuen, 1979), p. 13.

48 Payn and Morley, *The Noël Coward Diaries*, p. 596.

49 Lesley, *Remembered Laughter*, p. 228.

50 Clemence Dane, 'A Regiment of Women', in *Recapture, A Clemence Dane Omnibus* (London, Heineman, 1932). Reprinted by Virago, 1996.

51 Lillian Faderman, *Surpassing the Love of Men* (London, Junction Books, 1981), pp. 341–50.

52 Mitchell A. Leaska and John Phillips, *Violet to Vita, The Letters of Violet Trefusis to Vita Sackville West, 1910–1921* (London, Mandarin, 1991): see entries for 1 May 1920 (p. 209), 14 July 1920 (p. 225) and 28 October 1920 (p. 254). See also Violet Trefusis, *Don't Look Round* (London, Hutchinson, 1952) and Philippe Jullian and John Phillips, *The Other Woman, A Life of Violet Trefusis* (Boston, Houghton Mifflin Company, 1976).

53 Castle, *Noël Coward and Radcliffe Hall*, pp. 22–3.

54 See Gale, *West End Women*.

55 Clemence Dane, *The Women's Side* (London, John Herbert, 1926), p. 1.

56 J. C. Trewin, *The Gay Twenties* (London, Macdonald, 1958), p. 25.

57 Clemence Dane, 'Fair Play and Fair Pay', *Daily Herald*, 20 March 1941 and 'Revolution in the Home', *Daily Herald*, 5 September 1941.

58 Dane, *The Women's Side*, p. 129.

59 Chothia, *English Drama of the Early Modern Period*, pp. 90–102.

60 Dane, *The Women's Side*, p. 131.

61 Dane, *London Has a Garden*, p. 59.

62 Clemence Dane, *Approaches to Drama* (London, The English Association Presidential Address, 1961), pp. 1–7.

63 Clemence Dane, 'The Writer's Partner', in *Recapture, A Clemence Dane Omnibus*, pp. 3–26.

64 Kenneth Allsop, 'Why I Put Clemence Dane on the Scales', *Daily Mail*, 10 March 1960.

65 Basil Dean, *The Theatre at War* (London, George G. Harrap and Co. Ltd, 1956), p. 295. See also Basil Dean, *Seven Ages* (London, Hutchinson, 1970), and *Mind's Eye* (London, Hutchinson, 1973), for descriptions and analysis of Dane's work with Basil Dean.

66 Katherine Cockin, *Edy Craig (1846–1947), Dramatic Lives* (London, Cassell, 1998), pp. 11 and 177.

67 Peter Dacre, 'Ripe For Trouble', *Sunday Express*, 14 May 1961.

68 Dane, *Approaches to Drama*, p. 9.

69 *Ibid.*, pp. 10–11.

70 Dan Rebellato, *1956 And All That* (London, Routledge, 1999), p. 120.

71 Laura Marcus, *Autobiographical Discourses* (Manchester, Manchester University Press, 1994), p. 180.

72 Stanley, *The Auto/Biographical I*, p. 219.

8

WORKSHOP TO MAINSTREAM: WOMEN'S PLAYWRITING IN THE CONTEMPORARY BRITISH THEATRE

John Deeney

The work of women practitioners in contemporary British theatre has, since the early 1980s, engendered an important body of scholarly research, a development which has occurred alongside the appropriation of feminist theory by theatre studies and the reclamation of women's theatrical histories. The transatlantic proportions of this expansion provide their own arenas for debate. However, it is within such a context that this chapter considers the hitherto absent analysis of a particular occupancy, that of women's playwriting in the contemporary British theatrical mainstream – an area too often sidelined by analysis of and separation from subsidised theatre. The chapter aims to provide an analysis of the relationship between the idealistic expectations of feminist theorists and academics, and the achievements of some contemporary female playwrights whose plays have, with more comfort than perhaps expected, crossed over into a mainstream commercial or mainstream subsidised context.

> For a feminist to succeed in the mainstream in Britain, it is often necessary to underwrite feminist content with 'larger' messages, and to employ a format or style which does not emphasize the connections between the personal and the political. These problems are not limited to feminist theatre work; in fact they are common to most fringe theatre work and even some mainstream work.[1]

> [I]n the late seventies, when plays of protest by women started seeing the light of day, they were still about same thing, very narrow, domesticated. And I thought, 'This really is insidious', because not only is it the only thing that's encouraged, but because it's the only thing that's encouraged women are writing it. And where is the work by women that addresses the big, broad issues of our time? Well, they're there, certainly.[2]

The above observations are clearly articulated from particular professional positions. They reveal, at first glance, a problematic relationship between concerns within the academy and those within the theatre profession. Lizbeth Goodman pinpoints some of the problems facing 'feminist' dramatists accessing the 'mainstream', and specifically the necessity 'to underwrite feminist content with "larger" messages'. Conversely, Phyllis Nagy speaks of the need for 'work by women that addresses the big, broad issues of our time'. Their stances are not simply oppositional; both point to the problem of how particular subjects are critiqued within existing theoretical and critical paradigms. The intersection of feminism and theatre has permitted academics such as Goodman to assess the contribution of 'feminist theatres' to an extended political struggle. However, as Maggie B. Gale notes, as part of a project which aims at an analysis of the re-evaluation of women's playwriting, 'a great many studies of plays by women are framed by the question of whether the plays could be considered to be feminist or not' as a matter of course.[3] Gale's own study of women playwrights on the mid-twentieth-century London stage problematises the employment of a closed contemporary 'feminist agenda' when considering the role of women in theatre history, concluding that, 'using this as the primary basis for historical categorising limits the depiction and analysis of history to the extent that it becomes a discipline used to verify or justify our own contemporary position. It is arguably just another way of *fixing* history'.[4]

It may be evinced that Gale's analysis has partial relevance in a study of contemporary women dramatists – dramatists who cohabit the theatrical, cultural and political spaces where feminism has made its impact. However, whilst distinctions between 'feminist theatre' and 'women's theatre', or 'feminist dramatists' and 'women dramatists', are climacteric in the practice and study of feminist theatre, such distinctions arguably propitiate existing investigative and theoretical paradigms at the expense of attending to the emergence and development of women practitioners whose work problematises those very paradigms.

In *Feminist Stages* (1996), a collection of interviews with women in contemporary British theatre, Goodman acknowledges the diversity of women practitioners working from 1968 to the present, and proposes that 'consideration of their perspectives across generations and within their own definitions of "feminism" is enlightening'.[5] The section dedicated to the 1980s asserts, 'a new generation of women playwrights took up their pens',[6] whilst the next section begins with the observation, 'Perhaps the most important development of the 1990s was a move away from "drama" (scripted plays, often published) to more experimental, non-text-based and therefore more ephemeral forms of feminist work'.[7]

Goodman's arrangement of the interviews is predicated on a generational model, purportedly engendering 'less mediation and no pretense
of a uniformity of views'.[8] The extent to which this is 'enlightening' is
arguable. Such a strategy clearly characterises any particular decade by
the work of those practitioners who originate within it. The result is a
disengaged attempt to 'periodise' British feminist theatre post-1968,
carrying *en route* several significant exclusions. Goodman clearly owes
some debt to aspects of the New Women's History movement of the
1970s and early 1980s, an aspect of which was the employment of oral
recollections as a means of challenging 'traditional history to understand
periodization as the organization of value and meaning'.[9] *Feminist Stages*
successfully challenges the male-biased 'canon' of contemporary British
theatre, but in so doing implicitly replicates those aspects of traditional
history which its very methods seek to dispute, most notably the concept
of 'periodisation'. Further, there is no extended attempt to address the
relationship and distinctions between concepts of the 'alternative' and
the 'mainstream', through which much feminist theatre has defined
itself, or more importantly for the purposes of my argument, come to be
defined. The combined result is a negation of the historical continuum
and the absence of informed analysis of ways in which positionings of
women in the 'mainstream' impact on the established 'canon' in terms of
both production and reception.

For Elaine Aston plays by women, 'which break into the mainstream
tend to reflect the respectable face of bourgeois feminism'. As such,
'Canonical values more readily endorse the figure of the single playwright, but fail to acknowledge multi-authored, collaborative theatre-
making – especially when it is made by women'.[10] The 'mainstream', the
'canon' and 'bourgeois feminism' formulate a triptych here, embodying
the figure of the single (successful) woman playwright. Aston's strategy is
a useful tool in rescuing feminist theatre practice from, in this case, critical marginalisation; but, in so doing, it leaves the triptych generalised
and unproblematised. Whilst statistical surveys concerning the status of
women working in contemporary British theatre testify to persistent
under-representation in both creative and management roles, such
surveys invite, as Carole Woddis suggests, 'more sophisticated questions
of context and relativity'.[11] The statistical pattern for produced plays
written by women is possibly the most worrying; one of decreased representation between the mid-1980s and mid-1990s in both building-based
and touring companies funded by the Arts Council of England.
For building-based companies in 1985/86, 17 per cent of main stage

productions and 20 per cent of studio productions were by women. In
1994 the figures stood at 12 per cent and 25 per cent respectively. For
touring companies in 1985/86, 54 per cent of work produced was by
women compared to 35 per cent in 1994. Taking these statistics together,
22 per cent of all work performed in 1985 was written by women
compared to 20 per cent in 1994. These statistics include new plays,
adaptations and revivals.[12] Conversely, the period in question has seen
women both emerging and sustaining careers as playwrights. These
playwrights – which include Caryl Churchill, Pam Gems, Sarah Daniels,
April de Angelis, Sarah Kane, Charlotte Keatley, Sharman Macdonald,
Clare McIntyre, Phyllis Nagy, Winsome Pinnock, Diane Samuels and
Timberlake Wertenbaker – have been produced at the Royal Court
Theatre in Chelsea, the Royal National Theatre on the South Bank, the
Bush Theatre in Shepherd's Bush, and a number have had successful
West End transfers and international productions. For example, Claire
Luckham's *Trafford Tanzi* (1978) began its life touring clubs in Liverpool
and by 1981 was playing to West End audiences. Nell Dunn's *Steaming*
(1981) transferred to the West End from the Theatre Royal in Stratford
East – the home in the 1950s and 1960s of Joan Littlewood's Theatre
Workshop. Caryl Churchill's *Cloud Nine* (1979), in its original produc-
tion by the Joint Stock Theatre Group, had two successful runs at the
Royal Court and a new version of the text was produced in New York in
1981 directed by Tommy Tune. The original Royal Court production of
Churchill's *Top Girls* (1982) transferred to the Public Theater, New York,
and returned to the Royal Court in 1983. Again, Churchill's *Serious
Money* (1987), originally produced at the Royal Court, successfully transferred to the West End. Pam Gems's *Piaf* (1978), a biopic of the French
singer and originally produced by the Royal Shakespeare Company
(RSC), was revived in the West End in 1993 as a vehicle for the musical
theatre star Elaine Paige. Both RSC productions of Gems's *Camille*
(1984) and *The Blue Angel* (1991) also had West End transfers. Sharman
Macdonald's *When I Was a Girl I Used to Scream and Shout* (1984) had a
West End showing in 1986, as did Diane Samuels's *Kindertransport*
(1993), both in productions by small-scale companies – the Bush Theatre
and Soho Theatre Company respectively. That such primary activity
occurs within a five-mile radius of London's Trafalgar Square, and at
some of the theatres identified – 'powerhouses' of new writing, or
'cultural flagships' – produces an immediate picture of circulation in
metropolitan theatrical culture, of a positioning within Aston's notional
'mainstream'.[13] Loren Kruger points out:

a feminist theatre based on the *idea* – in the 'concern for gender relations' or the 'urge to politicise sexuality' – expressed in dramatic *texts*
forgets that the site on which these texts are performed and watched is a
theatre institution that renews itself by turning such 'concerns' into the
trademarks of a new commodity, 'plays by women' ... [14]

Kruger's analysis, as perspicacious as it may seem, masks the actuality
of all theatre as constituents of an industry which are part of an economic
system that relies on the generation of new commodities. Thus, can we jet-
tison the historical impact of feminist theatre which demonstrates a 'concern for gender relations' when it uses the only site available to it? That
stated, the post-war renaissance of new theatre writing has provided an
important aperture for feminist questioning – of the exclusion of women
playwrights in this project, and of the gendered content of male-authored
works.[15] Once women playwrights enter the project, the general tendency
has been to appropriate dominant critical methods to describe such a presence, principally as a connective storyline in a developing grand narrative.
This is how David Edgar describes it:

> I see the recent history of British theatre ... as a series of conversations
> between waves of playwrights and their audiences about the nature of
> the post-war world. So at the Royal Court in the late 1950s, angry young
> male playwrights debated the cultural consequences of the democratisa-
> tion of British society that occurred after the war ... Then, in the early
> 1970s, graduates of the youth revolt of the 1960s wrote big, public plays
> claiming that the welfare state had failed and that Britain was ripe for
> social revolution, while the extraordinary upsurge of women play-
> wrights in the 1980s challenged male writers and male subject matter ...
> bringing hitherto invisible relationships – notably those of mothers,
> daughters and sisters – to the centre of the stage ... However, they
> [women writers] may also have been the opening statement of a differ-
> ent debate. The decline of the dominant role of men – in the workplace
> and in the family – is probably the biggest single event of the past 30
> years in the West. If the initiating event of the theatre of Osborne and
> Wesker was the second world war, the movement that begins with the
> late 1970s work of Pam Gems and Caryl Churchill surely responds to the
> women's liberation movement of the late 1960s.[16]

If one sets Kruger and Edgar alongside each other, the former reading seems highly persuasive, particularly in its analysis of the 'masculinist strategies of legitimation' which marginalise alternative and certain
types of feminist theatre practice.[17] However, Kruger's proposition of the
'legitimate' and 'illegitimate' ('mainstream' and 'alternative') displaces

important questions of theatrical context and historiography, which Edgar most evidently fails to attend to. Kruger's emphasis on the 'site' of the theatrical event naturally foregrounds audience receivership, but this is at the expense of any informed analysis of the machinations of theatrical production. Further, whilst Edgar's description of the recent history of British drama appears as an unproblematic and conveniently periodised account of a mainstream movement, Kruger's project, not unlike Goodman's, also presupposes a degree of fixity in the methods of categorisation, singly qualified by 'masculinist strategies of legitimation'. Ironically, this replicates those aspects of traditional theatre history which seek to signify the mainstream and alternative as *distinct* entities of theatre practice.

The artistic directorship of Max Stafford-Clark at the Royal Court, which coincided with Caryl Churchill's critical and commercial recognition – 'legitimation' in Kruger's terms – brought to this theatre certain collaborative methods of play-making Stafford-Clark had developed with the Joint Stock Theatre Group, where he had begun working with Churchill. The approach consisted of playwright, director and actors researching a particular subject during a period of improvisation and workshops, followed by a writing interval and then rehearsals which would involve further rewriting. That such an approach – a repositioning of the playwright in the creative process, from a seemingly straightforward provider of a text, to a more complex co-collaborator producing an authored work – gained credence at the Royal Court in the 1980s is important for a number of reasons. Alan Sinfield has argued that, 'The significance of the Royal Court and *Look Back in Anger* was partly institutional: the principle that the state should finance 'good' culture was reinforced and extended …'.[18] However, the success of what Sinfield terms post-war 'Left-culturism' also required, from the theatre's position, the literary recognition of the playwright – something which of course George Bernard Shaw and the Stage Society had already attempted earlier on in the century. That the Royal Court was conceived as a 'writer's theatre' was therefore central to its cultural status. The importation of alternative practices into such a space, like the Joint Stock method, challenge, or at least complicate, the received role of the playwright within the institution.

Charlotte Keatley's *My Mother Said I Never Should* (1987), which was assured canonical status through its Royal Court production, followed by numerous international productions and translation into seventeen languages, carries a history which reveals some important processes at work.

Keatley's play gained initial recognition through North West Playwrights, a playwrights' support and development organisation based in Manchester since 1983. From here, it went on to be produced by Manchester's Contact Theatre. Keatley had continued dramaturgical support from Brigid Larmour, the play's director, through the entire pre-production process. Keatley has said of this, 'it was crucial to have Brigid Larmour directing. If I hadn't quite got there with a scene, she wouldn't try to make it in another scene. Instead, she'd be able to see through the net of words to what I was trying to do'.[19] Whilst such an observation perhaps reinforces the institutional and artistic power of the director, and by deduction the playwright's dependency, it is significant to note that Keatley's preference for a collaborative process-based approach may be the reason for the lack of subsequent full-scale productions of her other plays. The success of *My Mother Said* was clearly tied in to an extended period of dramaturgical development in which Keatley was permitted to forge certain relationships, something which might not have been afforded her at the Royal Court. It may be argued that this merely demonstrates a metropolitan reliance on regional theatre. However, the example reveals, as with Churchill and Joint Stock, how changing perceptions of the playwright's institutional and artistic role may impact on the repertoire.

The playwright Paul Godfrey compares the contemporary relationship between the theatre and the playwright 'to a degraded version of the parent–child relationship in which the parent is mistrustful of the child and weary of the responsibility, while the child resents its dependence yet craves approval from the parent'.[20] The examples quoted exceptionally, yet significantly, challenge this model. The emergence and impact of women's drama in the late 1970s and 1980s can be all too conveniently located, as in Edgar, as a response to the political and social impact of the second wave women's liberation movement. That such a response should take some twenty years to acquire theatrical realisation in the subsidised mainstream begs questioning. The emergence of women playwrights in this context is equally, and demonstrably, part and parcel of internal theatrical manoeuvrings and small-scale shifting opportunities which women playwrights have successfully embraced. This emphasis on the background to theatrical production also complicates the concept of 'legitimation'. It suggests that the 'illegitimate' is invariably open to appropriation and that it must therefore redefine itself in the face of such. As Gale notes, 'the majority position is defined in relation to its ideological other which, in turn, defines itself in terms of its difference to the majority position'.[21]

The tendency towards periodisation already noted serves to quantify women's dramatic writing through the intractability of gender demarcation. This usefully serves feminist thinking and criticism, but, as has been suggested, may also decontextualise the theatre practice in question. Edgar's periodisation of post-war British drama draws attention to the concerns of subsequent generations of playwrights, and in the process foregrounds the drama's developing thematic concerns in an art-form constantly seeking public attention in ever-increased competition with other media. This claim on public attention, underwritten by public subsidy, is founded on a pseudo-Brechtian utilitarianism; or, as the Arts Council of England describes it, the production of 'radical work which articulates society's contemporary development'.[22] However, the historical trajectory and the multifarious aspects of women's drama suggest closer analysis.

Richard Boon has observed that Margaret Thatcher's administration was critical in shaping the work of the dominant 1970s 'serious' *male* dramatists post-1979. He argues:

> these writers were at their most expansive and vociferous when working in a climate when the left was still dominant, and criticising and attacking socialist failures formed the bulk of their subject matter ... Yet, faced with the 'real enemy', with what they see as the most dangerously right-wing government of recent times, their work seems to have lost some of its momentum and their voice some of its authority.[23]

Boon is clearly reading a particular subject here. However, the loss in 'momentum' of 'their voice' – hence its 'authority' – can also read as the cleft upon which women's drama achieves greater attention. Further, the alignment of mainstream women's drama with the rise of Thatcherism usefully satisfies the labelling tendency which permits this drama to be described as 'contemporary', and therefore 'relevant' in the theatre's configuration in socio-political discourse. In this context, plays about 'mothers, daughters and sisters' satisfy an all too familiar interpretative pattern:

> Not only shrinking funds, but also gender attitudes as revealed in Clause 28, the moral panic about AIDS and the Thatcher Government's evocation of Victorian family values, indicate a move away from public feminism, which is affecting the nature of women's drama as presently performed, particularly in major venues.[24]

This all too neat configuration by Trevor R. Griffiths and Margaret Llewellyn-Jones treats an aspect of the recent history of women's drama as a synchronic phenomenon. This tendency, in both feminist and non-feminist criticism, not only limits the range of interpretative possibilities, it fails to account for important reconfigurations within a constantly changing theatrical context.

Courting women

Caryl Churchill's position in contemporary British theatre is indicative of the problems of critiquing a feminist presence in the mainstream. Churchill's ambivalence about her own feminism is reflected in a career that has seen her move from work with the feminist group Monstrous Regiment in the 1970s to West End success in the 1980s.[25] More recently, she has turned her attentions to collaborative theatre-making with dance practitioners and composers, suggesting a heightened interest in formal experiment.[26] Interestingly, her socialist penchant still prevails in a play like *The Skriker* (1994), which although infused by an 'other worldliness' is deeply rooted in a critique of social and cultural displacement and global/ecological promulgations.[27] Such experiment has been a sustaining feature throughout Churchill's continuing career.

Cloud Nine, originally conceived for Joint Stock, helped to ensure Churchill's position via its mainstage Royal Court showing in 1979 and 1980 and its subsequent international success.[28] The play employs cross-gender, cross-racial and cross-generational role-playing to discourse the impact of colonialism as a historical and contemporary predicament of politico-sexual significance. The various gender/role/character configurations in the play permit Churchill to explore the pervasiveness of colonialism as a system of political and sexual oppression. Act 2 is set in London in 1979, some one hundred years after the first Act, but for the characters of Betty, Victoria and Edward, now cast according to their assigned gender roles, it is just twenty-five years later. The looser structure of this Act reflects changing sexual mores, yet the attachment to colonialism threatens any advances which have been made. We learn of the death of a soldier in Northern Ireland, and Churchill has Cathy, a young child, played by a man, emphasising the continued construction of gender identities.

Criticism of *Cloud Nine* has frequently centred on Churchill's perceived position as a socialist feminist during this period, and the play's employment of a socialist-feminist dynamic in Act 1 which is diffused in Act 2. Michelene Wandor argues that:

The speed and wit of the first half structurally reinforce the socialist-feminist dynamic in the interconnection between class and gender. In the second half the libertarian lifestyles demonstrate the radical feminist dynamic of women determining their own sexuality and ways of living. But the second half lacks any sense of class (and socialist) dynamic, and the atomised structure reinforces this partial political disintegration. The relationship between the two halves is thus up for question. It could be argued that the second half is 'deliberately' open-ended, and will push the audience to come to its own conclusions ... or draws back from seeing the implications of its own hypothesis.[29]

It is important to note that Wandor is writing in 1984, a proximity to the play's original production which is significant. Wandor's suspicion of the 'open-ended' form is set within a concern at the lack of programmatic development along socialist-feminist lines. This supposes of course that the playwright's political position is stable and 'fixed', and to a certain extent that Churchill should fulfil a pre-ordained agenda. The play's structure and theatrical production further complicates this possibility; the 'neat, theatrical form' suggests that 'we can put the past into order ... and analyse it in terms of both class and gender cause and effect, but that we cannot do the same with the present'.[30] Wandor's criticism might actually suggest that Churchill's formal strategies serve to problematise the socialist project in contemporary drama, and this is something which both feminism and socialism need to negotiate. The first performances of *Cloud Nine* in early 1979 were at Dartington College of Arts, a college originally founded on the principles of an alternative educational philosophy in the early twentieth century. By the time the production reached the Royal Court Margaret Thatcher had been elected into office. Unlike many of her male contemporaries, Churchill was already dramatising a politico-sexual-familial terrain which, as the 1980s progressed, would provide a significant site for Thatcherite intervention.

In *Top Girls* Churchill develops her interest in history through the rise of the modern 'superwoman'.[31] Marlene has recently been promoted to managing director in the 'Top Girls' employment agency. The opening scene is a dinner party, where real and fictional historical 'superwomen' are invited to join in Marlene's celebration of her promotion, a seemingly transhistorical circumstance which foregrounds Marlene's own desire to transcend her assigned gender role. The arrival of Angie, her illegitimate teenage daughter, and the final tumultuous exchange between Marlene and her working-class sister Joyce complicates and disrupts the temperate 'how' of capitalist achievement and individualism.

Top Girls, like *Cloud Nine*, refuses to present a possible, let alone coherent programme for change around Marlene's future decisions about Angie. Such absence has led to the criticism that the play is underpinned by a bourgeois-feminist dynamic, embodied in the characterisation of Marlene as a self-determining individual.[32] This is questionable. Although Marlene may not be dependent on men, she is dependent on an incumbent ideology which has permitted her rise to power on male territory. It is this too, specifically through the character of Joyce, which Churchill is critiquing, and the impossibility of women such as Marlene negotiating the terrain of the 'superwoman' alongside that of motherhood.

Churchill's successes at the Royal Court in the early 1980s were clearly indebted, as has been noted, to her work with companies such as Monstrous Regiment and Joint Stock. However, both *Cloud Nine* and *Top Girls* form part of a another significant shift in the Court's position at this time. David Hare has noted, 'the Court in the early seventies was primarily an aesthetic theatre, not a political one':

> there was … only one reason why writers chose, as they did in great numbers, to give their work to the Court first, and that was the likelihood that it would be better *presented* than anywhere else. Here the text would be respected, the rehearsals would be serious …[33]

That the Court's constitution, and most importantly its *image* as a 'writer's theatre' did not necessarily make it a 'political theatre' is revealing in the shifting context of the 1980s. The presentation at the Royal Court of Churchill's work, and of critically acclaimed and popular plays such as Andrea Dunbar's *The Arbour* (1980) and Sarah Daniels' *Masterpieces* (1983), suggests that women's drama was integral to the Court's (*re-*)politicisation. The implications of this reading extend further. Whilst male playwrights such as Edgar and Hare – interminably described as *the* political dramatists – were utilising the resources of the Royal Shakespeare Company and the National Theatre to continue their analysis of the 'state of the nation', it was women's drama which was key to extending the *boundaries* of political theatre. This historical moment has been facilely overwritten by the subsequent economic and cultural crisis in the subsidised theatre, frequently invoked to characterise the 1980s. In 1991, Michael Billington, the lead theatre critic of the *Guardian*, complained that 'the crisis in new writing … is mainly to do with scale and connection: a manifest decline in big plays capable of addressing a large audience and tapping a vibrant communal response'.[34] Billington's observations clearly emulate a hegemonic propensity, rooted in the 1970s, of what new drama does best. However, when 'big plays' did emerge in the 1980s, it was, significantly, two plays by women which problematised such a model.

Caryl Churchill's *Serious Money*, an exposé of the City, a small geographical area of London which is the centre of the British financial and banking system, and the effects of the Big Bang, originated at the Royal Court and made a successful transfer to the West End.[35] Prior to writing the play, Churchill had taken part in a two-week workshop which involved visiting and researching London's financial markets, followed by her own period of intensive research. It was during this period that deregulation of the City occurred. The play pays enormous attention to the complexities of this world; the business of 'takeovers' and the roles of 'arbitrageurs', 'brokers' and 'jobbers'. Several plotlines, one concerning the attempted takeover of an English company by an American conglomerate, and another following Scilla Todd's investigation of her brother's mysterious death, disclose a network of corruption from which, it appears, no one is immune. Churchill's choice to write the play in verse drives the narrative with inundating and comic theatrical effect. The currency of the subject matter of *Serious Money* undoubtedly contributed to its commercial success, and particularly its appeal to the City. The critic of the *Daily Telegraph* noted, 'Designed by Ms Churchill as a savage attack on the City, the same rough-edged dealers have flocked to see it in their hundreds, organising parties, taking the whole office, and having fun identifying themselves on stage.'[36] That the generally favourable critical response was qualified by such observations is indicative of the problems of critiquing women's drama in the mainstream. Michael Ratcliffe's assertion in the *Observer* that the play 'is not a feminist critique of a male world' would seem to support this.[37] However, the foregrounding in the play's critical reception of the potential disparities in audience response reveals the (masculinist) journalistic tendency towards uncovering a play's 'meaning', which the audience reception of *Serious Money* would not hold to. The play's notoriety is therefore established, prefigured by Churchill's perceived identity as a feminist playwright. Hence, Churchill's position in the mainstream cannot be discarded as a straightforward matter of 'breaking in'. It is contingent on the subsequent 'problem' of *Serious Money* as a theatrical event.

Unlike Churchill's play which carries local topical interest, Timberlake Wertenbaker's *Our Country's Good* (1988) has enjoyed both West End and international success.[38] Based on Thomas Keneally's novel *The Playmaker*, it follows the late eighteenth-century British colonial conquest of Australia, where the military masters direct a group of convicts in a production of George Farquhar's *The Recruiting Officer* to celebrate the King's birthday. Again, the play was a Royal Court production which began its life as a workshop. It was also placed in repertory with a production of Farquhar's play. The critical success of *Our Country's Good* clearly resided in its dramatisation of the theatre's efficacy to transform both individuals and communities. Susan Carlson has observed that the play's reception as 'self-reflexive theatre', together with its pairing with *The Recruiting Officer*, left 'scant space in which to consider the twentieth-century play's abundance of extra-theatrical ideas', particularly the overarching theme of colonisation. However, Carlson goes on to describe the play's changing reception:

> The narrative move towards one theatrical community and the predominance of men in the cast list means that the play is not so clearly marked as either feminist or woman-centred ... After three London productions, the play was no longer the cohesive and intense product of a tight community of actors, writer and director, but a play less notable for its theatrical rewards than for its exposure of volatile issues of power, self and nation.[39]

Carlson's observations, as with the reception of *Serious Money*, point to an absence of indelible commodification. What these plays are 'about' is thus problematised in a theatrical culture which had lost its cohesiveness in the late 1980s. In foregrounding the arena of reception, both *Serious Money* and *Our Country's Good* are indicative examples of interventions by women dramatists in debates over the contemporary theatre's purpose and direction, then being argued out in both the subsidised and commercial mainstreams.

The problem with mothers and daughters

If plays by women about mothers and daughters were prominent in the 1980s, the emergence of such a genre seemingly provided an antidote to absence and crises elsewhere in the playwriting community. The presentation of this model is not only in danger of generalising the theatrical present, but of neglecting the theatrical past – ignoring previous periods in theatre history where plays by women discoursing the mother–daughter relationship were produced. The benefits of making these connections can reveal the shifting ideological contexts in which motherhood is discoursed; not only from one period to the next, but from one culture to another. Equally, considering dramatisations of the mother–daughter relationship in tandem with continuing developments in women's dramaturgy questions the superficial deftness of generic commodification, which is also in danger of devolving the plays from their theatrical context.

Caryl Churchill's *Top Girls* exposes the question of the mother–daughter relationship in its contemporary reference, discoursing how entry into patriarchy requires the negation of the maternal bond. Charlotte Keatley's *My Mother Said I Never Should* – again, with an all-woman cast – develops a device employed by Churchill, the manipulation of chronology, to explore the historicity of the mother–daughter question as it belongs to women's experience.[40] Keatley disrupts this chronology by dovetailing scenes in the women's lives to illustrate the cyclical pattern of inter-generational conflict where new opportunities give way to fresh challenges. The playwright also includes three child scenes, set in a 'patch of wasteground', where the four actresses play the girl-children of the women's respective generational origins. Whilst the themes of *My Mother Said* are multifarious, the play's perceived originality draws attention to a feminine morphology in its breaching of a linear time structure. Keatley's play clearly has its antecedents and referents here, not only in women's dramaturgy, but in the theorisation of women's experience from, particularly, the French feminist school, led by such figures as Cixous and Irigaray. Sue-Ellen Case summarises the collective theatrical relevance of such theoretical positionings:

> [The form] can be elliptical rather than illustrative, fragmentary rather than whole, ambiguous rather than clear, and interrupted rather than complete. This contiguity exists within the text and at its borders: the feminine form seems to be without a sense of formal closure – in fact, it operates as anti-closure … Without closure, the sense of beginning, middle and end, or a central focus, it abandons the hierarchical organising principles of traditional form that served to elide women from the discourse. Women can inhabit the realm of the outsider … and create a new discourse and form that exhibit the field of female experience.[41]

However, what Case pinpoints as 'the realm of the outsider' does not effortlessly translate into the theatrical mediation of texts such as *My Mother Said*. This 'realm' is negotiated in no single domain, but in the various environs of institution, production and reception. The play's critical reception at the Royal Court was by no means unanimous. A 'little sentimental', the 'audience's tear ducts are attacked', 'It is feminist but not polemical', it 'confirms the myth of maternal instinct'; these were just some of the comments made, across the gender divide, to qualify the play's strengths.[42] The canonical status of the play is not therefore as straightforward as might seem apparent. For, in this particular arena of theatre reception, the question 'what is a woman's play?' is subjugated for the more immediate question, 'what is this play's subject?'. Whilst this may support a theory of collusion between a male-dominated theatre and a male-dominated media, the suggestion that women's interventions in the mainstream engender legitimation is a theorised position which denies how theatre is manufactured as a cultural form.

This was manifestly illustrated by an 'event' at the Royal Court in early 1995. *Blasted* by Sarah Kane is set in a hotel room in Leeds whilst civil war is raging on the city's streets.[43] As Ian, a dying tabloid journalist seeks to seduce Cate, a mentally disturbed young woman, scenes of human degradation unfold involving rape, eye gouging and cannibalism. *Blasted*, viewed by some as a metaphor for the Bosnian war, opens on conventional dramatic terrain which, as Kane states, 'collapses into one of Cate's fits … the time and action are disrupted while unity of place is retained'.[44] However formally innovative the play is, it was the initial press outrage at Kane's graphic depiction of violence – ensuring front page, radio and television news coverage – which helped guarantee its position. The Royal Court production also engendered comparisons with Osborne's *Look Back in Anger* (1956) and Edward Bond's *Saved* (1965).[45] Tom Sellar went as far as to suggest that, 'We must address those [ugly social] truths with the same urgency that *Blasted* has reawakened in theater.'[46] Aleks Sierz groups the play with a number of others – all, significantly, by men – as 'examples of Cool Britannia', each distinguished by both 'popularity' and 'controversy'.[47] *Blasted* played for just three weeks at the Theatre Upstairs to sixty-five people a night, casting a somewhat different light on the perceived significance of the event. Here, both journalistic and academic criticism has proved unable to disencumber the notions of popularity and media curiosity.[48]

The manipulation of time in Keatley's *My Mother Said* is seen in other plays examining the mother–daughter relationship, such as Sharman Macdonald's *When I Was a Girl I Used to Scream and Shout* (1984) and Diane Samuels's *Kindertransport* (1993). The grouping of such plays, predicated on both theme and form, usefully enforces critical segregation which passes over the plays' marked differences. *When I Was a Girl* takes as its setting a beach on the east coast of Scotland where Fiona, her mother Morag and her friend Vari are holidaying.[49] The employment of flashbacks highlights the girls' sexual awakening, their sexual experimentation with one another and Fiona's teenage pregnancy, used by Fiona as a tactic to stop her divorced mother marrying and deserting her. An abortion has rendered Fiona childless, meaning that Morag's desire for grandchildren cannot be satisfied. Claire Armistead criticised the play on its West End opening for 'drawing an essentially negative picture … that it seems to become trapped by its own reductiveness'.[50] Significantly, reviews of the West End showing actually paid little attention to the play's Scottish location and idiom. This was most evident in the casting of Julie Walters – a leading English television actress and personality – in the role of Fiona. However, the play's Scottish context is foundational in Macdonald's formulation of the central relationship between Fiona and Morag. When Fiona is discovered 'jigging' (masturbating), Morag rebukes her: 'He (God) looks down and he says to himself, "That wee Fiona's a naughty, naughty girl and I thought she was one of my better efforts. Ttt. Ttt. Ttt," he goes … '.[51] This passage illustrates more directly the rarefaction of religious puritanism which is part of Macdonald's broader discourse. Armistead's 'reductiveness' more accurately reflects the play's performance in a West End theatre which she too noted had a 'flattening out' effect.[52]

Samuels's *Kindertransport* places the mother–daughter story in a very different frame from the previous two plays.[53] Prior to the outbreak of the Second World War, the Kindertransport movement organised the evacuation of over 9,000 Jewish children from Nazi Germany to England, most of whom would never see their parents again. Young Eva is from a wealthy Jewish family who, when evacuated to England on the Kindertransport by her mother Helga, is fostered by the endearing Lil in Manchester. We soon come to realise that Eva is sharing the stage with her older self, Evelyn. She too has a daughter, Faith, who is also leaving home. Faith discovers possessions which connect her mother to a forgotten history and a different self. The young Eva had changed her identity once she realised that her parents had not escaped Nazism. The dual time-scale of *Kindertransport* not only foregrounds the familial implications of denial of identity, it permits Samuels to dramatise a layer of history within the Holocaust in a form which rescues it from its perception as something past, something gone, as documentary. Lyn Gardner makes the germane observation that it 'is not issue-based drama' but 'a domestic and highly personal play which leaves room for the audience to supply a broader political framework'.[54]

Phyllis Nagy's *Butterfly Kiss* (1994), originally produced at the Almeida Theatre in North London, is strikingly different from the other plays discussed here.[55] Although the play considers a mother–daughter relationship, a complex structure of multiple time-scales and the question of a seemingly motiveless incident of lesbian matricide has helped to ensure that this playwright remains firmly ensconced in the subsidised sector. It is indeed possible to argue that, in its representation of the lesbian as 'outsider', *Butterfly Kiss* succeeds in problematising the stability of the 'mother–daughter play' as a category.

Trevor R. Griffiths has suggested that a number of West End successes by women in the 1980s, in which he includes Macdonald's *When I Was a Girl*, have 'depended on an element of eavesdropping and voyeurism':

> This relates in most cases to the still widespread assumption that an audience should be united by the dramatic strategies of the performance in a common view of the events and characters on stage, and to the structural conditions of watching plays in proscenium arch theatres, which is inherently voyeuristic.[56]

Griffiths neglects the perfectly acceptable suggestion that all theatre depends to some extent on voyeuristic tendencies and exposes the somewhat dangerous essentialist/gender-ised notion of reception, reflective of Billington's 'communal response'. Most crucially, Griffiths supposes a set of limitations placed on women playwrights where negotiation of the mainstream is concerned. However, these limitations effectively extend to all playwrights seeking to contravene the rules governing current dramatic conventions. It remains significant that the majority of the plays discussed here were not conceived for the spaces in which they ultimately found commercial success. This is less a comment on the individual plays than on the economic conditions of a theatre industry which looks to the regional and subsidised sector for inexpensive regimen. Equally, the commercial exploitation of such plays became a necessity in the 1980s as arts funding policies threatened the survival of the subsidised sector. To suggest that the 'mother–daughter play' asserts itself at a moment of crisis in the British theatre performs a useful critical and historical function. It disowns, however, the more difficult question of how such plays were able to articulate this crisis, through placing centre stage subjects and concerns which had largely been denied.

Significantly, Phyllis Nagy has questioned the proposition that the 'crisis of feminism' was 'the preoccupying concern of late 1970s through mid 1980s [serious] drama'. Nagy argues that this was and remains part of the contemporary theatre's tendency towards 'literalism' in both its creative and critical endeavours, that new plays are defined by reduction 'to their literal, factual components for the benefit of any potential audience'. 'This is how and why', she continues, 'the question of what our plays are "about" has come to be confused with what our "themes" are. Plots, no matter how fractured or fragmented, can be conveyed literally and very nearly objectively.'[57] Nagy's critique can be read as an attack on both feminist and non-feminist strategies which identify 'movements' in playwriting, yet are unable to attend to certain dramaturgy which, by its inclusion, might problematise the fecundity of such critical *modus operandi*.

This chapter discusses just a handful of plays by women, some of which encountered mainstream commercial success – not always mirrored in the dramas' critical reception – over an extended period of time. That period suggests no definitive interpretative category, but a mutating context in which women's drama, created within a cultural framework of developments in feminism and feminist thinking, made a particular impression on the contemporary theatrical map. The drawing of this history points attention to both the foreground and background to theatre production, and the reception of such drama in a frequently incognisant cultural domain. The playwrights mentioned, in the main, bestride two seemingly polarised contexts for theatrical production. Others such as Denise Deegan, Nell Dunn and Mary O'Malley form part of a larger project, emphasising the capacious challenge of locating women's drama, not only as an ongoing theoretical exigency, but an all too often disregarded and precarious historico-contemporary actuality.

Notes

1 Lizbeth Goodman, *Contemporary Feminist Theatres: To Each Her Own* (London, Routledge, 1993), p. 216.
2 Interview with Phyllis Nagy, in Heidi Stephenson and Natasha Langridge, *Rage and Reason: Women Playwrights on Playwriting* (London, Methuen, 1997), pp. 19–28, p. 27.
3 Maggie B. Gale, *West End Women: Women and the London Stage 1918–1962* (London, Routledge, 1996), p. 59.
4 *Ibid.*, p. 60.

5 Lizbeth Goodman and Jane de Gay, *Feminist Stages: Interviews with Women in Contemporary British Theatre* (Amsterdam, Harwood, 1996), p. 7.

6 *Ibid.*, p. 97.

7 *Ibid.*, p. 191.

8 *Ibid.*, p. 9.

9 Charlotte Canning, *Feminist Theatres in the U.S.A.* (London, Routledge, 1996), p. 15.

10 Elaine Aston, ed., *Feminist Theatre Voices* (Loughborough, Loughborough Theatre Texts, 1997), p. 12.

11 Carole Woddis, 'Back to the Future: A View from 1997', in Lizbeth Goodman with Jane de Gay, eds., *The Routledge Reader in Gender and Performance* (London, Routledge, 1998), pp. 125–8, p. 125.

12 Caroline Gardiner, *What Share of the Cake? The Employment of Women in the English Theatre* (London, Women's Playhouse Trust, 1987), Jennie Long, *What Share of the Cake Now? The Employment of Women in the English Theatre* (1994), report commissioned and circulated by the Women's Playhouse Trust, London. Both are reproduced in part, in Goodman and de Gay, *The Routledge Reader in Gender and Performance.*

13 The English Stage Company at the Royal Court operates both mainhouse (Theatre Downstairs) and studio (Theatre Upstairs) spaces. The Bush operates in a 'room' above a public house. The policy and programming for both the Theatre Upstairs and the Bush emphasises the production of work by new writers. Both geography and programming, particularly at the Bush, would suggest 'fringe' status. *Time Out*, the London entertainment guide, lists both as 'Off-West End'. The existence of such a category not only indicates the problems of how to identify London venues, it also points to shifting and nebulous definitions of 'subsidised mainstream'.

14 Loren Kruger, 'The dis-play's the thing: gender and the public sphere in contemporary British theatre', *Theatre Journal*, 42 (1990), pp. 27–47, p. 28.

15 See Catherine Itzen, *Stages in the Revolution: Political Theatre in Britain Since 1968* (London, Eyre Methuen, 1980), Michelene Wandor, *Carry On, Understudies: Theatre and Sexual Politics* (London, Routledge and Kegan Paul, 1986); and Michelene Wandor, *Look Back in Gender: Sexuality and the Family in Post-War British Drama* (London, Methuen, 1987).

16 David Edgar, in *The Sunday Times*, 7 September 1997.

17 Kruger, 'The dis-play's the thing', p. 28.

18 Alan Sinfield, *Literature, Politics and Culture in Postwar Britain* (Oxford, Blackwell, 1989), p. 249.

19 Charlotte Keatley, interviewed by Lizbeth Goodman, 'Artform or Platform? On Women and Playwriting', *New Theatre Quarterly*, 22 (1990), pp. 128–40, p. 139.

20 Paul Godfrey, 'The Artist and the Institution: The Playwright and the Theatre', unpublished lecture delivered at the conference 'Arts and Education: Responding to Cultural Diversity', organised by the British American Arts Association at the South Bank Centre, London, 8/9 February 1995.

21 Gale, *West End Women*, p. 10.

22 *The Policy of Drama for the English Arts Funding System* (London, Arts Council of England, 1996), p. 16.

23 Richard Boon, 'Retreating to the Future: Brenton in the Eighties', *Modern Drama*, 33, 1 (1990), pp. 30–41, p. 32.

24 Trevor R. Griffiths and Margaret Llewellyn-Jones, eds., 'Introduction', *British and Irish Women Dramatists Since 1958: A Critical Handbook* (Buckingham, Open University Press, 1993), p. 8.

25 See Caryl Churchill, interviewed by Geraldine Cousin, 'The Common Imagination and the Individual Voice', *New Theatre Quarterly*, 13 (1988), pp. 3–16.

26 For example, Churchill's work with the director/choreographer Ian Spink, composer Orlando Gough and the company Second Stride. Co-authored with David Lan, *A Mouthful of Birds* (1986) was produced by Joint Stock with Spink and Les Waters co-directing. Second Stride collaborations include *The Lives of the Great Poisoners* (1991) and *Hotel* (1997).

27 Caryl Churchill, 'The Skriker', in *Plays: 3* (London, Nick Hern Books, 1998).

28 Caryl Churchill, *Cloud Nine* (London, Nick Hern Books, 1989).

29 Wandor, *Carry On, Understudies*, pp. 171–2.

30 *Ibid.*, p. 172.

31 Caryl Churchill, *Top Girls* (London, Methuen, 1982).

32 Wandor, *Carry On, Understudies*, p. 173.

33 David Hare, *Writing Left-Handed* (London, Faber and Faber, 1991), p. 63.

34 Michael Billington, *One Night Stands: A Critic's View of Modern British Theatre* (London, Nick Hern Books, 1993), p. 363.

35 Caryl Churchill, *Serious Money* (London, Methuen, 1994).

36 Neil Collins, in *Daily Telegraph*, 7 July 1987.

37 Michael Ratcliffe, in *The Observer*, 29 March 1987.

38 Timberlake Wertenbaker, 'Our Country's Good', in *Plays 1* (London, Faber and Faber, 1996).

39 Susan Carlson, 'Issues of Identity, Nationality and Performance: The Reception of Two Plays by Timberlake Wertenbaker', *New Theatre Quarterly*, 35 (1993), pp. 267–289, pp. 276–9.

40 Charlotte Keatley, *My Mother Said I Never Should* (London, Methuen/Royal Court, 1988).

41 Sue-Ellen Case, *Feminism and Theatre* (Basingstoke, Macmillan, 1988), p. 129.

42 Claire Armistead, *The Financial Times*, 4 March 1989; Milton Shulman, *Evening Standard*, 6 March 1989; Lyn Gardner, *City Limits*, 9 March 1989; Maureen Paton, *Daily Express*, 15 March 1989.

43 Sarah Kane, *Blasted & Phaedra's Love* (London, Methuen, 1996).

44 Interview with Sarah Kane, in Stephenson and Langridge, *Rage and Reason*, pp. 129–135, p. 130.

45 See Tom Sellar, 'Truth and Dare: Sarah Kane's *Blasted*', *Theatre*, 1 (1996), pp. 29–34.

46 *Ibid.*, p. 34.

47 Aleks Sierz, 'Cool Britannia? "In-Yer-Face" Writing in the British Theatre Today', *New Theatre Quarterly*, 56 (1998), pp. 324–33, p. 328.

48 Sarah Kane committed suicide in 1999. Productions of subsequent plays – *Phaedra's Love* (Gate Theatre, 1996), *Cleansed* (Royal Court Theatre Downstairs, 1998) and *Crave* (Paines Plough Theatre Company, 1998) initiated some critical reassessment of *Blasted.*

49 Sharman Macdonald, 'When I was a Girl I Used to Scream and Shout', in *Plays 1* (London, Faber and Faber, 1995).

50 Claire Armistead, *The Financial Times*, 10 December 1986.

51 Macdonald, 'When I was a Girl', p. 19.

52 Armistead, *The Financial Times*, 10 December 1986.

53 Diane Samuels, *Kindertransport* (London, Nick Hern Books, 1995).

54 Lyn Gardner, *The Guardian*, 19 April 1993.

55 Phyllis Nagy, *Butterfly Kiss* (London, Nick Hern Books, 1994).

56 Trevor R. Griffiths, 'Waving not Drowning: The Mainstream, 1979–88', in Griffiths and Llewellyn-Jones *British and Irish Women Dramatists Since 1958*, pp. 47–83, p. 49.

57 Phyllis Nagy, 'Hold Your Nerve: Notes for a Young Playwright', in David Edgar, ed., *State of Play: Playwrights on Playwriting* (London, Faber and Faber, 1999), pp. 121–32, pp. 124–5.

9

Feminists perform their past: constructing history in *The Heidi Chronicles* and *The Break of Day* [1]

Charlotte Canning

HEIDI   Although Sofonisba [Anguissola] was praised in the seventeenth century as being a portraitist equal to Titian, and at least thirty of her paintings remain known to us, there is no trace of her or any other woman artist prior to the twentieth century in your current Art History Survey textbook. Of course, in my day, this same standard text mentioned no women 'from the Dawn of History to the Present.' Are you with me? Okay.[2]

APRIL   No one talks about women like me. Particularly not in your magazines, Tess … We may not consume much, but we contribute a lot. We work. I think I live with dignity and some grace. I try to behave with decency. I feel lonely sometimes … but I keep going. My life is full. I want you to write a song about that, Nina, I want you to write a song about me.[3]

One assumption underlying women's history produced in the 1970s and early 1980s was that the need for the recuperation of women erased from history would cease to exist once women had been successfully instated. Books such as *Hidden From History* (1974), *Becoming Visible* (1977), and *The Majority Finds Its Past* (1979) explicitly mark this project in their titles.[4] Concomitantly, this work raised questions about the writing of history itself. Feminist historians found that putting women in history led to a 'reevaluation of established standards of historical significance'.[5] This 'compensatory' project, putting women in history, was expected to fade in light of the historiographical one that would prevent the subsequent erasure of women from history.[6] What many have found, however, is that this initial project has not disappeared with time and that the task of placing women in history has not ended with those efforts in the 1970s and 1980s. Instead,

[a]s feminists documented the lives of women in the past, provided
information that challenged received interpretations of particular periods or events, and analyzed the specific conditions of women's subordi-
nation, they have encountered the powerful resistance of history – as a
disciplined body of knowledge and as a professional institution.[7]

The operations of power revealed in the challenges feminism offered to
history's 'body of knowledge' and 'professional institution' confronted
women with the realisation that neither putting women in history, nor
re-envisioning history itself was going to be unchallenged or progres-
sively successful. Instead, these efforts were going to be repetitive and
fraught with disagreements, contradictions and controversy. Nowhere is
this more clearly illustrated than in the increasingly complicated and
contentious endeavour of constructing the historical narrative of second
wave feminism.

Heidi, in her eponymous chronicle, finds that feminism was not a
simple answer to a direct question. She marks the shift between what she
experienced as a student, no women in art history 'from the dawn of
time to the present', to what her students experience, 'no women prior to
the twentieth century' as she lectures about women artists, who are not
in the textbooks but who did work 'prior to the twentieth century'.[8]
While she acknowledges the changes since her student days, she simultaneously acknowledges their insufficiency and continues the same labour
– placing women in history. Wasserstein marks the difficulties in historicising women in the face of a relentlessly resistant dominant narrative
which would at most exclude women and at least marginalise them.

Similarly, April, at the end of *The Break of Day*, foregrounds the
ongoing erasure of women, one that did not cease with maturing of
second wave feminism. Her life – not a traditional one as she has no
lover, children or husband – is not represented in any of the places she
looks. Tess's glossy women's magazine wants to ignore that women like
April exist; however, when Tess protests weakly 'I'd change that but –',
she marks the disempowerment of some women by dominant political
and cultural discourses and their complicity with the erasure of women
from historical narratives.[9] April's call for attention to the diversity of
women's experiences could also be understood as a call for a new historiography that would put the diversity of women in history and keep it
there.

Paradoxically, both these characters are accomplishing the very thing
they desire – the presence of women in historical narratives – through
their existence in performance. As Antoinette Burton has indicated

'[h]istory has become virtually indispensable to feminists in the last decade'. [10] Both these plays provide entry points into the many ways in which the importance of history to feminism is increasing. This is not to argue, however, that feminists have not always been concerned with the workings of history – to the contrary as the editors of the two-volume play anthology *Herstory* noted that 'the Women's Liberation Movement of the 1960s and early 1970s … demand[ed] that women start to appear on the maps of the world – the cultural, historical, political ones, for example'.[11] It is instead to argue that as second wave feminism has persisted there has been increased reference to and construction of a 'feminist past' in current debates and discussions.[12] This growing focus on history is not tangential to feminist inquiry but part of the recognition that despite powerful efforts the changes wrought by feminism are subject to the vicissitudes of the historical moment, as well as significant debate over what these changes mean and how they came about.

As Heidi's and April's remarks which frame this chapter demonstrate, reclaiming women and putting them into history is a perpetual task, not one that can be completed and abandoned. If, as Burton indicates, 'history is not simply what happened in the past but … the kinds of knowledge about the past that we are made aware of', then feminists cannot rely on history to stay made once it is constructed or that the diversity of feminist endeavours will necessarily be fully delineated.[13] The construction of feminist historical narratives is itself a process of history – steeped in the struggles, investments and desires of a particular historical moment – which must be 'continuously revealed as the historical process it is'.[14] These two plays are caught between the compelling nature of the past moment and the difficult task of evaluating it in the light of the present one.

Feminists who have tried to articulate what the 1970s meant to them have been hard pressed to characterise those extraordinary times.

> Everywhere you turned, we were marching, writing, performing, striking … occupying newspapers … arguing with each other and everyone else. What's hard to grab hold of and pass on at a distance of twenty years is the sheer exhilaration and excitement of the times. The Buzz. The feeling – the knowledge – that what we were doing was *the* most important political and social movement … [15]

Gillian Hanna describes a past that had a greater effect on its participants than characterising it simply as a new set of ideas or new possibilities can begin to evoke. Instead, she calls up a range of memories – of labour, of joy, of doing something that mattered – and the power of those memories, both in their first experience and in their later recall. The dizzying array of activities and venues for action elicits a sense of a moment so compelling that it is difficult to deal with its legacy. It is easy to understand, however, how the assumptions of the durability of the actions and ideas of that time might have arisen. Developments from that moment must have appeared so forcefully compelling that there could be little doubt about their lasting impact. It was possible to assume that women's place in history, if not assured, was not going to remain marginalised and oppressed.

By the time of the two plays in question (1989–95), however, such assumptions were difficult to maintain. By this time there was talk in a variety of venues from mainstream media to academia of 'post-feminism'.

> [T]he irony is, however, that the proclamation of 'post-feminism' has occurred at precisely the same moment as acclaimed feminist studies demonstrate that not only have women's real advancements been limited but also that there has been a backlash against feminism of international significance. Could it be that 'post-feminism' as a concept is derived within the backlash?[16]

This sobering vision of a double-bind – losses for women at the same time they are being told that feminism is no longer necessary – is a sharp contrast to Hanna's vision of exuberant joy. What begins to be erased from history is the very feminism that fought so hard to revise history. These negative efforts are not absolute, of course. Sue-Ellen Case described a sense of feminist achievement in 1996 when she viewed Judy Chicago's remounted 1970s *Dinner Party*. 'I imagined something hopeful, the coming ... of those women to the table. I felt moved in a way I did not in the 1970s in one way I realized, that many women had already eaten quite well from that table ... '.[17] She traces several possible historical trajectories: Hildegard Von Bingen who has been followed by the development of feminist musicology and Sappho who 'has birthed numerous lesbian and gay studies programmes in many major universities'.[18] Theatre, too, has enjoyed an explosion of activity from Broadway and the West End to performance art and elsewhere. Case's sense of where feminism is and its connections to the past is an alternate view of the present to the one Vicki Coppock describes. The two versions, however, do not negate each other but do give a sense of the complexity of characterising feminism through the relation of its past to its present.

The Heidi Chronicles and *The Break of Day* struggle similarly to understand and narrativise these conflicting kinds of experiences and information to explore the dramaturgical narrativisation of feminism in
history.

Both plays participate in the 'historical process' of determining and
defining a 'feminist past'.[19] These plays have their characters, who were
young women full of the excitement of feminism in the 1970s, look back
at the heady early days of second wave feminism and evaluate it in terms
of their current lives and experiences. In that process of looking back
and assessing each play offers a history of feminism and it is that history
I will discuss and evaluate. The plays clearly ask: how do we remember
women and keep them in history? What are the effects of these actions?
Less overtly, the plays also ask whose history is it? How do conflicting
stories, ideas and memories coalesce or resolve into history, or do they?
Finally, each play invites the question: who is empowered to write the
history of feminism and what version(s) will become central? Both *The
Heidi Chronicles* and *The Break of Day* refer to the same moment in time
and both attempt to convey a dissonance between past and current
moments and yet employ divergent dramaturgy, different perspectives
and discrete conclusions.

Most of *The Heidi Chronicles* takes place in the past – the rarely seen
present is defined as 1989 in three of the thirteen scenes. Wasserstein
quotes events and locations as universal experiences – the high school
dance, the consciousness-raising session, or the television talk show – as
a way to summon up the setting, experience and politic of a particular
historical moment. These moments are evoked in four ways: popular
music (e.g. *Shoop Shoop Song* or *Imagine*), properties (e.g. McCarthy for
President placards or filofaxes), costume and casual asides referencing
current events (e.g. the Lennon assassination or the aerobics craze), but
there is little engagement with the complexities of these times and the
further complications of their relation to the present moment of the
play.

Heidi's academic lectures frame the play. She is presenting work
from women artists who have been left out of history. Her tone, however,
is not very respectful, rather it is jocular and overly familiar ('Hello
girls'), and her analogies to the current day trivialise the historical differences between the paintings and the current moment.[20] The connection
Heidi makes between the content and technique of the paintings and her
life compares the women portrayed to wallflowers at a high school dance
and then later to being disempowered and without agency. Heidi

describes the women in the painting, and by extension herself, as a highly informed spectator.[21] This typifies Heidi throughout the play. Everything happens to her, she does not drive the action of the play. With this dramaturgy Wasserstein suggests that women are not active historical agents – history happens to them but they have little effect on it. Unlike the women characters in *The Break of Day* who, while struggling between history as a reflection of an individual's experiences or as intersections of a variety of discourses, effect and drive the action of the play, Heidi cannot seem to be more than a passive presence in her friends' lives.

In the first two scenes Wasserstein introduces Heidi's friends, Susan, Peter and Scoop, who comprise the central characters. In scene one (1965) Susan, who shortens her skirt at the high school dance to attract boys' attention, urges Heidi to move away so 'it won't look like you just wanna hang around with your girlfriend. But don't look desperate. Men won't dance with desperate women.'[22] Despite Heidi's attempts to reduce and demystify male and female differences, Susan soon abandons her for a boy who can 'twist and smoke at the same time'.[23] Peter, who will become a paediatrician and come out of the closet in 1974, moves over when Susan leaves. He and Heidi bond instantly and throughout the play Heidi will find more in common with him than with any of the women.

In the next scene, 1968, Heidi meets Scoop who, throughout the scene and subsequently the play, works to maintain his superiority to Heidi. His voice, as it is established here and reinforced throughout the play, is one of prescience. It is he who accurately predicts Heidi's fate.

> Heidi, you don't understand. You're the one this is all going to affect. You're the one whose life this will all change significantly. Has to. You're a very serious person. In fact, you're the unfortunate contradiction in terms – a serious good person.[24]

Wasserstein empowers this male character much more than she will her title character. All the other characters adapt to changing conditions – especially Susan who represents the clichéd mainstream choices for women. She makes law review and clerks for a Supreme Court judge in the early 1970s, moves to a women's health and legal collective in the late 1970s, and by the mid-1980s has moved to Los Angeles to become a successful producer of television situation comedies. In contrast, Heidi is paralysed by her analytical groping for happiness and satisfaction. While she rejects Susan's notion that it was all in error – 'I don't think we made such big mistakes' – she does not seem animated or empowered by her critique of current conditions or the choices she has made.[25] Taking a Fulbright in England or a job in Minnesota are both moments of retreat, not triumph or exploration.

The only concerted act of will Heidi makes throughout the play is to adopt a daughter, constructing a contradictory ending for the play. Heidi is emphatic that the adoption is not what completes her.

> HEIDI Wait a minute, why is my baby my ten and your work is your
> ten?
> SCOOP I didn't mean it that way.
> HEIDI Well it certainly came out that way. I'm not some empty vessel.[26]

Heidi vigorously rejects Scoop's characterisation, but two factors mitigate her denial. Wasserstein's last scene is a man, a woman and a baby and, while they are not an actual nuclear family, the image reinforces that traditional bond. The final image is of Heidi in a rocking chair, holding her daughter, and singing Sam Cooke's 1957 *You Send Me*. The image itself is the second mitigating factor – it is one of strong resolution. Heidi is finally depicted as content, unreservedly hopeful and confident. Unlike the end of *Break of Day* where the characters are together in a group facing the past and the future as a community, Heidi is alone, a single mother, concerned only with the future – she murmurs to her daughter 'A heroine for the twenty-first [century].'[27] She has stepped out of the struggle instead of demonstrating a renewed engagement.

All the characters, ideas and storylines in *The Break of Day* are imbricated with history: Nina's hope for an adopted daughter with the fall of communism and recent events in Eastern Europe; Tess's and Jamie's lives with recent developments in medicine (whether in treatments like in vitro fertilisation [IVF] or economic and cultural shifts in practices); and all the characters with the tensions brought about by the past's relationship to the present and the effects of that relationship to future possibilities. The connections between the personal and the historical inform every aspect of the play. This is the starting point of the play as Tess, a successful editor of a large women's magazine, and Nina, a singer-songwriter, have a friendly argument over their own and feminism's past.

Before the action of the play begins Wertenbaker provides a glimpse of the three women in the heady days of 1970s feminism playing in a rock and roll band. They sing: 'The present is mine for the asking / The future's a moment away ... / And now it belongs to me / I'm going to change the world.'[28] Tess remembers this feminist past – their song resonates with Gillian Hanna's memories quoted earlier -but attributes it to their youth and not to larger forces. They were young and therefore ripe for such excitement. Now that they are older it is logical that those days have faded. Nina disagrees and suggests that it is not so much one's age or point of life but the historical moment that determines one's sense of power.

> Tess is raking up the past – how we stood in front of life with all those possibilities – not because we were young but because it was that moment. I don't feel powerful at all, is that because of this moment? But since you only see with the eyes given to you by the moment you live in, how can you fight it? Who'll give you the map showing the passage out?[29]

Nina's challenging questions set the agenda for the play. She refuses such an individualised view of history, but in her recognition of the power of the historical moment to prescribe actions and agendas she is paralysed. Although she tentatively attributes her paralysis to her current experiences, it becomes clear that for all the characters the demands of the past and its influence on the present create paralysis.

The complicated influences of the feminist past on the current moment are foregrounded when Marisa (Nina's stepson's girlfriend) announces she is pregnant, returning the three friends to their earlier argument. Nina and Tess counsel Marisa to abort and she flings back to them, 'So I can end up like you, married to ambition, bitter and childless … .'[30] April, an academic and Nina and Tess's friend from the earlier days, reminds Nina that because of her illegal abortion Nina can no longer have children – is this what feminism has led older women to wish on younger ones?

This stark and horrible moment circles back to the opening evaluation of feminism and its legacy. April accuses Tess of 'betraying feminism' because of her work on a woman's magazine.[31] Nina defends Tess, but April tries to get them to understand that magazines like that are complicit with an agenda that works against women. 'You had one of the best minds – your deconstruction of just the kind of magazine you're editing. How it held up an image of happiness that was unattainable.'[32] Tess has been 'corrupted', losing her political critique and her defence against the forces that reduce women to disempowered wombs.[33] Tess, however, disagrees, and despite April's assertion that having a child is not 'the only purpose of a woman's life', Tess reveals her obsession with bearing a child that she will pursue throughout the play.[34] Nina urges Tess to relinquish this focus and come to terms with childlessness, but Tess connects her need to her sense that the personal determines the historical. The empowerment she experienced in the past has been translated into the belief that she can achieve anything she works at diligently.

But the act does not end with the personal or individual. Wertenbaker intervenes in the discussions of parenting with a reminder of larger political, social and cultural struggles. Mr Hardacre, Tess's neighbour, offers homegrown tomatoes but cannot stay. He is 'going on a march with my suitcase', the same suitcase his wife, a Jewish refugee from the Second World War carried when she escaped from the Nazis in France.[35] Disturbed by recent events, and seeing a stark similarity between the floods of refugees during and after the Second World War and the present moment, Mr Hardacre declares his solidarity with these refugees. He argues for connections among people ('we are all one') rather than the atomisation of late, multinational capitalism (we are each consumers).[36] 'I'm going to protest against history', he states and offers a stark contrast between Nina's paralysis and Tess's self-absorption with his own sense of empowerment in the face of overwhelming odds.[37]

The second act is about the making and getting of babies. Working to illustrate Mr Hardacre's forceful introduction of a sense of the larger world, it alternates between Nina and Hugh's struggles in an unnamed Eastern European country to adopt a child and Tess's in London to complete IVF successfully. Tess's life slowly disintegrates – her job, home and lover all slipping away as her obsession increases. She ends up objectifying women precisely as the patriarchy does. 'Women used to be my sisters. They're objects: egg vessels.'[38] Wertenbaker's comparison of the two women's situations clearly favours Nina's struggle for a transnational adoption. Nina is an active agent in realising her desire to be a mother while Tess passively narrows her focus until her life is defined by the expensive, elitist and rarely successful technology of artificial fertilisation and implants.

The play's end reunites the seven main characters of the first Act. The hopes and plans the others had have changed. Marisa is depressed after the birth of her child, Jamie's hospital has closed and Tess has not conceived. Robert wishes Tess would abandon her attempt to get pregnant and that they could rekindle their relationship but Tess's understanding of the myth of progress is a debilitating one – anyone can achieve anything if they work at it and are willing to pay the price – and it cuts her off from productive relationships.

It is April who is the most hopeful and satisfied with her life. Marriage and romance do not 'curtain' April from 'the world', but it is her life that is in danger of going unrecorded, uncelebrated.[39] Hugh notes that April's life is interesting but April responds, 'I think so, but no one talks about women like me.'[40] She demands that discourse and representation shift to attend to women like her, implying as well that they shift away from their current practices as exemplified in magazines like Tess's. April's description of her life is also a cry for feminism and for the revision of the ways in which women are historicised. But it is Tess who asserts at the end, 'We only want to try and understand what's happened' and with this Wertenbaker avoids an anti-feminist dismissal of Tess or an artificial resolution of history.[41] She gestures toward a 'hopeful' ongoing struggle to understand the past as the struggle in which the characters have engaged and which will move them into the future.

The Heidi Chronicles was received by the mainstream theatre establishment (critics and producers alike) with overwhelmingly positive enthusiasm. Besides the glowing reviews it also received several prestigious awards, including a Pulitzer and a Tony.[42] But the play also met with stinging rebuke. Some critics felt it was hackneyed and trite, others that it was overly simplistic.[43] There was a strong rejection of the play by a variety of feminist critics who saw it less as a play about women than a rejection of feminism that put men at its core.[44] Overall the play received much attention and debate. *The Break of Day* received a very different critical reception and most critics intensely disliked the play. While the basis of the play is almost unanimously praised (a contemporary version of Chekhov's *Three Sisters*), critics took Wertenbaker to task for being unable to integrate what they saw as an awkward intersection of disparate and unconnected ideas.[45] The supportive reviews were the exception.[46] Wertenbaker found this dismissive reception both troubling and puzzling, telling one interviewer that the critics 'didn't make the effort to understand it, which shocked me actually, because I think they should have made the effort'.[47] The reception of both plays has been contentious although, as the reviews demonstrate, for very different reasons.

Despite their interesting and controversial receptions, neither play suggests, either through dramaturgy or content, a particularly radical new vision of feminism's past. Several assumptions about that past can be extracted from the plays. Women experience a considerable gap between their past expectations and their current situations and their present discontent can be attributed to the promises the past seemed to make to them. Subsequently, women are suspicious of current feminism's utility. Finally, both plays suggest, although differently, that feminism has obfuscated women's central and defining purpose – child-rearing. While these are generalisations, and *The Break of Day* is more sophisticated about these assumptions, they can be reasonably extracted from the plays.

Significantly, the treatment in both plays of sexuality and race recalls the historical struggles of feminism around those issues. The feminist past one might construct from *The Heidi Chronicles* and *The Break of Day* in many ways reasserts misleading narratives which have dominated feminist discourse – that feminism was largely theorised by, fought for and laboured on by white heterosexual women and that lesbians and women of colour were not significant contributors. This is not, however, to prescribe content or approach for these playwrights nor rebuke either playwright for a play she did not set out to write. It is, instead, to point out that the ways in which these issues are simultaneously invoked and ignored recollects the ways in which racism and homophobia have long been significant problems within feminism as heterosexual white women often have positioned themselves as typical and unquestioningly used their own lived experiences as bases for feminist theory and action.[48] If one reads these plays as accounts of the feminist past and that past's impact on the present it is very important to understand each play's approach.

In both plays lesbianism is presented as a source of humour or embarrassment for heterosexual women. While the depictions are divergent, the two plays position heterosexual women as reasonable and moderating forces burdened with the responsibility of attending to the dependent lesbian. The heterosexual position is centred and normalised so that spectators see lesbians through heterosexual perspectives rather than as a discrete and distinct category independent of heterosexuality.

Fran, the most overt lesbian in *The Heidi Chronicles*, wears army fatigues, uses profanity every time she speaks (the only character to do so), and is generally critical of and intimidating to the other women, all of whom are heterosexual.[49] The youngest member of the consciousness-raising circle, Becky, compares Fran to her overbearing, abusive boyfriend. Fran reassures Becky that 'no one in the group hates her' and shows no reaction to the homophobic and sexist comparison of a lesbian to an abusive heterosexual man.[50] Susan does offer a half-hearted defence of Fran ('Fran is one of the most honest people I've ever met.

She's a great friend') but it does not contradict Becky's comparison, allowing the characterisation of lesbian as abusive and domineering, to stand as authoritative.[51]

Natasha, Tess's Eastern European servant, assumes April is a lesbian because she is writing a book on the poet Sappho. Natasha 'lunges at April and kisses her'.[52] April's response to this attack is to explain that Sappho 'wasn't gay, at least not in the way we understand the word, it's a historical misunderstanding …', supplying a scholarly response as if to rescue Sappho (and herself) from inaccurate popular misunderstandings, wheras Tess's is to offer to fire her.[53] That the kiss is preceded by a 'lunge', taking April by surprise, offers a vision of lesbian sexuality that is predatory. April does rally to Natasha's defence, countering Tess's doubts that Natasha is not a refugee but from 'Cardiff', telling her not to dismiss her, pointing out that being 'gay and a war victim' is not a contradiction in terms.[54] Ultimately April's solution is to apologise to Natasha. The apology, however, is not based on the sexual misunderstanding but the cultural one. April tells Tess that she must apologise:

> Because we don't know where she's from, and her life has ceased to interest us, although we cry for her on television, because our imagination has been depleted by this terrible century – because words like compassion and humanity have cracked in the last fifteen years and we've let it happen … .[55]

This view of a lesbian character is far more complex than in *The Heidi Chronicles*. Wertenbaker displaces the straight liberal guilt from sexuality on to the disintegration of communism and capitalism's disregard for the suffering that ensued. One could argue that by making the character a lesbian Wertenbaker refuses to construct a world where heterosexuality is the norm and disrupts expectations about refugees as sexuality is rarely discussed around refugee issues, as well as that the moment does not put the heterosexual characters in a particularly sympathetic light. One could counter-argue, however, that the elision of lesbian with the geopolitical situation allows the characters to avoid confronting sexual issues further exoticising lesbian as foreign (either Eastern European or Welsh) and an inconvenient source of guilt for heterosexuals.

Race is more difficult to track in the two plays and they diverge widely in their construction of the category. *The Heidi Chronicles* does not acknowledge race at all, interesting in a play dedicated to critiquing feminism for the ways in which it failed women. There is one opening at the end of the play for a gesture towards the struggles within feminism around race. Heidi has adopted a daughter, an adoption she reveals to be transnational and transracial. When asked her daughter's name she replies, 'Peter suggested Panama Hattie in honor of his favorite musical and her place of birth.'[56] This line is tossed off and never referred to again. Given that the movie itself includes no actual Panamanians, that the character 'Panama Hattie' is European American, and that the people of colour who do appear in the movie are definitively segregated, Heidi's reference is less a gesture toward the complexities of race and racism for feminism than a reinscription of pervasive US racism.[57]

While *The Break of Day* does not grapple with race directly it does focus on ethnicity. Ethnicity is crucial to the play as the effects of the fall of communism are struggled over. But the Eastern European country that Nina and Hugh visit is not specified. This elides the particular histories of these diverse countries, suggesting an absence of differences among them. This creates an imbalance between the specificity of England's political and social problems (health care, education and the arts are specifically referenced) and the vague difficulties caused by the end of communism for former Soviet bloc nations.

In examining how she writes lesbian and gay history Jennifer Terry notes that rather than trying to reveal homosexuality throughout the ages, 'I look for the conditions that make possible, and those that constrain, the emergence and vitality of "lesbians" and "gay men" who populate our present.'[58] Her argument is that both the past and its construction make possible the present. Thus histories that claim, for example, that there were no lesbians support 'the present circumstances of widespread homophobia'.[59] Partial views of the past can licence exclusion in the present. Similarly, versions of the past that elide racial differences and experiences act, as Hazel Carby describes it, 'within the relations of racism'.[60] The power of history is such that it can naturalise present-day exclusion by creating a past in which the excluded do not appear. This is not to say that either playwright consciously intended to occlude lesbians or women of colour but that their marginalisation in these plays could be read as 'proof' of their marginalisation in the historical moment. The stakes of writing history are extremely high and no more so than when trying to understand the effects of an emancipatory political movement like feminism.

It is not surprising that the task of placing women in history described as part of the feminist historical agenda in the 1970s has not faded but been inscribed into feminist debate over its past. The terms have changed, it is no longer solely about how others have omitted or included women and the effect of these choices on history, but how feminism theorizes and constructs its own past. This task, as Antoinette Burton sees it, is part of the 'claims about the situatedness, renegotiation, and contestability of knowledge which remain, together, at the heart of feminist inquiry'.[61] *The Heidi Chronicles* and *The Break of Day*, while different plays, could both be placed at this heart.

The Heidi Chronicles and *The Break of Day* offer different versions of the feminist past, its meanings, and its influences on the future. Wertenbaker ultimately embraces feminism and its achievements: 'Wertenbaker's women do not represent their feminism as a mistake but as a way of looking forward'.[62] For Wasserstein, however, feminism may ultimately be a mistake, given the way she denigrates and denies feminism and its achievements. Both plays and playwrights, however, offer significant and compelling forays into performed historiography, that is into the task of staging the insertion of women into history. They are texts for performance which need performers and audiences to realise their full potential – as such the plays are really starting points – these histories should be read as possible, rather than definitive, accounts and the critical reception of both plays demonstrates that audiences have not been shy to challenge, disagree or embrace these narratives. *The Heidi Chronicles* and *The Break of Day* are in dialogue with their audiences evoking the experiences, memories and pasts of those audiences. Each spectator must compare the staged construction of the feminist past with the one that she has experienced, remembering that '[c]onflicting understandings of the uses of the past have been intrinsic to the project of feminist history', and make choices about how she will narrativise her own and feminism's history.[63]

Notes

1 This article was originally presented as a paper in the Feminist Research Working Group in the 1998 World Congress of the International Federation for Theatre Research at the University of Kent in Canterbury. I would like to thank the working group, especially Elaine Aston, for their insightful comments.

2 Wendy Wasserstein, *The Heidi Chronicles* (New York, Dramatists Play Service, 1990), p. 7.

3 Timberlake Wertenbaker, *The Break of Day* (London, Faber and Faber, 1995), p. 93.

4 Sheila Rowbotham, *Hidden from History* (New York, Pantheon, 1974); Renate Bridenthal and Claudia Koonz, *Becoming Visible: Women in European*

History (Boston, Houghton Mifflin, 1977); and Gerda Lerner, *The Majority Finds Its Past* (New York, Oxford University Press, 1979).

5 Joan Wallach Scott, *Gender and the Politics of History* (New York, Columbia University Press, 1988), p. 17.

6 Meenakshi Ponnuswami, 'Feminist History in Contemporary British Theatre', *Women and Performance: A Journal of Feminist Theory*, 7–8, 2–1 (1995), p. 289.

7 Scott, *Gender and the Politics of History*, p. 18.

8 Wasserstein, *The Heidi Chronicles*, p. 7.

9 Wertenbaker, *The Break of Day*, p. 93.

10 Antoinette Burton, '"History" is Now: Feminist Theory and the Production of Historical Feminisms', *Women's History Review*, 1, 1 (1992), p. 25.

11 Gabrielle Griffin and Elaine Aston, *Herstory: Plays By Women* (Sheffield, Sheffield Academic Press, 1991), p. 7.

12 Burton, '"History" is now', p. 25. I will use 'feminist past' in the singular throughout not because I believe a monolithic, unified narrative of feminist history is possible or desirable but because the plural implies a solution to the debates over the recent past of feminism – if everyone's version can be put forward with equal weight and import, why debate? It is precisely because versions have different weight and make competing claims to the past rather than pasts that I maintain the singular for the purposes of this particular argument.

13 *Ibid.*, p. 26.

14 *Ibid.*

15 Gillian Hanna, 'Introduction', in Gillian Hanna, ed., *Monstrous Regiment: A Collective Celebration* (London, Nick Hern, 1991), at the 1998 World Congress, p. xv.

16 Vicki Coppock, Deena Haydon and Ingrid Richter, *The Illusions of 'Post-Feminism': New Women, Old Myths* (London, Taylor and Francis, 1995), p. 3.

17 Sue-Ellen Case, lecture, Sweden, 1997, n. p.

18 *Ibid.*

19 Burton, '"History" is now', p. 25.

20 Wasserstein, *The Heidi Chronicles*, p. 7.

21 *Ibid.*, p. 41.

22 *Ibid.*, p. 9.

23 *Ibid.*

24 *Ibid.*, p. 16.

25 *Ibid.*, p. 58.

26 *Ibid.*, p. 73.

27 *Ibid.*, p. 75.

28 Wertenbaker, *The Break of Day*, p. 95.

29 *Ibid.*, pp. 6–7.

30 *Ibid.*, p. 32.

31 *Ibid.*, p. 33.

32 *Ibid.*, pp. 33–4.

33 *Ibid.*, p. 35.

34 *Ibid.*, p. 34.

35 *Ibid.*, p. 42.

36 *Ibid.*, p. 39.

37 *Ibid.*, p. 43.

38 *Ibid.*, p. 71.

39 *Ibid.*, p. 93.

40 *Ibid.*

41 *Ibid.*, p. 94.

42 See, for example, Mimi Kramer, review of *The Heidi Chronicles,* in *The New Yorker,* 26 December 1988, pp. 81–2 and Robert Brustein, review of *The Heidi Chronicles,* in *The New Republic,* 17 April 1989, pp. 33–4.

43 See, for example, Richard Hornby, review of *The Heidi Chronicles, Hudson Review,* 42, 3 (Autumn 1989), pp. 459–66 and review of *The Heidi Chronicles,* in *New York,* 2 January 1989, p. 49.

44 See, for example, Gayle Austin, review of *The Heidi Chronicles, Theatre Journal,* 42, 1 (March 1990), pp. 107–8 and Phyllis Jane Rose, 'An Open Letter to Dr. Heidi Holland', *American Theatre* (October 1989), p. 26. For more scholarly feminist analysis and critique see Jill Dolan, *Presence and Desire: Essays on Gender, Sexuality, and Performance,* (Ann Arbor, University of Michigan Press, 1993) and Helene Keyssar, 'Drama and the Dialogic Imagination: *The Heidi Chronicles* and *Fefu and Her Friends', Modern Drama* (March 1991), pp. 88–106.

45 See, for example, Michael Billington, review of *The Break of Day, Guardian,* 3 November 1995, p. 13; Paul Taylor, review of *The Break of Day, Independent,* sec. 2, 30 November 1995, p. 13, and Shena MacKay, review of *The Break of Day, Times Literary Supplement,* 22 December 1995, p. 18.

46 See, for example, Clare Bayley, review of *The Break of Day, New Statesman and Society,* 1 December 1995, p. 33.

47 Interview with Timberlake Wertenbaker, in Heidi Stephenson and Natasha Langridge, eds., *Rage and Reason: Women Playwrights on Playwriting* (London, Methuen, 1997), p. 144.

48 Charlotte Canning, 'Constructing Experience: Theorizing a Feminist Theatre History', *Theatre Journal,* 45, 4 (1993), pp. 533–4.

49 I say 'overt lesbian' because there is a suggestion that Susan is a lesbian when she lives in Montana on a women's health and legal collective but that is never developed or directly articulated: Wasserstein, *The Heidi Chronicles,* pp. 32–3.

50 *Ibid.*, p. 21.

51 *Ibid.*

52 *Ibid.*, p. 23.

53 Wertenbaker, *The Break of Day,* p. 23.

54 *Ibid.*

55 *Ibid.*, p. 24.

56 Wasserstein, *The Heidi Chronicles*, p. 73.

57 *Panama Hattie* is a 1942 movie musical based on an earlier play by Herbert Fields and B. G. DeSylva, and stars Ann Sothern, Red Skelton and Virginia O'Brien. The music is composed by Cole Porter. The movie has several 'exotic' South American musical numbers featuring African American performers, particularly Lena Horne (in her screen debut) and the Berry Brothers. Their numbers are not integrated into the plot, nor do we see them in the club where Hattie headlines and they all ostensibly work. Instead they are completely segregated from the action and the white characters.

58 Jennifer Terry, 'Theorizing Deviant Historiography', in Ann-Louise Shapiro, ed., *Feminists Revision History* (New Brunswick, NJ, Rutgers University Press, 1994), p. 284.

59 *Ibid.*

60 Hazel Carby, 'White Women Listen! Black Feminism and the Boundaries of Sisterhood', in Heidi Safia Mirza, ed., *Black British Feminism* (London, Routledge, 1997), p. 51.

61 Burton, '"History" is now', p. 33.

62 Elaine Aston, '"Millennium mothers": the politics of non-reproduction', International Federation for Theatre Research World Congress, 1998, n.p.

63 Joan Wallach Scott, 'Introduction', in idem, ed., *Feminism and History* (Oxford, Oxford University Press, 1996), p. 4.

NO SPACE OF OUR OWN? MARGARET MACNAMARA, ALMA BROSNAN, RUTH DODDS AND THE ILP ARTS GUILD

Ros Merkin

'Every known dramatist yet has had to make their initial appearance, some after years of heart-breaking struggle and neglect', ran a 1928 review of Ruth Dodd's *The Pressed Man*. Over fifty years later, Ruth Dodds alongside Alma Brosnan and Margaret Macnamara are still struggling to make an appearance in historiographies of women and theatre. In part, their neglect may be attributed to the fact that all three are bound together by their work for the Independent Labour Party (ILP) Arts Guild during the 1920s, a period summed up by Michelene Wandor as one in which 'organised feminism was far less visible ... theatre work controlled by women, linking feminism and aesthetics, ceased to command its own space'.[1] Yet, whilst it was true that the Arts Guild did not offer women a theatre space of their own, limiting a field of analysis to work which links 'feminism and aesthetics' is problematic. Large numbers of women were involved in the work of the Arts Guild from the outset. At the Guild's inaugural meeting, in 1925, messages of support were read from Sybil Thorndike, Edith Craig and Irene Rooke, an actress identified with the 'new movement' in English drama, and by the end of the month all three also found themselves on the National Administrative Council of the Guild alongside Kyrle Bellew (the actress wife of Arthur Bourchier), Kathleen Dillon, Evelyn Hope, Evelyn Sharp and the dancer Margaret Morris. Nor was their contribution to the theatre of the Labour movement confined simply to messages of support or sitting on committees. At the Sunday evenings held at the Strand Theatre in 1925 and 1926 – an initiative undertaken with the help of Bourchier and Kyrle Bellew which provided some of the impetus for the establishment of the Guild – performances were given free of charge by bountiful, well-established performers. Margaret Morris and her pupils made several appearances as did Marjorie Gullein's Scottish speaking choir who performed rhythmic movement to poetry. Sybil Thorndike's performance in the trial scene from *The Merchant of Venice* elicited seventeen curtain calls and Mary Raby, Martha Vanne, Moyna MacGill and Elizabeth Arkell appeared in a performance of Miles Malleson's anti-war play *Black 'Ell*. Nor were the professional performers alone in working for the Guild; in many ways focusing on their involvement misses the real point of the Guild – which was largely to encourage 'amateurs' to discover a path to socialism through theatre. At its height, the Guild boasted over 130 active local groups and whilst tracing information concerning the activities (and also the hopes and aspirations they had for the Guild) of 'ordinary' women is difficult, the columns in the *New Leader* which reported on the work of the Guild make it clear that women were involved in the work of the Guild in a variety of ways.[2]

Tracing the number of women playwrights performed by Guild groups is an easy task and a glance through the Guild's repertoire shows evidence of performances of plays by Susan Glaspell or Elizabeth Baker's *The Price of Thomas Scott* and Clemence Dane's *Bill of Divorcement*. Others were written by amateurs or those on the fringes of professionalism – the distinction is sometimes a hard one to draw – specifically for use by the Labour movement, including the five plays by women (out of a total of nineteen) which formed part of the series 'Plays for the People' published between 1920-1927. The series was edited by Monica Ewer, one-time drama critic for the *Daily Herald* and author of *Play Production for Everyone* and it included her own full-length play *The Best of Both Worlds*.

Margaret Macnamara

One of the most popular pieces from the series was Margaret Macnamara's *Mrs Jupp Obliges* (1925). Interestingly enough, even those most fundamentally involved in the work of the Guild itself were as likely to dismiss Macnamara's plays as 'slight trifles' resembling 'Miss Gertrude Jennings' bright and harmless efforts' as they were to uphold them as examples of plays which the ILP should be producing.[3] It may have been Margaret Macnamara's involvement with the Women's Institute and the British Drama League – for which she served on the Community Theatre Committee from 1921 and as Secretary until 1926 – which led to such views, but it did not prevent four of her plays appearing with some regularity in the Arts Guild repertoire (she was a far more prolific writer than this suggests).[4] All are 'well-made' comic one-acters dealing with issues close to the heart of the ILP – all pointed to a Labour moral. The 'slightest' of the four might be *Love-Fibs* (1920), a rustic comedy about the truth and lies of love in which the young maid is seduced by the prospect of a new Sunday hat; this leads her to lie to her mistress about losing some money so she can still afford to buy her fiancé a watch with a crocodile strap. Two of the others deal with issues around housing, and in both of these working-class women are seen to outwit their adversaries with the help of great deal of natural ingenuity. Mrs Hodges, in the play of the same name, outmanoeuvres the members of the local Housing Committee including Mrs Clam-Digby of 'county importance' and 'commanding headgear', who believes that the new cottages being proposed are another instance of 'the deplorable habit we've got into of pampering the working-class'. The committee all want to ignore the recommendations of the Women's Institute as too expensive; cheap housing is their priority and water butts, despite the attendant health hazards, cost less than proper surface drainage. It is left to Mrs Hodges' ingenuity and a series of comic contrivances involving the architect going to stay at her house to ensure that the women win out.

Rural housing, or the lack of rural housing for local workers, is at the heart of *Mrs Jupp Obliges* in which Mrs Jupp outwits both the weekender Miss Hickman, who has been ordered to spend time in the country by her doctor on account of her nerves, and the disorganised and servantless Mrs Poynder. Having been forced out of her own house when her husband lost his job and unable to find suitable housing in the village because of the demand of weekenders, Mrs Jupp has no choice but to rely on her wits in order to keep her family together and ensure that she can move into Miss Hickman's cottage; as she tells Miss Hickman, 'I regret having to push in where I'm not welcome … but right's right. I have to have a home fit for my family'.[5]

The issue at the heart of *Light Gray or Dark* (1920) is the question of illegitimacy and the hypocrisy of the church. For the curate the question is black and white; 'it would be very unjust to treat an unmarried mother on the same footing as the married' and 'without the one virtue that is called "virtue" in a woman, how can she begin to be a … er … worthy of the name of mother?'. He has the power to decide if 'Mrs' Bridger's children can go to the Church orphanage, not an ideal solution for the hardworked, poverty-stricken mother worn out by the age of 35, but one which is infinitely better than the Poor Law Cottages with 'the improperbehaved and the foul-mouthed'. For this to happen the curate must sign a document verifying that he has seen the mother's marriage certificate, which of course does not exist. It is the lodger, Miss Pelling, who is left to argue the mother's case. She tells the details of the story ('Mrs' Bridger left her first husband when he went to prison and lived with the kind and respectable lodger, Mr Bridger, until his death), but she also argues passionately for the importance of natural affection between the mother and children 'which takes no notice of a service in church' and of the significance of 'mother-love' which should be the foundation of religion. In the final instance, it is 'Mrs' Bridger who throws the curate out for, 'outcast as she is, she despises him'[6] and the church's hypocrisy, and it is in this final silent moment that the curate changes his mind and signs the forms.

Alma Brosnan

Another of the plays published in the series was by Alma Brosnan, a leading member of the ILP Arts Guild in Bath where she was the producer for the Green Park Players. In comparison to the witty comedies of Margaret Macnamara, Brosnan was a bleak writer and her first play, *The Street* (1926), shows the downward spiral that leads women into prostitution. Set in the Blisters' one-room apartment near the London docks, she depicts the life of an impoverished young couple. Joe struggles at the docks day after day to get a precious token that will mean work. Their son is in the hospital, 'ruptured through bad feeding' and Nell is reduced to shoes full of holes and a feeling of being shut in 'like a rat in a trap'. 'Why can't they fix it diff'rent?', she asks her husband, 'They seems as if they can do whatever they want to do. Look at them big places they put up and the food in the shops. Whatever they want they can get. Why don't they *want* to fix things diff'rent for them as do the work?'. His reply is bitter. He is as trapped as she is because 'nobody cares about the want in another man's belly'.[7] The only offer of help comes from Moll Dangers, Nell's neighbour, who will show her the way of the streets. At first Nell is horrified and adamantly refuses. She is respectable and has been brought up differently from Moll and, anyway, Joe has 'put 'is foot down flat'. Moll laughs off all her objections; what right has a man got to 'keep a woman all to 'imself if 'e shuts 'er up in four walls and starves 'er?' she asks. She is older than Nell and has 'learned some. My man and I tried b'in respectable … Flush for a few days, but longer and longer spells o'stoney broke … We ain't fools, that's all; we ain't goin' to starve, that's all; we ain't goin' to sit down in the mopes and die, that's all.

We'd be respectable if it paid, but it don't, see?'[8] The situation in which the characters find themselves drives their actions; in the end, it is not Moll's words, but the fact that Joe is hurt fighting to get his hands on the precious work token – left weak and helpless as a child – which finally drives Nell to put on some rouge and go on to the street.

The Street truly is 'a shilling shocker', a 'ghoulish play' which, despite Moll's defiant voice, seems to offer little hope. The Bradford Pioneer predicted frequent performances of the piece 'by the less enlightened Socialist amateur societies' arguing (rather oddly) that prostitution 'has a particular fascination, especially for really austere and active women', but it is the play's sense of weariness and helplessness (as with Brosnan's other plays) which really opened it to criticism. 'If labour players could play this play to wealthy audiences who know too little of these things it should prove valuable propaganda for it is sincerely written', declared H. Weston Wells, but he was doubtful about its value as a 'play for the people', uncertain if people want or need to be depressed by realities they know too well. Men are not made stronger by despair and 'if it be art to hold a mirror up to Nature' he doubted if the play was as true to life as it pretended to be.[9] This accusation of defeatism and despair (when the socialist movement was optimistic to the bone), it is part of a wider debate that occurred within the ILP Arts Guild about the type of plays they should be looking for. In this instance, though, the plays found an unlikely defender, in the shape of Huntley Carter, writing from the side of the Workers' Theatre Movement – the side quickest to attack ILP plays for their imitations of bourgeois art and for their defeatism. Although Carter would have preferred a note of struggle rather than resignation, and he is talking here not just of the work of Alma Brosnan but of all the Plays for the People, he thought they did express socialism from the point of view of the common people, offering a good picture of 'certain aspects of the transitional socialist world' and he praised, in particular, The Street for bringing to people's notice the fact 'that a clean working woman is driven to prostitution by economic conditions'.[10]

Alma Brosnan's next play, Scrapped (1927), was as downbeat as her first, showing the downward slide of the Berger family as one after the other they 'become the victims of unemployment or the other oppressions of our present capitalist system'. Set in the 'small villa home' of the lower middle-class Berger family, she emphasises the impact unemployment has on people's lives by concentrating in the first Act on their triumphs and achievements. The daughter, Ellen, wins her much worked for scholarship to college. The father, John, is absent for much of the Act at the firm's dinner, returning proudly with an initialised suitcase and an illuminated framed address, the reward for thirty-five years' dutiful service to the *Mercury*. The only discordant note comes from Aunt Annie, John Berger's unmarried sister who lives with the family and works as a shop assistant. Thirty-five years of seeing the reality of business has made her more sceptical than the others; it has taught her that it is 'pounds, shillings and pence' that are the real master and she sees little reason to be proud of a framed address when 'a bundle of shares' or making him a director ' 'ud be more to the point, I'm thinking'.[11]

By the beginning of Act Two, the Bergers' night of triumph has faded and the harsh world of Aunt Annie and unemployment takes hold. The rest of the play shows the disintegration of the individual family members and of the family as a whole as it slides into bickering and squabbling. The impact is greatest on John Berger; as his newspaper merges with the town's other paper and he finds that, despite his years of hard work, he is no longer needed, he changes from a 'loyal husband, loyal worker, loyal churchman, non-smoker, non-drinker' into a human wreck. After months of fruitlessly searching for work, he smashes the illuminated address, a symbol of his own destruction, and by the beginning of Act Three, as a result of a stroke, he is a 'shell' of a man; 'he has no memory and takes no interest in anything, except food and warmth ... for all the part he takes in what follows he might be a domestic pet'.[12] Nor is he the only member of the family to lose his job and to be altered by the experience. Jack, the 'foolish' and cheerful son of Act One, who enjoys nothing better than singing comic songs, very quickly becomes a bitter, angry and, at times, tearful man as his seven-year apprenticeship ends. Instead of being employed by the company he finds his job taken by a new apprentice. Even Aunt Annie suffers the same fate, turned away from the shop because she is too old and will not be quiet about the manager's son getting one of the young assistant's 'into trouble'. From being a smart, confident woman, she becomes unkempt and, like Jack, bitter, her bitterness centred on not being able to keep her niece Ellen at college, and thus being unable to fulfil her own hopes through her.

Alma Brosnan constantly tries to bring into the Bergers' small living room both the reasons for all this suffering and the stupidity of a world that creates such pain and waste. The outside world intrudes directly in two interludes inserted between scenes (played in front of the curtain): a scene outside the dole office showing the men queuing to get their money and a scene in the shop where both Annie and Ellen work. Whilst

these both contribute to an understanding that it is the world outside the
house which creates problems, her main method of exposing the causes
is confined to bringing the larger world into the living room. All that
passes does so because of what Aunt Annie sees as the dominant role of
money. John Berger's paper mergers with its arch rival, the *Gazette*, for
profit, apprentices get Jack's job because they are cheaper and Ellen has
to give up hopes of becoming a teacher because the family cannot give
her sufficient money to stay at college. Much of the railing against the
world comes from Jack. His experiences lead him to attack the stupidity
of a world that says engineers are not wanted; 'why, even in a town like
this, look at the things we could do if they'd let us get at it … things that
want doing … and we're tramping the streets!'. He learns about the rules
of 'business' from an article in the newspaper by Major-General Hughes,
an article about,

> the 'Won't-works' and the 'Work-shies'. I know something about Major-
> General Hughes; he's a director of Jones'. Well Jones' have just turned off
> fifty hands – knowing they'll want 'em back in six months. Somebody's
> got to keep 'em; and they're kept – the dole; parish relief; charity … And
> Mr Blasted Jones and Company, living on the dibs, sneer at them, know-
> ing quite well the minute they want 'em the whole crew'll come rushing
> back, cap in hand, cringing for jobs … 'Business', they call it. Anything's
> alright as long as it's 'Business'.[13]

He also has plenty to say about his father's attitude of 'honest service for
honest pay' – an attitude which the action of the play shows to be
completely misplaced. Yet when it comes to finding a solution neither
Jack nor Ellen have an answer. The younger generation sees that the only
way to survive is to play the world at its own game. If anything is all right
as long as it is 'Business', Jack reasons, 'why should we be any different …
Work! Why the devil should they! Why don't they follow the example of
their masters and rob?' This is exactly what both children set out to do.
Jack sets up a mail order business buying articles cheaply and selling
them as 'bargains' for twice the price. Ellen becomes a sales assistant,
using her charms to marry the manager's son and gain control of the
company but, in Alma Brosnan's eyes, such solutions do not save the
younger generation from being 'scrapped' alongside their elders, for they
have to give up any principles or ideals or hope of happiness to survive.
At the start of the play, Ellen is a guileless and idealistic young girl. By the
end of it, she is a hard-faced shop girl, who smokes and preens in front
of the mirror and who is prepared to marry Ronnie Carlesden (without

even telling her mother) solely so she can walk into the shop as mistress of the business.

No solution is forthcoming either from the one character who stands outside the impact of 'Business' by virtue of living her life entirely inside the house – Mrs Berger. She spends the play fussing round the other family members, cleaning, cooking, looking after them, never lifting her nose from her job and whilst the enclosed protection of the house means she is not 'tainted' by the outside world, it also means she is ill-equipped to deal with its impact. Yet by the end there is a small glimmer of light. Faced with Jack's description of how he intends to con people, she attempts for the first time in the play to respond critically, at the same time as recognising her own shortcomings. Unhappy with his plans, she wishes she 'hadn't gone pottering about the house' so she could argue with him and show him he is wrong. Whilst Jack all but ignores her and whilst Mrs Berger can do no more than wish Mr Berger had been spared his health so he could show Jack the error of his ways, the final image of the play leaves her as the central character amidst the wreckage.

> Mrs Berger crosses and sits down. On one side of her old John Berger smiles and twitters, on the other old Annie Berger, with no sound, cries … Mrs Berger looks from one to the other. From the other room comes the sound of the piano, and of a rollicking comic song, and of Jack and Babs laughing gaily … Very quietly, the curtain comes down.[14]

C. P. Trevelyan left the performance feeling 'far more vividly than before how decent, how simple men and women could be if they were only given a fair share of security' and how 'it is our present economic system which denies this to them'. The play clearly succeeded in angering Lever Brothers, the owners of the Blackfriars, where the play was performed by the Guild in 1926, who prohibited them from using the theatre for future performances stating that *Scrapped* was too 'red', although it clearly did not put off the management of the Arts Theatre where the play received five performances in 1927.[15]

A month later, Alma Brosnan's *At No. Fifteen* (1927) appeared for one performance only at the Arts Theatre, having previously been performed by ILP groups. The house of the title belongs to the Putmans, who, having fallen on hard times, are forced to let all their rooms and to share their kitchen with 'quarrelling women and squalling kids'. It is 'hell with the lid on'. In common with Brosnan's other plays we see a family whose spirit is cramped by poverty, lack of work and stifling housing conditions, who search for a 'dummy' to soothe the pain. The father, who has been turned into a dead and worthless man by the army and then through unemployment, claims to be a 'thinking man' but spends his time reading cheap paperbacks. Grandfather is a 'fatt-alist' who restorts to playing a whistle to take his mind off things – and who is banished to the yard for his pains. The son Dick loses his job as a van driver as soon as they have to insure him and sinks to the point where he wishes he had never been born. Haunted by his memory of having once been to the moors where the space made him feel strong, as if he could do anything, he is driven to steal, arguing that everybody who has got money steals and 'it's only the way you steal that gets you into trouble – if it's a little you steal'. Mrs Putnam has no solution and no choice except to 'keep toiling on'. Her daughter, Myra, starts the play with more hope than anyone else. She dreams that she can pass her shorthand and typing classes at the local night school and get a job in an office and she dreams she can marry Pawson, a slick, good-looking man she has met at her classes who lives in a family house without lodgers and who has a good job. But her dreams are rudely shattered when Pawson visits Myra at home to find himself surrounded by the squalor and argument of the shared kitchen and who, as a consequence, does not stay around for very long. Myra is crushed; her dreams shattered, she gives up night school and contents herself with going out dancing every night so she does not have 'to see too clear that everything's rotten'.[16] As with her earlier plays, there is little hope to be found here. Rather it is a heartfelt indictment of a world which crushes the life out of people.

Ruth Dodds

Further north, dramatic activity was also very much in evidence. Ruth Dodds was one of the mainstays of the Gateshead ILP Players from its foundation in 1919, when she joined the ILP, until her death in 1976. Active in the dramatic group (which became known as the Progressive Players in 1924) in 'almost every conceivable way', she not only wrote three plays for the Players but was also for a long period their chief producer. Along with two of her sisters, Sylvia (who was wardrobe mistress and actress for the Players) and Hope (a more prolific if less original writer than Ruth), she assisted them financially in 1939 when the group had to move from their original premises in Westfield Hall. Ruth was manager of the subsequent Gateshead Little Theatre from 1943 until 1965 and even performed, on at least one occasion, in her own play, *The Hilltop* (1925), taking the part of Maud Ancroft. Born in Gateshead in

1890, Ruth Dodds was shocked into serious social and political activity in 1910 when she canvassed for the Liberal candidate amongst the slums of the city, joining first the Gateshead branch of the National Union of Women's Suffrage Societies in 1914 and, later, the ILP. Originally a supporter of the war, she soon became a pacifist, joining the Quakers in 1925 and her pacifism led to her resignation from the Labour Party at the outbreak of the Second World War, although not before she had served as a Labour councillor from 1929–39. She was also an active member of her ILP branch, spending time on the propaganda committee and acting as assistant secretary. To these activities she added, between 1925 and 1935, the editorship of the monthly *Gateshead Labour News* (later the *Gateshead Herald*) contributing many articles under the byline of 'Redcap'.[17]

Of Dodd's three plays performed by the Players, the most successful (and designated as the 'club's greatest venture' by Hope Dodds) was *The Pitman's Pay* (1922). The title was taken from a popular poem about a miner's life by the local writer Thomas Wilson and she subtitled it 'Scenes from the life of Thomas Hepburn, showing the history of the first Miners' Union'. Yet we are introduced to the world of the play, not through the eyes of the union leading Hepburn but from the perspective of Robert Shafto, a colliery owner from County Durham smarting from the first victory the union has been able to impose on the bosses. He is intent on stamping 'out these agitators like vermin' and to this end has arranged to meet secretly a Home Office-sponsored spy in a local pub – Charles White alias Wilson, whose job it is to crush the mutinous spirit that is abroad and to try and catch Hepburn out in the process. We know from the outset that there is trouble brewing. It is from their point of view that we first get a picture of Hepburn, a picture which paints him as a passionate educator, a political reformer and a man fairly worshipped by the workers in the district. We later learn that he is inspired by the Biblical principle, '[t]hey shall plant houses and inhabit them; they shall plant vineyards and eat the fruit of them; they shall not build and another inhabit; they shall not plant and another eat', but above all else he is inspired by a passionate belief in non-violence. 'We canna beat them by fighting', he tells a group of workers, 'but we can beat them by bearing whatever they put upon us like men, by standing together like brothers and by obeying the union rules – no violence but stand fast'. [18] Such high ideals make him hard for Wilson to 'frame'. But this is not a story of unfettered heroism. The struggle to win people over to a peaceful and honourable path of change is not straightforward and during a number of bitter disputes, Hepburn loses the respect and support of the majority of the miners, finding himself hawking tea to earn a living until he agrees with one mine owner to take a job on the condition he never gets involved with unions again. Whilst Wilson is eventually unmasked for the spy that he is, Hepburn is not an unqualified victor.

In the course of the play he finds an unlikely ally. Shafto's Uncle Forster is a magistrate and part-owner of Felling Colliery. Never part of his nephew's plans to use spies to break the union and imprison the leaders, he is an old-fashioned, paternalistic boss who believes he can keep the pitmen in their proper place by showing them he is a gentleman and therefore their natural superior. On their first encounter, the two men have a fiery exchange. 'You think you're fighting against the masters but you're wrong. You're fighting against the laws of nature – and that's a losing battle', Forster tells Hepburn, but Hepburn is not to be shaken from his belief that the 'law of human nature teaches men to unite with their mates and work together for the good of all'. For all their supposed opposition, the two men share a desire for truth, honesty and fairness – they are both 'men of their words' – and such a way of working is shown by the play to be the right one.

Of the women in the play, it is only Bess, Hepburn's sister who stands out. His wife, Mary, hardly appears (and when she does she barely speaks) and his mother is a representative of the old world when the workers kowtowed to the bosses. Bess by contrast is fiery and defiant; she contradicts Forster at her wedding when he tells her she should wish for a husband who is humble but happy, she is an avid supporter of the union and is the first to declare she will not leave her house, unless they carry her out when the magistrates arrive in the village to evict the locked out miners. And it is Bess who gets the final words of the play. Announcing her pregnancy, she replies to her mother's wish for a boy by asking God to send her a girl, 'a scolding, unchancey woman like myself' who will 'know the great hope like me'. But despite Bess's feisty spirit, little of the play focuses on the role of women. Apart from a short exchange in which Hepburn tells Bess's husband not to let his wife meddle in the union, for women cannot take a calm view, nor can they be expected to, he goes on to argue, for a woman's life is 'just wrapped up with the bit things at home'. Little is shown or said about the role of women in the miner's fight; rather, Ruth Dodds chooses to focus on the battle between the workers and the bosses.[19]

In 1922, the play was entered for a competition held by the Sheffield Playgoers Society (the forerunner of the Sheffield Repertory Theatre) for which first prize was a production of the play by the society. She did win first prize, but this 'eminently bourgeois body ... refused to produce it on the grounds it would be too difficult'. Undaunted, the ILP dramatic group tackled their comrade's work with far less money and fewer resources than Sheffield possessed – they were still struggling with having to take down their stage after each performance so the hall could be used for the more profitable whist drives and dances and with a local authority who refused to licence the hall so audiences had to be let in free. However, with the men making the scenery and the women the costumes, the 'play was most successfully produced' even having a real-life miner (Norman Harrington) playing the part of Hepburn. The play ran for six performances in Gateshead and three in Newcastle, as well as going on tour to local villages, even though 'it was not easy for workers to find time to go on tour'. It was aptly revived in 1926 to raise money for the miners and once again in 1937 whilst the Miners' Federation were balloting over strike action against non-union labour.[20]

Six years after the first performance of *The Pitman's Pay*, Ruth Dodds won the Sheffield Playgoers' competition for a second time. On this occasion the play, *The Pressed Man; or the Sailor's Revenge* (1928), was performed by the Playgoers, although according to the reviewer from the *Amateur Stage*, 'the play probably lost something by reason of its inter-pretation ... instead of rough looking fishermen one saw fine-speaking men in fishermen's clothes'. Once again, this 'eminently bourgeois' soci-ety had failed the Gateshead writer. A romantic comedy set in Alnmouth at the time of the Napoleonic wars, the play tells the story of press gangs, smuggling and betrayal. Although not so obviously a play of labour interest as its predecessor, which no doubt accounted for the Playgoers' willingness to produce it, reviews of the performance suggest certain points which may have recommended it to an ILP audience – not least the central ideas of self-sacrifice and the ability of people to change for the better with the help of love. It focuses on the betrayal of Andy Fairweather to the press gangs by Jem Stanton, a sailor who returns from sea to discover his betrothed in the other man's arms. Yet, as soon as he has handed Andy over to the gang and his jealousy has subsided, Jem is full of remorse. He sets out to make amends by helping his victim's mother and sister, becoming, over the following year, their sole support. When Andy returns a year later, having escaped the press gang's ship to warn his smuggling friends of a trap that has been set for them, Jem who is now, in part, driven to make good his past behaviour by his growing love for Andy's sister, gives himself up in Andy's place.[21]

In between the two prize-winning plays is Ruth Dodds's industrial comedy, *The Hilltop* (1925), set in the imaginary Upton Dryfield, centre of the equally imaginary leatherware industry. In her introduction, she explains that she has chosen a non-specific setting for the play so that the picture of 'modern industrial conditions and methods' would be seen in a general way, and (unlike *The Pitman's Pay*) 'no workers or employers in any particular trade can suppose it to apply to them either more or less than to those engaged in other trades'.[22] On the surface, the play tells the story of Bill, the Secretary of the United Brotherhood of Leatherware Workers (the Lewers) who inherits £100,000 from an uncle in South Africa. At first he plans to spend the money on building a new Labour Hall in the town, a focus for the lives of the working people to attack the dirt, disease and injustice of society complete with a theatre for the girls (who have already performed *The Mikado*), a library and a billiards room. But he is sickened by the constant arguments between the union and Labour Party members and their distrust of him now he has money. He is driven to take a holiday 'amongst the good things in life' and for a while he is seduced by his 'holiday dream', by Lucy (the banker's daughter) and by the persuasions of the bankers and managers (who think they can avert industrial unrest if they prevent Bill from returning to Upton) to forsake the dirt and squalor of the town forever. In the event, Lucy inadvertently persuades him to return, jolting him out of his dreams when she quotes from the Bible: 'All these things will I give you, if you will fall down and worship me'. The words are a message from his mother, words she spoke to him long ago, before she was killed in a factory accident and buried beneath the sooty grass, words which remind him that he has to,

> go back and help – all those folks down there; to fight against the dragon and to go on fighting as long as I live. If you and I find it so good to come out into the sunshine and the green world, wouldn't it be good to give it to those others, to bring them out of the smoke and grime onto the hilltop? ... I love you and I love your life – that's why I want it for my own people. But I've no right to all these things, I'm not worthy of them, unless I try to share them – to give everyone a chance. [23]

Underlying Bill's story is a tale of trade unionism and of the need for unity in the face of an attack from the employers. The Lewer girls are led by Maud Ancroft, a 'sturdy, determined little woman', who wants 'to join things up'. In the course of the play, her big problem is how to join the men and women in the union so that when they strike over a pay cut they know is in the offing, they will stand together and the girls won't be driven back to work before the men. The big sticking point is the Strike Fund, for the girls have less money to put in and during an argument at the Negotiations Committee, Ruth Dodds uses the opportunity to air a number of arguments about the need for unity between men and women in trade unions. From the mouth of Gibson, one of the lewers, comes a string of objections; 'girls needn't starve' because 'they've got no families dependent on them', the men are not 'going to give them our Funds to buy new hats with', if the bosses cannot 'get the girls cheap' how 'can they afford to give us a living wage?', the girls want the men to do all the giving because 'their one idea is to get a chap to keep them – or a lot of chaps in this case'.[24] He is answered, not only by the girls and Maud (who insist they are not asking for anything 'out of reason' like equal pay or equal benefits!) but also by a fellow lewer who argues that,

> The girls will bring us unity … and a good heart for the fight – I tell you their spirit's worth a dozen Strike Funds … I only wish the chaps had half their keenness. See where we stand. The masters will turn down our proposals next week, that's certain. Then they'll enforce the reduction. Now let's say we don't amalgamate but men and girls both strike together. The girls will be on the rocks a couple of months before us. Say they're forced in at the new rates. What'll happen? They'll simply cut us out … most of us will never get back in this world, not on any terms.[25]

In the end, Gibson is the only member of the Committee against the merger (and his position is further undermined in the eyes of the audience by the fact that he has been leaking 'smear' stories about Bill to the newspapers). But his view is that of the majority of the men, hovering outside the Committee room door in a mass meeting. Maud, however, is confident that the Committee always has the 'power to stir up the inert masses' and to 'drag tham along after us in the end'. As it turns out, the situation is saved, not by the Committee's power with words but by the return of Bill who is in time to give his money to the girls' Strike Fund and to save the day.

The exploration the work of these three women playwrights challenges, in part, the predomination of feminist focused histories and analyses of women and politics in twentieth-century British theatre. Such predominance, whilst it has uncovered a wealth of exciting and significant material, has in its own way constructed false frameworks, a view of women, theatre and politics which parallels Sheila Stowell's recent comments that 'suffrage theatre critics understood their job to be the interpretation of plays and productions from a specifically suffrage point of view'.[26] Limiting a study of women and politics to that work dominated by a feminist ideology can constrict our view, creating false histories, a false 'canon'. As Gerry Harris has pointed out, the concept of 'herstory' and the creation of a 'prescriptive political correctness' has often offered 'interpretations that failed to acknowledge their own partiality in terms of sexuality, race, class and ethnicity'.[27] Such prescriptive approaches outlaw the work of women like Margaret Macnamara, Alma Brosnan and Ruth Dodds – in all the plays touched on above, the common enemy is capitalism, the key concern, class. Although some include female protagonists or touch on issues of concern to women, this is not necessarily their primary concern and this makes one recent suggestion that in order to challenge the dominance of the 'prescriptive political correctness' we should make the 'criterion for inclusion in a feminist history of women's theatre that a play in some ways either examines or criticises the position of women within a given culture' a problematic starting point which still privileges some women over others.[28]

These three playwrights may well have been ignored for reasons other than the content of their work. In terms of form, they all use the 'well-made' play formula, and this can be seen as conservative. Some of the plays are One Act(ers), a form which fitted perfectly into a branch evening or into the limited resources of amateur groups but one which is generally seen as slight. Certainly the basic realism of the plays offered no exciting stylistic challenges – although the same could be said for the men writing for the Guild, with the possible exception of Yaffle's satirical *Foiling the Reds* (1926). In this way, they may have fallen foul of a current tendency to assert that the 'best' of women's theatre practice must present an aesthetic challenge to realism, following Sue-Ellen Case's urging that we must 'cast realism aside – its consequences for women are deadly'.[29] Equally, Susan Bassnett's assertion that part of the problem in theatre scholarship is its emphasis on text-based theatre at the expense of other forms of performance and a wider understanding of women's role in the theatre, has signalled a shift in focus of research, which whilst it has thrown up new and exciting work, is in danger of ejecting the text and the writer altogether.[30] Similarly all three could be seen as 'amateurs', who might make the occasional foray on to the professional stage. However, the great emphasis in much research on the social, cultural and individual problems which met women who worked in the professional theatre, should suggest to us that there may be a large body of work by women on the amateur stage which could shed some light on women's theatrical work.

At best, those working in areas of political theatre outside the 'feminist', have been ignored and the three dramatists written about here are only the tip of a larger ILP iceberg that might include Monica Ewer, Evelyn Sharp and Josephine Knowles. At worst, their work has been denigrated. Gertrude Jennings, for example, is applauded for her contribution to the Actresses' Franchise League (in the shape of *A Woman's Influence*), yet the vast bulk of her fifty plus plays – many popular with Clarion Dramatic Societies – are dismissed. Nor should the Arts Guild be taken itself as setting boundaries for looking at women's involvement in political theatre. Stretching backwards we find fascinating glimpses; the near appearance of Mary Ann Walker, the Chartist celebrity, as Gertrude in a production of *Hamlet* at the Globe Theatre in 1843, the theatrical benefits held by the Women Matchmaker's Union in the 1888s, Delia Larkin's Irish Workers' Dramatic Company based at Liberty Hall, Louise Michel's play *The Strike* published in the Socialist league's newspaper *Commonweal* and the better chronicled contributions made by both Eleanor Marx and May Morris to the entertainments of the same organisation. Reaching forward from the Arts Guild is the work of the Masses Stage and Film Guild, which, as many other organisations did, drew Edith Craig into its orbit, the Workers' Theatre Movement, Unity Theatre and Left Theatre. All these offer possibilities for work which could yield fruitful insight into women's work in the theatre despite its seeming lack of an underpinning 'feminist' agenda.

Notes

1 Fred Chadwick, 'Dramatic Talks', *Northern Democrat*, January 1928; Michelene Wandor, *Carry on, Understudies: Theatre and Sexual Politics* (London, Routledge and Kegan Paul, 1986), pp. 3–4.

2 *New Leader*, 12 June 1925, p. 7 and 3 July 1925, p. 14. The programme of the Sunday performances at the Strand Theatre (which became known as the 'theatre of ideals') can be found in the *New Leader* between 16 January 1925 and 26 March 1926 and it is listed in full as an appendix in Ros Merkin, 'The Theatre of the Organised Working Class 1830–1930'(unpublished Ph.D. thesis, Warwick University, 1993) which also includes a fuller history of the work of the Guild. More information on the ILP Arts Guild can also be found in Ros Merkin, 'The Religion of Socialism or a Pleasant Sunday Afternoon?: The ILP Arts Guild', in Clive Barker and Maggie B. Gale, eds., *Interwar Theatres* (Cambridge, Cambridge University Press, 2000), Raphael

Samuel; 'Theatre and Socialism in Britain 1880–1935', in Raphael Samuel,
Ewan MacColl and Stuart Cosgrove, eds., *Theatres of the Left 1880–1935*
(London, Routledge, 1985); Morag Shiach, *Discourse on Popular Culture*
(Cambridge, Polity, 1989).

3 Miles Malleson, *New Leader*, 8 January 1926, p. 13; J. F. Horrabin, *Lansbury's
Labour Weekly*, 3 April 1926, p. 5.

4 The catalogue for the Women's Theatre Collection at the University of
Bristol, England, lists some thirty-one typescripts and published plays by
Macnamara including those mentioned here but not including *George and
Jenny* (performed at the Etlinger, 1 June 1917), *Enjoying the Business* (London,
Joseph Williams, 1924), and *Mum's the Word* (London, Joseph Williams,
1939). For biographical details see her obituary by Geoffrey Whitworth in
Drama: Quarterly Review, 20 (Spring 1951), p. 33.

5 Margaret Macnamara, *Mrs Jupp Obliges: A Small Domestic Comedy in One
Act* (London, Labour Publishing Company, 1925), p. 8.

6 Margaret Macnamara, *Light Gray or Dark?* (London, C. W. Daniel, 1920),
pp. 8–26.

7 Alma Brosnan, *The Street* (London, Labour Publishing Company, 1926),
p. 10.

8 *Ibid.*, p. 9.

9 H. Weston Wells, 'Short Plays for the People', *London News* (December 1926),
p. 4; idem, 'Labour Plays: A Frank Criticism', *Bradford Pioneer*, 20 December
1926, p. 6; *Lansbury's Labour Weekly*, 25 December 1926, p. 10.

10 *Sunday Worker*, 14 November 1925, p. 8. For a wider discussion of the debate
surrounding defeatism in the ILP Arts Guild, see Merkin, 'The Religion of
Socialism'.

11 Alma Brosnan, *Scrapped* (London, Sidgwick & Jackson, 1928), revised by
Miles Malleson, p. 14, *New Leader*, 24 December 1926, p. 12. The play was first
performed at the Blackfriars Theatre in December 1926 under the auspices of
the Central ILP Players, a 'company' which drew its members from the
twenty-five London groups of the Guild and which only existed for a few
short months and three performances.

12 Brosnan, *Scrapped*, p. 44.

13 *Ibid.*, p. 56.

14 *Ibid.*, p. 80.

15 *New Leader*, 24 December 1926, p. 12 and 25 December 1927, p. 15.

16 Brosnan, *At No. Fifteen* (London, Sidgwick & Jackson, 1927), pp. 40 and 42.

17 Maureen Callcott and Margaret Espinasse, 'Ruth Dodds: Socialist and
Labour Councillor', in J. H. Bellamy and John Saville, eds., *Dictionary of
Labour Biography*, Vol. VII 1972–1987 (London, Macmillan, 1976), pp. 63–7;
Gateshead Post, 18 April 1976, p. 1; interview with Councillor Ruth Dodds
(n.d.) in *Gateshead Personalia*, Gateshead Public Library.

18 Ruth Dodds, *The Pitman's Pay* (London, Labour Publishing Company, 1923),
pp. 33 and 35.

19 *Ibid.*, pp. 36 and 80.

20 M. H. Dodds, 'Socialism and the Drama', *Labour Magazine*, 2, 3 July 1923, pp. 109–10.

21 *Amateur Stage* (December 1928), p. 343; *Northern Democrat* (January 1928).

22 Ruth Dodds, *The Hilltop* (typescript, Gateshead Public Library), p. 4.

23 *Ibid.*, pp. 70–1.

24 *Ibid.*, pp. 78–9.

25 *Ibid.*, p. 78.

26 Sheila Stowell, 'Suffrage Critics and Political Action: A Feminist Agenda', in Michael R. Booth and Joel H. Kaplan, eds., *The Edwardian Theatre* (Cambridge, Cambridge University Press, 1996), p. 173.

27 Gerry Harris, 'Introduction to Part Two: Women Taking the Stage', in Lizbeth Goodman, ed., *The Routledge Reader in Gender and Performance* (London, Routledge, 1998), pp. 55–9, p. 56.

28 Maggie B. Gale, 'A Need for Reappraisal: Women Playwrights on the London Stage, 1918–1958', in Goodman, *The Routledge Reader in Gender and Performance*, p. 84.

29 Sue-Ellen Case, *Feminism and Theatre* (London, Macmillan, 1988), p. 297. Much of Maggie B. Gale's work presents a welcome challenge to this view. See for example, Maggie B. Gale, *West End Women: Women and the London Stage 1918–1962* (London, Routledge, 1996).

30 Susan Bassnett, 'Struggling with the Past: Women's Theatre in Search of a History', *New Theatre Quarterly*, 18 (May 1989), pp. 107–12.

11

COMIC MILITANCY:
THE POLITICS OF SUFFRAGE DRAMA

Susan Carlson

I would like to begin with two familiar narratives of the Edwardian and pre-First World War suffrage campaign. The best-known recounting of the escalations in activism begin with the taunting civil disobedience of Christabel Pankhurst and Annie Kenney in 1905, and establish the Women's Social and Political Union (WSPU) as the centrifugal point of civil disobedience as well as daring acts of violence against property. The heroic efforts of suffragettes on the streets and in the prisons have provided the most vivid and lasting images of the struggle for women's suffrage. Though known to a much smaller audience, the most familiar narrative of pre-war suffrage theatre traces a similar heroism in the aesthetic realm, as the Actresses' Franchise League (AFL) supervised the writing of hundreds of suffrage plays and encouraged a provocative theatrical presence on platforms and in protest marches. In parallel ways, however, such familiar narratives mask other aspects of the early twentieth-century suffrage campaign and its theatre. I would like to examine the pre-war suffrage theatre with an eye to that theatre's variety of venues and participants and to suggest that its connection to radical politics is but one part of its story. We have perhaps too eagerly accepted narratives of suffragette activism and suffrage theatre which privilege the most radical and valorise the most disruptive politics. There are other ways to tell the story.

Narratives of the campaign

Indeed, historians and literary scholars have recently interrogated the ways in which the British suffrage campaign has been understood for the greater part of the twentieth century. In my own review of these revisionary efforts below, I would like to highlight the ways these changing narratives can help shape a reoriented history of suffrage theatre.

The work of several scholars reflects a broad-based rethinking of women in the modernist period, primarily from post-structuralist and feminist perspectives. With a focus on the most radical suffragists (in the WSPU and the Women's Freedom League (WFL)), Barbara Green argues that femininity and specularity are aligned in the suffrage movement where the 'performative discourse of suffrage' encourages a public response at the same time as it challenges a standard 'public gaze'.[1] She notes that suffragists successfully conscripted multiple public venues in their campaign, most with a theatrical nature: 'The pageants of the WSPU were highly produced and featured an alliance between feminism and the theatre ... Suffrage plays, carefully planned interruptions of government officials' speeches, and deputations to parliament, though they worked in very different ways, shared a distinctly theatrical character'.[2] In the course of her study, however, Green focuses on non-theatrical texts and argues that actual theatre pieces written for the suffrage campaign – pageants, plays, and skits – are usually ineffective as tools of the 'performative'. Green's work is invaluable as it brings a broadened understanding of the performative to suffrage activism, and as it groups hunger strikes, biographies and archivists in the same study. But ironically, her study of spectacle and performance devalues actual theatre and dramatic performance, largely because she finds that they are less politically proactive than other kinds of public events. Similarly, Jane Eldridge Miller, in arguing for a new integration of women's writing into our understanding of the modernist novel, also demotes the importance of women's theatre, finding that to focus on pageants, comedies, farces and fantasies is to avoid the 'ongoing and complex rebellion' of the suffrage era.[3] Both Green and Miller revalidate some forgotten aspects of pre-war feminism and literature, but acknowledge the theatre only as a weak participant in political aesthetics.

Janet Lyon and Laura E. Nym Mayhall, however, offer a way out of such devaluing of both suffrage theatre and its general optimism, and from them I hope to pattern out my own revaluations. While studying the public realm of political protest, both find an inclusive way of looking back at the events of suffrage activism. Lyon proposes that we align the public women of the suffrage movement not with a 'telos of attenuation and decline' – i.e. not only with suffering and trauma – but also with an avant-garde which valorises 'transgressive patterns of modern individual expression'.[4] Mayhall also stresses the need to move beyond the tragic 'meta-narrative' of suffrage activism, a narrative 'in which authentic suffrage militancy became the precursor of radical feminism', a narrative in which other less radical activism is devalued or ignored.[5] Mayhall's proposed reconstruction of the suffrage narrative, in fact, most closely resembles my own proposed revision of our narratives of suffrage theatre: Mayhall notes that suffrage 'militancy' took several forms, and that the tragic trajectory of the force-fed, law-breaking suffragettes is but one of them. She suggests that we revalidate the work of suffragists whose politics and tactics were more centrist. As all of these scholars acknowledge, our understanding of the suffrage campaign is conditioned by our own late twentieth-century politics; that should not prevent us, however, from recognising the full scope of pre-war feminist activism, including the contribution of protestive behaviour not obviously radical.

Narratives of suffrage theatre

The lacunae in the study of suffrage theatre are not so glaring, but here too a critical adjustment can allow us a fuller recognition of the range of dramatic efforts. While the dominant narratives of suffrage activism have highlighted the commitment to violence and the potential for tragedy, accounts of suffrage theatre have centred on the work generated by the AFL during the same pre-war years. Julie Holledge's groundbreaking account of the organisation has been followed by the efforts of Sheila Stowell, Claire Hirschfield, Viv Gardner, Linda Fitzsimmons, Christine Dymkowski and others.[6] In turn, their scholarship has spawned important publication of the plays themselves, including the volumes by Gardner, Spender and Hayman, and Fitzsimmons and Gardner, in addition to the initial plays in Holledge's book.[7] Yet a significant aspect of such scholarship has always been a recognition that the AFL, while the centre of political drama by women between 1905 and 1914, was not the sole generator of women's plays or of suffrage theatre. In her book, Holledge includes a final chapter on Edy Craig and her work with the Pioneer Players; Fitzsimmons and Gardner publish plays written outside the auspices of the AFL; and Stowell puts her chapter on 'Suffrage Drama' in the context of the careers of Elizabeth Robins, Cicely Hamilton, Elizabeth Baker and Githa Sowerby, only some of whose careers intersect significantly with suffrage activism.

Yet even with such judicious investigation, scholars continue to focus on plays with more radical politics, plays with a more recognisable feminism. In an attempt to expand our current thinking about suffrage theatre in the pre-war years, I suggest we look past the dominant visions of both the suffrage movement in general and the suffrage theatre in particular. In the pages that follow, I have focused primarily on the journalistic theatre of the suffrage movement – plays published in suffrage newspapers – with the goal of re-examining the ways in which they promoted the cause and also reflected its various politics. As I have written elsewhere, most of the plays connected to the suffrage cause were comic in nature; I would like to propose further, below, that with this look at journalistic drama, we can see how the comedy offers a politics of its own, a politics I have (somewhat) ironically labelled 'comic militancy'. While not as audacious as brick throwing or arson, it is protest which promotes political change as it protects most social realms from change. Like much comedy, it is both politically progressive and socially conservative. It is the buoyancy of such comedy, in fact, which encouraged activists to go on with their difficult work and which accounts for the popularity of suffrage theatre. Even in times of force-feeding and bitter politics, comic plays reminded those weary from their political struggles that optimism was possible. Of a play about a new MP and his suffrage wife (produced by the AFL in 1910), a reporter for *Votes for Women* notes the welcomed joy of its happy ending:

> [the wife] ends in laughing all his anti-suffrage principles out of him proving her own capacity both in politics and in affairs. Her assertion that even a suffragette liked a man to show affection for his wife produced loud applause from a Suffragist audience, and explained in a subtle sort of way, perhaps, why the rest of the programme, though arranged for a Suffrage matinée, dealt almost entirely with love and laughter and the more obviously human side of life.[8]

Comic militancy I: conversions to the cause

In 1910, as she was campaigning for the vote at the Scottish Exhibition, theatre producer Edy Craig stressed that plays are one of the most effective of persuasive tools, 'I do think plays have done such a lot for the Suffrage. They get hold of nice frivolous people who would die sooner than go in cold blood to meetings. But they see the plays, and get interested, and then we can rope them in for meetings. All Suffrage writers ought to write Suffrage plays as hard as they can. It's great work'.[9] Playwright Cicely Hamilton, like Craig a primary force in suffrage theatre, echoes these thoughts just a few years later, in 1913, at a meeting of the Women Writers' Suffrage League, arguing that the theatre overcomes differences of politics and intelligence as well as inertia: 'Miss Cicely Hamilton spoke of the difficulty people of average intelligence experienced in realising entirely new idea[s] presented to them, and said she hoped those not already in sympathy with the Women's Movement could be got into the Woman's Theatre even by false pretences, so that they might be convinced by the plays'.[10] Craig and Hamilton are clearly energised by what they have seen of the persuasive power of political theatre. Both women, most likely, are thinking of the rally platforms on which so many performances of suffrage plays occurred and to which so many conversions were anecdotally traced. But many suffrage plays had a life outside of the platform. Venues like the Royal Court, the Little Theatre, and the Kingsway Theatre (with the help of suffragists like Lena Ashwell, Gertrude Kingston, Lillah McCarthy, and others) supported suffrage theatre in particular and the growing role of women in theatre in general. But the prominence of plays, dialogues and theatre reviews in the major suffrage newspapers suggests that such newspapers also constitute a significant platform for the persuasive power of suffrage drama.[11] The journalistic drama encouraged particular types of plays, but more importantly, it dissected ideas in original ways, ways not realisable in other theatre venues.

Each of the major suffrage newspapers of the pre-war years offered prominent display of theatrical events related to the cause. *Common Cause*, the organ of the centrist National Union of Women's Suffrage Societies (NUWSS), was the most internationally-oriented of the suffrage papers, but the local (London) theatre still maintains a high profile through theatre reviews and announcements about events ranging from AFL 'At Homes' to performances in Annie Horniman's theatre. Two other major papers also offered detailed reporting and, in addition, published a significant number of suffrage plays. In *Votes for Women*, the paper of the WSPU, theatre takes its prominent position through the writing of major theatre figures (like Christopher St John and Laurence Housman), as well as through the publication of plays. By late 1912, the paper had also instituted a 'Plays of the Week' section in every issue.[12] The writing is upbeat and supportive, though often critical of established theatre. St John, for example, takes the West End theatre to task for the absence of suffragists on the stage,[13] and the praise lavished on a production of *Lysistrata* implies an equally clear critique of most standard West End fare.[14] *The Vote*, the organ of the Women's Freedom League (WFL), offers a complementary focus. In addition to publishing a substantial number of plays, it includes a series of feature articles on theatre figures (Edy Craig, Madeleine Lucette Ryley, Decima Moore, Gertrude Elliott, Laurence Housman, Eva Moore, and others).

All of these papers offer readers close reporting on theatre. But more notably, they make plays a frequent vehicle for political persuasion, vehicles which take on a comic format as they press towards political conversion. As I detail the centrality of conversion in the plays, I hope to reveal a cautious approach to other social or political change. Obviously, creating converts to the cause was at the heart of the suffrage campaign, and many of the best known suffrage plays are driven by conversions (*The Apple*, *How the Vote Was Won*, *Lady Geraldine's Speech*, etc.). The journalistic focus on conversion adds to that focus a particular attention to the interplay of social protocol and political change.

In many of the plays, the conversion is a matter of rational, intellectual adjustment, removed from social context.[15] In 'The New Socrates', by H. S., a dialogue between Phaedrus and Socrates begins with Phaedrus asking Socrates what he thinks of 'these wild women – militants'. Socrates manoeuvres Phaedrus to think of the women's choices with an appeal to common sense, and Phaedrus ends the play acknowledging his changed opinion, 'Indeed, Socrates, I think you are perfectly right. And I am very glad I met you this morning, for I begin to see that if I wish to keep my character as a sensible man in my own estimation, I shall have to revise entirely my opinion on the whole matter'.[16] The same author turns the same trick with 'A Speech: Justice to Women', a monologue modelled on Antony's 'Friends, Romans, Countrymen' oration in *Julius Caesar*. The speech is driven by the idea that votes for women make common sense, and the speaker, 'a woman loquitur', concludes on the plea for equal justice, 'I only speak right on; /I tell you that which you yourselves do know, / And beg you make the justice which you love / A thing for women also'.[17] Though much more elaborate, G. Watkinson's 'Women and Suffrage' also moves the characters and audience to conversion through intellectual abstractions. In this 'Moral Play' the figure of 'Suffragia Feminina' brings abstract representations of 'Justice', 'Humane Conscience' and 'Utopia' to battle against the misguided arguments of 'Ancient Prejudice', 'Conventionality' and 'Frivolity'. The main character, named 'Woman', is persuaded to join the cause and declares her commitment with these words to Suffragia Feminina,

> Lo, now, Suffragia, thee take I by the hand!
> And stalwart by thy side I'll have my stand!
> So we'll bring about blessings unheard of in history,
> And tread in triumph the path of glory,
> Filling to the fullest Woman's vocation![18]

While these brief dialogues and monologues all climax with conversion, the works which take on a fuller dramatic format and more developed characters allow writers to examine the social response to conversion. In 'Mr. Peppercorn's Awakening', the titular character is moved from his initial opinion that independent women are 'unsexed viragoes' to full support of a daughter who wants to train for a career.[19] His conversion is prompted by dream-like visitations from a host of working women and is supported by the women in his family. In Isabel Tippett's 'Woman, Old or New?' the focus is also on socially contextualising the conversion of a man who longs for his wife to assume the behavioural traits of his conventional mother. However, the wife Dolly and family friend John are easily able to trick the stodgy Bill into a full acceptance of his wife as a new woman. For a while, Dolly mimics her stepmother in buying frivolous and expensive clothes and in flirting with men to accrue position; when Bill recognises this is not what he wants in a wife, he fully assents to his wife's claim to her own education and politics. Notable in this play is the assumption of middle-class affluence and the assurance that marriage will continue for politically committed women.[20] In other words, votes for women are more palatable because they threaten neither class hierarchy nor patriarchal institutions.

Many of the plays that focus on conversion do, in fact, couple conversion to the cause with central relationships between men and women. In A. L. Little's 'The Shadow of the Sofa', all of the main characters are so stunted by convention that they all happily flock behind the excitement of the suffrage cause when it presents itself; the converts include Aunt Rachel and Uncle Jeremiah, young Beatrice and her soon-to-be-beau Philip as well as the maid Louise. They collectively vow to support the cause and to withhold taxes, but the joyousness of the moment seems certified by the fact that both men and women convert. In other words, the cause is not just for radical women, but also for men; it does not disturb marriage but cements it.[21] This trumpeting of heterosexuality is most clearly set out in Edith M. Baker's 'Our Happy Home', where the political recruiters are men, not women. Both Miss Verreker and her niece Sybil begin by labelling the vote a 'dangerous notion',[22] but the suave and spirited persuasion of Harry Leicester and Sir Joseph Wilmot brings the women to a recognition that the cause of suffrage deserves their time. Sir Joseph is the most convincing: 'Well I can assure you that even as regards their most militant and desperate plans, the case for the defence is very strong, and I know that an intellectual, enlightened woman like yourself is always determined to hear both sides of a question ... A woman's place is wherever there is work to be done and evils to be redressed'.[23] The play ends with all four characters at a suffrage demonstration, proud to take public part in its performative nature. But again these conversions are delivered in the safety of heterosexual ties. Not only do the men engineer the conversions, but – through the cause – the women strengthen their alliances with men.

As a group, these plays show that political conversion builds communities, that people of all ages and both sexes come to see the cause as their cause. There is even one play, 'Little Jane and Grandmama', in which the convert is a child.[24] It is important to understand that these conversions build on the most common of comic structures, reversal. The standard comic reversal involves a situation in which the normal order is somehow upset, inverted so that unusual behaviour can occur. Most comedies, however, eventually move out of such liberating inversion and back to a status quo which is usually grounded in marriage and community. These plays focused on conversion draw from the comfort of such a comic reversal – that is, the expectation that order will return after disorder – at the same time they change that status quo, that order, by accepting women's vote. This combination means that the political change proposed – the vote for women – is coupled with an acceptance of standard social order, the family as an institution based on the primacy of marriage. Thus these comic plays allow the playwrights to argue for a change which is *not* socially threatening. So although the writers urge a change of political positions, they generally temper that change with a conservative social message. While the journalistic suffrage plays are not unique in offering such safe conversion, they stand as evidence that all the major suffrage organisations (as represented in their newspapers), even in their most radical years, relied on relatively conservative pleas in addition to their more flashy public protests. Their conscription of comedy allows a politically savvy promise of 'safe change'.

Two groups of plays do not offer this combination of social stability and political change. The addition of social instability in some of the plays or the lack or political conversion in others allows for additional speculation about the politics of conversion. In the first group, the writers couple political change with social *in*stability. In 'The Science of Forgiveness', Winifred St Clair presents Molly Burt's efforts to convince her husband Tony that men and women deserve equal treatment. Their debate centres on the love affair of Tony's first wife and his best friend Tom. While Tom has remained Tony's friend, the wife (and a child fathered by Tom) was abandoned by both Tom and Tony. The play, indeed, ends on a conversion, as Tony comes around to his wife's way of thinking that the indiscreet man and woman should be treated in a similar manner. The conclusion is bittersweet, however, for although Molly has won the debate through her logical approach, her husband's concession leaves him beaten, with his 'head on hand at mantelshelf'.[25] The politics of equality have won, but they are begrudgingly accepted. The comic joy so often coupled with conversion has also evaporated in 'The Stuff that 'Eroes Are Made Of' where playwright Isabel Tippett moves us to a working-class family in which a woman's adherence to the cause loses her a fiancé. Two sisters, Tilda and Liz, battle over both politics and over Liz's fiancé, Alf. Tilda finds the suffrage cause silly, and convinces Alf that it emasculates him. In response, suffragette Liz must defend her belief in equality, though her pleas fall on deaf ears. Alf tells her, 'I don't want a suffragette, I wants a wife', and her sister then manages to steal Alf, stating, 'E's a man, 'e is. 'E don't want no blooming Suffragette ter crow it over 'im. I don't want no votes for women, I don't. Come on out of this, Alf. Yer could do a pint, couldn't yer? So could I. We ain't blooming Suffragettes as 'as got to live up, and never put a drop down'.[26] The play ends with Liz in conflict, claiming her ongoing love for Alf and wondering whether her politics are worth the sacrifice. Both of these plays suggest the fragility of combining political change with social stability; both also offer an admission of how personally destructive political change can be. It is somewhat surprising that a paper as politically proactive and progressive as *The Vote* would include plays which raise basic questions the way these two do.

The functioning of conversion in suffrage plays is also better understood when compared to a second group of plays, anti-suffrage plays in which conversion is blocked and/or ridiculed. In these plays there is no political change or conversion, though there remains a large dose of social stability. Throughout the final years of the suffrage campaign, pro-suffrage plays – such as those in the suffrage newspapers – were answered with anti-suffrage plays which make suffragists the cause of laughter not the source of social reason.[27] The suffragists who appear in these plays are myopically focused on the vote, are dowdy and comically lacking in social skills. Their politics are also superficial, mainly expressions of this social ineptitude. In 'A Woman's Vote', Miss Darem gives up her commitment to the vote as soon as she has the chance to marry; and all suffragists are belittled in the figure of a suffrage doll who squeaks 'votes for women' at an increasingly diminished speed.[28] In Inglis Allen's 'The Suffragette's Redemption', the wife returns from a prison stint at Holloway to be proven illogical and petty. While she claims to her husband, 'Love, my dear Dick, is not the all-important thing to us women that you imagine', she gives up her suffrage commitment easily in a jealous effort to protect her husband from another woman.[29] The most sobering portrait occurs in George Dance's 'The Suffragettes', where the suffragists are illogical, sexually loose and underhanded. Captain Joe Blighter offers the play's final words, which certify that the suffragists are only using suffrage as a familiar leisure pastime: 'So it was afterwards with Eve from the time of the Garden of Eden. She starts a craze which carries her this way or that, but you can always bring her together with a diamond necklace'.[30]

Like many of the pro-suffrage plays, these three anti-suffrage plays focus on wealthy characters whose lives and values are only moderately changed by their commitment to the women's vote. In this backhanded way, these anti-suffrage plays emphasise that the comic format of pro-suffrage plays actually protects most of the status quo, while allowing for an isolated change, women's vote. In a chilling way, the two groups of plays are not so different. And it is ironic to note that many of these anti-suffrage plays are housed in the Lord Chamberlain's Collection right next to significant pro-suffrage plays. Dance's play, for example, is bound in the same volume as Elizabeth Robins's influential *Votes for Women*. Allen's 'The Suffragette's Redemption' appears immediately after George Bernard Shaw's pro-suffrage offering, *Press Cuttings*.

These anti-suffrage plays, together with the darker suffrage plays (like 'The Science of Forgiveness' and 'The Stuff that 'Eroes Are Made Of'), suggest how tenuous the use of comedy was for suffrage activists. The platforms and the suffrage newspapers all offered plays culminating in conversion: *The Vote* and *Votes for Women* published a steady diet of these persuasive dramas. As Craig, Hamilton and others argued, such plays promoted a change of heart among ideologically uncertain men and women, and reassured those already committed to the cause. The ways these plays conscript comedy, however, with the common coupling of political change and social stability, suggests that even at the height of suffrage activism, radical politics coexisted with socially conservative inclinations. I suggest that we acknowledge the theatrical activism of the suffragists as innovative and influential, but as oftentimes cautiously committed to change.

Comic militancy II: literary forms and occasional theatre

Just as the journalistic drama is cautious in its portrayal of conversion, it is also aesthetically opportunistic. As an 'occasional theatre' geared to specific moments, events and reactions, it had to make use of familiar formats to make new politics feel comfortable. The use of comedy is, of course, the most common reliance on standard literary form. But by relying on other popular formats, suffragist writers also find other ways to press their case. The goal was not generating original works of art but fostering commitment to the cause.

In 'The New Socrates', Platonic dialogue is enlisted as the author uses Socrates' careful, clear questioning to make the case for women's suffrage. As in so many of these plays, when the facts of women's situation are presented, the case for the vote is meant to be obvious. In 'A Speech: Justice to Women', the same author moves from classical dialogue to Shakespearean oration as a model, again drawing from a public literary rhetoric which uses familiar persuasive tactics to reach the truth. Covering some of the same argumentative ground as Socrates, the Woman Loquitur in 'A Speech' speaks against taxation without representation, legal double standards, and two-faced politicians as she recalls the many years of the campaign,

> Long years in patience we tried peaceful means
> But still we were denied all public voice
> Or utterance; now we rise in force,
> Determined that we'll gain the public ear,
> The public eye, and reach the hearts of men.[31]

Another literary template, the morality play, with its figural representation of abstract ideas, is used to assert the righteousness of the cause in two other plays. In 'Women and Suffrage', a stiff poetic line (often blank verse, sometimes rhyming) supports figures like 'Suffragia Feminina', 'Reason', 'Justice' and 'Conventionality'. The format assures the outcome of the debate: Woman will find suffrage her only logical end. 'Mr. Peppercorn's Awakening' also relies on such abstract figures, using metred speech and elevated language to suggest that a realm beyond the human is also in full support of the cause. In each of these plays, the authors use the familiarity of their formats to make the political ideas seem equally familiar. The ingenuity lies not in creating something new, but in reshaping the old.

More contemporary templates are also employed by these writers. Just as classical dialogue and Shakespearean monologue help make the case, so too does the Mad Hatter's tea party from *Alice in Wonderland*. In Helen McLachlan's 'The Mad Hatter's Tea Party up to Date', the words of anti-suffragists are given to the illogical characters and Alice's innocent questions reveal the ridiculousness of denying women the vote:

ALICE   My name is Alice. I was a little girl this morning but I've had so many adventures since then that really –

HARE   Have some votes for women.

ALICE   I don't see any votes for women.

HARE   There aren't any! We only have votes every other day!

ALICE   Every other day?

HARE   Yes! Votes yesterday, and votes to-morrow, but *never* votes to-day!

ALICE   Then it wasn't very civil of you to offer them.

HARE   It wasn't very civil of *you* to sit down without being invited. It's quite plain that this table is only intended for men.[32]

Like several other plays, this one also makes its appeal through popular songs, chants and dance. It ends with a song that invites others to join the Suffrage Dance, 'Will you, won't you, will you, won't you, join the Suffrage Dance?'[33] In Henry W. Nevinson's 'The Cabinet Concert', song also predominates as the members of Asquith's cabinet comically search for lyrics appropriate to their politics. They move from their flounderings with 'Sigh no more, ladies' and 'I'm sitting on the Fence, Mary' to 'Votes for Women Rag' in which they declare their support for the vote. Their inadvertent conversion to the cause also ends in a dance, the 'Votes Tango'.[34]

I would like to point, finally, to a variety of ways in which all such dramatic contributions to the suffrage cause not only drew from established forms, but also helped to shape the thinking of the day. Indeed, this is a variation on Green's argument that performativity was at the heart of suffrage activism. I have found the influence of the theatre on the patterning of non-theatrical events most demonstrable in Ethel Ayres Purdie's 'A Red Tape Comedy', a journalistic piece that refashions a non-fiction narrative as theatre. Purdie decides that the best way to demonstrate the absurdities of law as they apply to women is to narrate one representative case as if it were a comic drama. She tells the story of a woman doctor from New Zealand (where her legal position is protected by women having the vote) who refused to pay taxes on her income in England claiming that the law can only tax her husband. As Purdie tells the story of the court proceedings she supervised, she highlights her title, 'Red Tape Comedy', referring to the illogical turns in the action through reference to the theatre.

The comedy appears in *The Vote* in three instalments, which function as three Acts. In the first Part/Act Purdie introduces her 'Dramatis Personae' and ends with a climax appropriately labelled 'Pièce de Resistance', when Purdie turns events in favour of her client by producing a crucial document:

> The Surveyor looks pleased, as though he fancies he has scored at last. The other three appear to sympathise with me; even my client begins to look apprehensive, as if she fears I am done for. Because (as she tells me subsequently) she also thinks I cannot produce this thing, and that I have only been bluffing.
>
> Pièce de Resistance
>
> But I make a sudden dive down to my satchel, which lies open on the floor at my feet, and where, unseen by anybody else, the disputed form (No. 44 A) has been lying in wait.[35]

Part/Act Two also ends leaving readers hanging on a second dramatic disclosure, this one about secret documents. Throughout the drama, Purdie gestures to literary models in both Gilbert and Sullivan and *Alice in Wonderland*. Purdie and her client win the case in the third Part/Act, though not without some additional rises and falls in the action, and she acknowledges that both of them 'are glad to escape from the realms of topsey turveydom'.[36] Like the 'Mad Hatter's Tea Party up to Date', this account finds the logic for women's rights unbeatable. Like the host of other plays about conversion, this account gives experience a comic trajectory which leads participants towards the undeniable common sense of women's vote. 'A Red-Tape Comedy', more than any other work I have been able to unearth in suffrage journalism, shows not only that the comic drama was a significant political tradition, but also that it shaped thinking on political topics.

Beyond comedy, beyond convention

In closing, I would like to situate these plays I have focused on alongside a handful of others which do not share such familiar formats and strategies, again to reveal the complex range of efforts in suffrage drama. The vast majority of the plays appearing in suffrage papers were comic, and many drew power and appeal from their use of popular literary formats. This predominance of theatrical predictability and conventionality creates the necessary background for understanding a small number of plays which reject formulas and experiment with the presentation of the conflicting interests and tendencies that characterised so much of the debate on suffrage politics. Plays and dialogues that could never work at a public rally – because they have indeterminate conclusions, because they question basic assumptions in the campaign for the vote – can exist in the pages of a newspaper where they create a thinking space which accommodates complex political opinion. Earlier I discussed both 'The Science of Forgiveness' and 'The Stuff that 'Eroes Are Made Of' as plays which reject both the comic formula and political conversion. The raw and open quality of these plays marks a distinctive political contribution and suggests under explored directions in historicising suffrage theatre. Three other plays offer similar innovations as they deal with group energies and responses.

Just as Elizabeth Robins's *Votes for Women* – in 1907 – shocked audiences with its realistic rally scene, these plays, on a smaller scale, explore the confusions of public protest. W. Pett Ridge's 'A Good By-Election' is set at teatime in High Street, where campaigning ranges from 'advertisement cars' to the shouting of small boys. Readers are placed in the midst of the gritty work of campaigning. One boy turns away an eager aristocratic woman campaigner when she falls back on trite phrases, a 'Burly Man' campaigns by name-calling, and a 'Girl Speaker' shows her versatility by handling questions hostile to women's suffrage. Yet the play only poses questions; and instead of making the Girl Speaker's adaptability the climax, Ridge follows the girl's panache with three speeches which reiterate the unpredictable vicissitudes of campaigning. While the suffragist is the most accomplished speaker, her victory is not assured in the mix of voices and causes.[37] Lorimer Royston's 'Fair Play' also portrays the heat of debate at a village bazaar where a Sleek Man asks '*Why* do these women brawl and shriek and break the laws'.[38] He's supported by an 'Anti-Suffragist Lady' but cleverly challenged by a 'Modern Young Woman' who offers a common sense response to each charge he raises against the suffragists. Interestingly, the young woman's comments come in the middle of the brief play, after which the Sleek Man, the Anti, A Working Man, and others sift through her ideas, coming to varying conclusions. And the play ends with a cacophony of voices ranging from the Sleek Man's 'Order must be restored' to the Modern Young Woman's 'Votes must be given to women'.[39] As in 'A Good By-Election', we see a young suffragist holding her position of reason with social graciousness, even in the heat of debate; but in both plays such reasons and graciousness come up against a hard-nosed, immovable opposition. There is not conversion here, but stalemate.

Alice Chapin's 'At the Gates' offers an extended example of such a reflective and open drama. The full version of the play was licensed for performance at the Royal Albert Hall in December of 1909, and in the same month a one-page version of the play appeared in *The Vote*.[40] In both versions, Chapin presents a central suffragist character who – as in 'The Good By-Election' and 'Fair Play' – is tirelessly campaigning. Chapin's suffragette is sitting outside Parliament with a petition for members and a bundle of handbills for passers-by. She is kindly treated by the police officers on patrol, finds sympathy from a seamstress and is ostracised by a hostile man. In the short version as in the longer one, the complexity of the campaign is clear and conversion is never assured. While the irony of the suffragette's position is clear, comic buoyancy is missing. As all three of these plays deal with public group dynamics and partially unsympathetic audiences, they suggest the courageous leaps other authors made with their comic portraits of political conversions. The comic approach was not always easy, perhaps not always believable and certainly not always as progressive as we might hope, but it was a brave commitment to the belief that change was possible.

Conclusion

My hope is that this review of journalistic drama reveals a range of dramatic responses to the politics of the moment in pre-war suffrage drama. Just as the various suffrage organisations rallied a range of support for social and political change, so too did the drama give expression to socially conservative but politically progressive views as well as to admissions about the social costs of political commitment. In this essay, I have mined the narrow vein of the journalistic drama connected to the suffrage cause. My goal has been to suggest how broadly we must define suffrage theatre to understand its full presence and effect. Just as early twentieth-century feminist politics was a nexus of groups, opinions and varying successes, so too was the suffrage theatre a complex of politics and formats. And while my focus on comedy shows the limitations of that genre in political causes, it should also show that comedy remains a vehicle for expressing hopes and envisioning a changed world. Comedy need not be an escape, but can be conscripted as a persuasive tool. It rarely operates as a radical tool, but performs a militancy of its own.

Notes

1 Barbara Green, *Spectacular Confessions: Autobiography, Performative Activism, and the Sites of Suffrage 1905–1938* (New York, St. Martins, 1997), pp. 15, 5.

2 *Ibid.*, p. 5.

3 Jane Eldridge Miller, *Rebel Women: Feminism, Modernism and the Edwardian Novel* (London, Virago Press, 1994), p. 131. See also the work of Jane Marcus ('The Asylums of Antaeus: Women, War, and Madness – Is there a Feminist Fetishism?', in Aram Veeser, ed., *The New Historicism* (London, Routledge, 1989), pp. 132–51) and Angela Ingram and Daphne Patai ('Introduction', in Ingram and Patai, eds., *Rediscovering Forgotten Radicals: British Women Writers, 1880–1939* (Chapel Hill, University of North Carolina Press, 1993), pp. 1–22) who undertake similar efforts to stretch thinking about the suffrage era and its literature. These three, in particular, are calling for a stand against historicisms which erase women's politics and against post-structuralisms which confound women's subjectivity. Not surprisingly, theatre is not a central concern in their review of feminist politics.

4 Janet Lyon, 'Women Demonstrating Modernisms', *Discourse*, 17, 2 (Winter 1994–95), pp. 8–9, 17.

5 Laura E. Nym Mayhall, 'Creating the "Suffragette Spirit": British Feminism and the Historical Imagination', *Women's History Review*, 4, 3 (1995), p. 320.

6 Julie Holledge, *Innocent Flowers: Women in the Edwardian Theatre* (London, Virago, 1981); Sheila Stowell, *A Stage of Their Own: Feminist Playwrights of the Suffrage Era* (Ann Arbor, University of Michigan Press, 1992); Claire Hirschfield, 'The Suffrage Play in England 1907–1913', *Cahiers Victoriens and Edouardiens*, 33 (1991), pp. 73–85; idem, 'The Woman's Theatre in England: 1913–1918', *Theatre History Studies*, 15 (June 1995), pp. 123–37; Linda Fitzsimmons and Viv Gardner, eds., *New Woman Plays* (London, Methuen, 1991); and Christine Dymkowski, 'Entertaining Ideas: Edy Craig and the Pioneer Players', in Viv Gardner and Susan Rutherford, eds., *The New Woman and her Sisters: Feminism and Theatre 1850–1914* (New York, Harvester Wheatsheaf, 1992), pp. 221–33.

7 Viv Gardner, ed., *Sketches from the Actresses' Franchise League* (Nottingham, Nottingham Drama Texts, 1985); Dale Spender and Carole Hayman, eds., *How the Vote was Won and Other Suffragette Plays* (London, Methuen, 1985); Fitzsimmons and Gardner, *New Woman Plays*; Holledge, *Innocent Flowers*.

8 'Some Suffrage Plays: Actresses' Franchise League', *Votes for Women*, 27 May 1910, p. 561.

9 Margaret Kilroy, 'Helpers at the Scottish Exhibition: I. Miss Edy Craig', *Votes for Women*, 15 April 1910, p. 455.

10 'Other Societies: Women Writers' Suffrage League', *The Vote*, 12 December 1913, pp. 117–18.

11 Holledge's attention to journalistic suffrage plays is notable. Two of the three plays she publishes in *Innocent Flowers* originally appeared in suffrage newspapers.

12 The WSPU split into two organisations in 1912; after that time *Votes for Women* was edited by Emmeline and Frederick Pethick Lawrence. What remained of the WSPU, under the leadership of the Pankhurst family, began publishing *The Suffragette*. Both papers continued their coverage of drama after 1912.

13 Christopher St John, 'The World We Live In: Suffrage on the Stage', *Votes for Women*, 12 November 1909, p. 103.

14 'The Greek Suffragettes', *Votes for Women*, 17 March 1911, p. 386.

15 Some of the plays I discuss in this essay are authored by men, and several more have bylines with initials, so the gender of the authors is indeterminate. The vast majority of the plays are written by women, but I have included plays by men because I find that their work is driven by the direction set by the women writers; while there might be some differences to be identified between the work of the men and that of women, more to the point here are the similarities in their approaches.

16 H. S., 'The New Socrates', *The Vote*, 29 August 1913, p. 293.

17 H. S., 'A Speech: Justice to Women!', *The Vote*, 24 August 1912, p. 307.

18 G. Watkinson, 'Women and Suffrage', *The Common Cause*, 2 February 1911, pp. 701–3.

19 N. A., 'Mr. Peppercorn's Awakening', *The Vote*, 1 August 1913, p. 229.

20 Isabel Tippett, 'Woman, Old or New?', *The Vote*, 31 August 1912, pp. 325–6; 7 September 1912, pp. 341–2.

21 A. L. Little, 'The Shadow of the Sofa: A One-Act Play', *The Vote*, 24 December 1913, pp. 139–41.

22 Edith M. Baker, 'Our Happy Home', *The Vote*, 30 December 1911, p. 115.

23 *Ibid.*, p. 116.

24 Lorimer Royston, 'Little Jane and Grandmama. A Modern Dialogue', *Votes for Women*, 16 January 1914, p. 230.

25 Winifred St Clair, 'The Science of Forgiveness', *The Vote*, 28 November 1913, p. 72.

26 Isabel Tippett, 'The Stuff that 'Eroes Are Made Of', *The Vote*, 19 August 1911, pp. 208–9.

27 The anti-suffrage plays I refer to were not journalistic, but stage bound. All exist in the Lord Chamberlain's Collection at the British Library.

28 N. A., 'A Woman's Vote', Lord Chamberlain's Collection, British Library, 13 January 1909, Thraxton Corn Exchange.

29 Inglis Allen, 'The Suffragette's Redemption', Lord Chamberlain's Collection, British Library, 16 September 1909, Royalty Theatre, Glasgow.

30 George Dance, 'The Suffragette', Lord Chamberlain's Collection, British Library, 13 March 1907, Shakespeare Theatre, Clapham Junction.

31 H. S., 'A Speech', p. 307.

32 Helen McLachlan, 'The Mad Hatter's Tea Party up to Date', *The Vote*, 20 April 1912, p. 11. This is one of two plays that make use of Lewis Carroll's Alice to argue for *The Vote*. The other is Laurence Housman's *Alice in Ganderland* (London, The Woman's Press, 1911).

33 McLachlan, 'The Mad Hatter's Tea Party', p. 13.

34 Henry W. Nevinson, 'The Cabinet Concert', *Votes for Women*, 5 December 1913, p. 142.

35 Ethel Ayres Purdie, 'A Red-Tape Comedy', *The Vote*, 16 November 1912, p. 47.

36 *Ibid.*, 30 November 1912, p. 81.

37 W. Pett Ridge, 'A Good By-Election', *Votes for Women*, 8 April 1910, p. 441.

38 Lorimer Royston, 'Fair Play: A Dialogue', *Votes for Women*, 13 February 1914, p. 298.

39 Ibid., p. 298.

40 The play was not performed as scheduled, however, due to an overfull bill at the Albert Hall. So the play's more immediate impact was the published version ('Secretary's Report, June 1909–June 1910', AFL Archives, Fawcett Library, p. 6). See Alice Chapin, 'At the Gates: Being a Twentieth Century Episode', Lord Chamberlain's Collection, British Library, 13 December 1909, Royal Albert Hall; and idem, 'At the Gates', *The Vote*, 16 December 1909, p. 94.

12

The gender of russian serf theatre and performance

Catherine Schuler

Fundamental to a materialist historiography is the assumption that social institutions are marked by the laws, ideologies, social practices and culturally sanctified traditions peculiar to their historical moment. For the materialist theatre historian, then, theatres must be understood as social institutions, the material practices of which are marked by a particular legal, ideological and cultural context. In materialist historiography, the term 'marked' is deliberately neutral; the principal objective of a materialist historian is to understand and position, rather than to defend or condemn. Indeed, the term 'marked' implies judgement deferred. Although 'marked' is an exceedingly useful term of analysis, certain situations require less neutrality and concomitantly stronger language. In order to understand theatrical practice in Imperial Russia, for example, 'scarred' is both more useful and descriptive than 'marked.' For reasons that will become clear in the course of the following argument, in Russia the judicially mandated practice of serfdom did not simply 'mark' social institutions like theatre, it left wounds that even revolution could not heal.

Serfdom affected all aspects of ethnic Russian theatre, especially the profession of acting. Professional actors were drawn primarily from the serf class; for that reason, acting – as both art and skilled craft – suffered most from its connections to serfdom. Although critics often blamed the debasement of theatre on the ignorance of the reading and viewing public, actors and actresses were not regarded sympathetically. According to these self-appointed *raisonneurs* of respectable society, if members of the actor caste were on 'the margins of contemporary social life', they had only themselves to blame; completely indifferent to literature, intellectual development, current events or new ideas, actors frittered away their time quaffing kvass at public houses rather than attending edifying lectures and literary evenings.[1] The collective reputation of actresses was even more debased. Doubly oppressed by class and a rigid set of largely unreconstructed medieval gender conventions, actresses were exceptionally vulnerable to the effects of the serf system both before and after the emancipation of the serfs in 1861. Perhaps for that reason, even more so than actors, actresses were censured for their dubious anti-artistic preoccupations – especially their perceived devotion to toilette and coquetry rather than the art and craft of acting. But who could blame them? The rewards of coquetry were far greater than the rewards of art.

Although the emancipation freed serfs from centuries of bondage, the mentality of serfdom continued to infect institutions and individuals at all levels of Russian society. If the emancipation eliminated serf theatre and performance as a formal practice, the psychology of serfdom influenced the practice and reception of theatrical performance well into the post-emancipation period.

The context of Russian serfdom

Because the practice of serfdom affected all aspects of Russian life and art, the nature of pre-Renaissance Russian theatre cannot be fully grasped outside the context of serfdom as a mode of social and economic organisation.[2] Although certain practices associated with serfdom are peculiar to the Russian context, generally speaking the legal conventions and institutional practices of the Russian serf system do not differ significantly from those of other feudal or slave-owning societies. Readers familiar with the paternalistic authoritarianism of American slavery or the economic, religious and ideological practices of Western European feudalism, will find obvious parallels in the Russian situation. As a formal institution, Russian serfdom flourished from the seventeenth to the middle of the nineteenth century. In contrast, however, to slave-owning societies that imported racially distinct populations from foreign lands to perform work considered beneath the ruling classes, the Russian system of bonded labour evolved accidentally – perhaps even 'naturally' (if such problematic term may be used in a post-structuralist age) within the historical context of the Russian autocracy.

The shared interests of sovereigns and nobility in a stable, immobile serf population made serfdom both desirable and necessary. The serf system required a division of labour that categorised workers as either house or field serfs and, on most estates, two structures of life and labour were possible for the serf population: *obrok* and *barshchina*. Under the *obrok* arrangement, serfs who paid the estate owner either a 'quit-rent' or with labour in kind enjoyed relative autonomy. Under the *barshchina* arrangement, serfs lived and worked in the constant presence of the estate owner or his manager; for that reason, they were subject to closer surveillance as well as more frequent and severe punishments.[3] Although different in kind, *obrok* and *barshchina* arrangements shared an important feature: like the autocracy itself, both were unremittingly patriarchal and paternalistic.

The principles and practices of autocracy organised all levels of social, political and cultural life in Russia. The estate owner's authority over his or her serf 'children' mirrored the absolute authority of the tsar to rule the Russian people as s/he saw fit.[4] Maintenance of autocratic rule of law in Russia relied upon the selective application of extreme forms of correction and discipline, including corporal punishment. In *Politics and Culture in Eighteenth Century Russia*, Isabel De Madariaga observed that the eighteenth century in Russia was a 'brutal age';[5] certain classes were, however, more likely to be physically and psychologically brutalised than others. Although the terms of the autocracy allowed extreme forms of punishment to be visited on any citizen, collectively peasants and serfs were particularly vulnerable to abuse. Indeed, as Abby Schrader explains in 'Containing the Spectacle of Punishment', certain categories of punishment were used by the autocracy to establish social boundaries and construct 'firmer divisions between privileged and unprivileged subjects'.[6] In the eyes of Russian officialdom, members of the lower estates were 'amorphous rabble' incapable of higher moral development; for that reason, they had to be 'treated harshly if the social and state order were to be preserved'. Schrader argues that, from the state's perspective, the primitivism and ignorance of the Russian *narod* (people) made physical intimidation a legitimate and necessary form of social control.[7] Even more curious was the conviction, apparently common among members of the serf-owning classes, that corporal punishment encouraged creativity, intellectual development and artistic accomplishments in the peasant and serf populations.

Finally, the practices of serf theatre and performance were shaped by the social organisation of the provincial estate. During the sixteenth and seventeenth centuries, estates owned by the aristocracy and gentry proliferated in suburban and provincial Russia. Because estates tended to be isolated, hermetic and feudal, life on the estate was often savagely primitive. Estate life began to change after 1762 when Peter II issued a manifesto freeing the nobility from compulsory military and civil service. Peter's manifesto, which encouraged an increasingly Westernised aristocracy to migrate to their suburban and provincial estates, transformed the character and organisation of the serf system. Especially important for the purposes of understanding serf theatre was the formation during this period of a serf intelligentsia. Not to be confused with its bourgeois counterpart, the serf intelligentsia consisted primarily of skilled craftspeople and artisans, including, among others, physicians, architects, accountants, painters, musicians, dancers and actors. Although historical opinion regarding the origins of this class of educated peasants is not uniform, the presence of a serf intelligentsia was a decisive factor in the formation and proliferation of serf theatre and performance, and in the eventual emancipation of the serf population.

The origins of serf theatre and performance

Although the popularity of serf theatre and performance peaked in the late eighteenth and early nineteenth centuries, performances by serfs in the homes of Tsar Aleksei Mikhailovich's boyars were not unusual by the mid-seventeenth century.[8] Perhaps because theatre in Russia was largely *domashnii* and *liubitel'skii* – private and amateur – until the middle of the eighteenth century, there is little additional documentation of serf performance before Elizaveta Petrovna assumed the throne in 1741. In 1744, the first stage performance by serfs, *The Ballet of the Flowers*, was given to mark the occasion of Peter II's betrothal to the German princess and future Tsar of Russia, Catherine II.[9] Although serf theatre flourished and became the predominant genre of theatrical entertainment under Catherine, Elizaveta Petrovna, a passionate patron of court entertainments, prepared the way for future developments in serf performance by promoting increased Westernisation at court, chartering the Imperial theatres, and allowing Aleksandr Sumarokov to organise amateur theatricals in the Cadet Corps using male students from the nobility (*blagorodnye pitomtsa*). Because it produced a new generation of young aristocrats with a taste for theatre as well as the knowledge and skills to organise it, theatrical activity in the Cadet Corps was a prominent factor in the development of serf theatre under Catherine.[10] This process of development occurred in several stages.

Bolstered by the example of the Cadet Corps and by the progressive 'Frenchification' of the Russian aristocracy, a vogue for amateur theatre (*moda na liubitel'skogo teatra*) began to spread outside the closed circle of the court during Elizaveta Petrovna's reign. The manifesto of 1762 encouraged further geographical dissemination of theatre as the now liberated aristocracy migrated to their provincial estates, bringing with them their newly acquired taste for Western high culture, including art, literature and amateur theatricals. The ground was thus prepared for the active advocacy of Catherine II, whose neoclassic understanding of theatre as an essential tool of edification and amusement influenced attitudes both inside and outside court circles. Arguing that 'people who sing and dance do not think about evil,' Catherine called theatre the 'people's school' (*shkola narodnaia*). Her enthusiasm for theatre was not rhetorical: among her other accomplishments, Catherine wrote edifying comedies, encouraged instructors at the Smolnyi Institute for Noble Girls to incorporate theatre into their pedagogical practice, discussed dramatic literature and theatre with Voltaire, and further strengthened the still embryonic professional theatre in Russia.[11]

Catherine's taste for, and active advocacy of, Western art, literature and theatre moved wealthy members of the noble and merchant classes to imitate her example in their homes and on their estates. Some of these enthusiasts were motivated to the study and practice of the fine and performing arts by a sincere desire for self-improvement and a conviction that such self-improvement would advance the status of Russia in Europe; others were driven solely by the necessity to curry favour with the monarch. Hoping to please Catherine – thereby improving their positions in provincial society – provincial administrators and the local aristocracy devised plans to initiate 'noble and useful amusements'. As one observer wrote: 'Theatre became fashionable because the enlightened monarch and her colleagues considered it desirable.'[12] Regardless of social rank or measure of personal wealth, estate owners endeavoured to create miniature courts, complete with court entertainments, on their estates. By the end of the eighteenth century, most grandees (*vel'mozh*) maintained private theatres and orchestras. A second layer of society, consisting primarily of wealthy noblemen, rushed to imitate the grandees. Behind the second layer was a third – average estate owners (*pomeshchiki srednei ruki*) who did not possess sufficient resources to maintain a private theatre, but were driven to follow fashion until their ill-conceived adventures reduced them to bankruptcy.[13]

In the early stages of the *moda na liubitel'skogo teatra*, private productions were usually staged and performed by the owner and his or her family and friends. By the beginning of Catherine's tenure as head of the Russian state, the form and organisation of private theatre in Russia were fundamentally altered as productions by aristocratic amateurs were replaced in the homes and on the estates of many landowners by serf theatre. Although aristocratic amateurs continued to perform through-out the pre-emancipation period, even making occasional appearances on stage with both serf and professional actors, by the late eighteenth century the predominant form of private entertainment consisted of performances by trained serfs.[14] While it is tempting to ascribe the appearance of serf theatre to some amorphous notion of Russian 'national character' or to the peculiarities of Russian autocracy, it is impossible to know with certainty why this genre of performance flour-ished in Russia but was absent from those Western nations considered exemplary by the Russian intelligentsia and aristocracy. Several histori-ans argue that the origins of serf theatre are located in the tendency of the Russian aristocracy to laxity, class hierarchy and paternalism.[15] According to Liubov Gurevich, the enthusiasm of aristocratic amateurs for staging, designing and performing in their own productions dimin-ished as they acquired a deeper appreciation of the complexities of producing theatre – especially theatre that could satisfy the tastes of an increasingly sophisticated court with pretensions to European art and manners. In addition, although talented amateurs were not unusual, aristocratic actors and actresses usually fell far short of a rigorous artistic ideal. The virtual absence of exemplary models of stage artistry may account in part for the poor quality of amateur acting, but the root of the problem lay elsewhere. Even gifted aristocratic amateurs rarely undertook serious study of acting because the actual study of stage art was deemed to be beneath their dignity as members of the aristocracy. In this context, the idea to train serfs in the arts of acting, design and construction arose quite naturally.

The original impulse to train and educate serfs as replacements for aristocratic amateurs in the estates theatres was, however, soon corrupted by the discovery that trained serfs were valuable commodities who could be bought and sold for large amounts of money. Although the commercial exchange of serfs was common throughout the Imperial period, by the late eighteenth century the terms of the serf trade had changed significantly: ordinary serfs brought their owners between ten and eighty rubles, while literate serfs could fetch as much as seven hundred. In the same period, a serf actress was sold by her owner for 5,000 rubles, while a price of 20,000 was set on a particularly talented violinist.[16] Estate owners who kept their actors also made substantial profits. Prince Shakhovskoi, for example, cleared more than 10,000 rubles of pure profit by touring his troupe of serf performers to provin-cial cities and fairs.[17] By the end of the eighteenth century, trade in trained serfs flourished as owners sold their human property – not only individuals, but entire companies of actors, dancers and musicians – to each other, to provincial entrepreneurs, and to the Imperial theatres. Although the whole of Russian theatre suffered from its association with serfdom, the effects of this trade were particularly devastating for serf, and later free, actresses.

Serf theatre: a historiographical digression

Before focusing more narrowly on issues of gender and class in serf theatre and performance, several observations about the treatment – in both fantasy and fact – of the serf system by Russian and Soviet novelists, sociologists and historians are necessary. Since the early nineteenth century, the manifold complexities of the serf system have been treated at length in Russian fiction and non-fiction, including memoir literature. Even a dilatory topical survey of serfdom in any decent library in Moscow or St Petersburg will be rewarded by a surfeit of factually reliable secondary sources. M. D. Kurmacheva cautions, however, that although many of the sources are factually sound, the treatment of the data varies significantly by period and by the class of the author.[18] Many Soviet (and some late Imperial) social historians, for example, emphasise abuses of the system, arguing that serfdom had no redeeming value and that the serf intelligentsia consisted primarily of skilled craftspeople whose contributions to Russian art and culture were negligible. In contrast, in their frequent role as apologists for autocracy, many pre-revolutionary (and some late Soviet) historians argue that although the serf system was not ideal, reports of abuse were greatly exaggerated; oppressive owners were exceptional; the serf intelligentsia was a progressive – perhaps even revolutionary – force in Russia; and even if there were isolated instances of abuse, serfdom, as it developed in the post-Petrine era, had the positive effect of bringing enlightenment to the largely illiterate peasant and serf population. Two frequently cited secondary sources, one by Ekaterina Letkova and the other by Nikolai Evreinov, suggest the range of critical and historical views on the serf intelligentsia and serf performance.

Published in 1883, Letkova's 'Krepostnaia intelligentsiia' offered readers an emotionally charged account of the tragic lives of serf artists, actors and musicians. Setting out to demonstrate that serfdom was symptomatic of a serious illness affecting the entire social structure of Imperial Russia, she cites case after case of human deprivation and humiliation, including flogging, rape, and mental and emotional abuse. While acknowledging the occasional presence of genuine lovers of art among the landowning aristocracy and authentic talent among their bonded artists and performers, Letkova argued that the dubious accomplishments of the serf intelligentsia did little to redeem the institution of serfdom. Even more damning from her point of view was the mentality of serfdom that continued to poison Russian life and culture long after the emancipation in 1861 of the serf population. 'Dependence, and dominion did not', she argued, 'disappear with the fall of judicially mandated slavery. They exist even now, albeit in more muted, complex, and veiled forms.'[19]

The point of view in Nikolai Evreinov's monograph, *Krepostnye aktery,* is in marked contrast to Letkova's. Acting as an apologist for both autocracy and artistic privilege, Evreinov offered a familiar cooking metaphor to describe the legacy of serf theatre and performance: like bakers who must break a few eggs in order to produce tasty, beautifully formed cakes, serf owners had to break a few serfs in order to produce art. Taking a fundamentally Machiavellian perspective, Evreinov argued that the ends justified the means: the occasional brilliance of serf theatre justified its violent excesses and, even more importantly, provincial theatre owed its existence to serf theatre.

Available primary and secondary information on Russian serfdom reaffirms a fundamental principle of historical research: truth is not simple or singular. In the context of eighteenth- and nineteenth-century social organisation, Russians of all classes were simultaneously enlightened and savagely barbaric; serfs owned by enlightened masters flourished while those who served despots did not; and the quality of serf theatre and performance ranged from the sublime to the grotesque. The point is simply that existing sources offer strikingly different points of view on serfdom and serf theatre. The serf system did not encourage neutrality among the memoirists, social critics and historians who described it and polemicists on both sides of the issue tend to select the most spectacular, extraordinary and salacious examples of abuse and privilege to sway and titillate readers. For all of these reasons, sorting fact from critical frame is not always easy.

Serf theatre and the gender divide

From a progressive Western point of view, the irony of autocracy and serfdom in Russia is that together they created a peculiar illusion of gender equality in a society where gender inequality was a fundamental principle of the social order. Even today, fearful of encroachments by Western feminism, Russians will insist that institutionalised discrimination on the basis of sex and gender was not a significant aspect of daily life in Imperial Russia. According to this argument, men and women experienced oppression equally because neither enjoyed basic civil rights under the terms of Russian autocracy. Among the serf population, the master's lash fell on men and women indiscriminately, therefore neither sex was privileged over the other. But if the cult of abuse and suffering in Russia cut across lines of class and gender, women were particularly vulnerable and had fewer opportunities to escape through education or training in a skilled craft. Among field serfs, women had little market value; and although ordinary housemaids might bring as much as fifty rubles, the market for women rested primarily upon 'pretty young serf girls'.[20] Not surprisingly, serf actresses tended to be drawn from the available supply of succulent young beauties.

The consensus of opinion among Russian theatre historians is that a significant percentage of serf actresses performed the dual role of actress and concubine in the master's household, collectively constituting a sort of theatrical harem. Differences of historical opinion arise not about the reality of sexual exploitation, but about the consequences of the master/serf hierarchy for women and, more particularly, for actresses as professional artists and skilled craftspeople. From Evreinov's point of view, for example, whatever its excesses, serf theatre was a tool of enlightenment that brought the beauty and truth of art, literature, music and performance to the benighted masses, thus raising them from bestial to human status. If serf actresses endured sexual exploitation, acting still offered opportunities for social advancement otherwise unavailable to women of their class.[21] In contrast, Letkova argues that the vast majority of serfs were entirely indifferent to theatre, art and music and took part in them unwillingly and without understanding. For that reason, with rare exceptions, their work was hopelessly shoddy and unsophisticated.[22] With regard to serf actresses, Letkova insists that closer proximity to the master was hardly an advantage for women: locked away inside the four walls of their harem and forbidden to leave except to go to the theatre, serf actresses hardly exemplified the freedoms that should accrue to individuals with higher education and a skilled craft.[23]

The simple truth is that men derived greater advantage than women from changes in the serf system. Although Catherine II supported educational reform, the principal beneficiaries were noble girls and peasant and serf boys. At her urging, the aristocracy provided schools for their serfs and peasants, but only boys and men had access to formal education.[24] M. D. Kurmacheva explains that 'training for girls was considered unnecessary in these schools: if a man – the future head of the family – acquired the necessary education, then his wife and daughters could borrow whatever knowledge they needed from him'.[25] Access to higher education allowed male serfs entry to a wide variety of useful trades and professions that were closed to their sisters in bondage. Male serfs were trained as painters, musicians, designers, architects and technicians. Female serfs could become actresses, dancers and singers – professions that required little beyond physical attractiveness, grace and basic reading skills, and that were shunned by respectable free women.[26] In his memoir of life as a serf actor, Mikhail Shchepkin describes an incident that illuminates the conflicted relationship of women to theatre in the eighteenth and nineteenth centuries. Although born a serf, Shchepkin had the good fortune to attend a school for children from the nobility, civil service and the merchantry. One innovative instructor decided to incorporate theatre into his pedagogy, but when he tried to cast the play, outraged parents refused to allow their daughters to perform on a public stage – even in a school context. 'How,' the distressed parents cried, 'could our daughters be actresses!' In the end, boys played the old women and female servants, while Shchepkin's sister played the ingenue role because, as Shchepkin put it, 'she could be forced'.[27]

For most serfs, theatre was not a freely chosen profession. Although sympathetic historians and critics argue that the function of serf theatre as an agent of enlightenment justified its existence, few owners organised theatres with the goal of lifting their serfs from ignorance and servitude to enlightenment and freedom. Not surprisingly, serfs themselves – especially provincial serfs – were not particularly hungry for the kind of enlightenment offered by theatre and other fine arts. Serf girls and women rarely chose to be actresses; usually they were simply plucked from their families as children and adolescents and either trained for the stage or forced to perform with little or no preparation. Like all serfs, serf actresses were goods to be disposed of as their owners saw fit. Serf girls could be left in the fields or put on the stage; they could be bought, sold, traded, lost or won at cards, used to pay debts, or simply given as gifts. Serf actresses were distinguished, however, from their brethren in artistic bondage by their vulnerability to sexual exploitation and debased eroticism.

The Russian verb *ugodit* – to please or oblige – offers a point of entry into the function of serf performance. Influenced by a miscellany of Slavic and non-Slavic practices, social decorum in Russia embraced forms of hospitality found more commonly in Asia than in Europe.[28] Wealthy hosts were obliged by social decorum to afford guests access to all of the pleasures, comforts and amusements of her or his home. Thus, in the homes of the aristocracy, theatre, dance and music performed by serfs were offered as gifts to please or oblige invited guests. Unhappily for serf actresses, the act of giving often extended beyond the curtain line and the genres in which they were required to perform were not always strictly 'theatrical'. One of the most frequently cited examples of the 'collective concubinage' of serf actresses is Petr Esipov's theatre in Kazan. Apparently Esipov treated male guests not only to theatrical performances, but to 'bacchanalias' replete with private entertainment by serf actresses. Filip Filippovich Vigel, who visited Esipov's estate in the early nineteenth century, was astonished by the appearance at dinner of a dozen attractive, elegantly dressed young women who were promptly distributed among the men. As it turned out, the women were Esipov's serf actresses. Their function at dinner was to entertain the male guests with drinks, kisses and provocative doggerel that encouraged the men to 'embrace and kiss' their table companions.[29] Another such 'performance site' was located in the 'depths of the Vologodskaia province'. Evgenii Opochinin, who visited the Bulanov estate, reported: 'In the 1880s, an elderly local resident showed me a green house (*zelenyi domik*) with the remains of a stage and curtain. According to local legend, the estate owner arranged nighttime orgies with serf dancers. Transforming female members of a serf troupe into a harem was an ordinary occurrence. Pleasure houses, which were called "little heavens" (*raik*), "pavilions", or simply green houses, were commonly found on estates.'[30]

In the early nineteenth century, the tenor of the aristocracy began to change. Under Catherine's successors, enthusiasm for the ideals of the enlightenment diminished while the profit motive gradually replaced social decorum as the principal source of serf exploitation. Count Sergei Mikhailovich Kamenskii, one of the most eccentric producers of serf theatre and the target of much contemporaneous satire, maintained two theatres in Orel: one on his country estate and another on the public fairground.[31] Kamenskii's theatres were commercial enterprises; for that reason, the count carefully regulated the activities of his human property. The lives of his performers and house serfs were organised on a military model: entering and exiting the dining area to the beat of a drum and blare of a French horn, they ate rations while standing at a common table. During performances, Kamenskii sat with notebook in hand jotting down missed cues and bumbled lines; during act breaks, he hurried backstage with a whip to punish performers on the spot for their blunders. Cries of the beaten were audible in the auditorium. Although extreme, Kamenskii's attitude towards, and treatment of, his serf actresses were not unusual. Far from offering his serf actresses to male visitors, Kamenskii isolated them from the rest of the household in a sort of harem.[32] When the count watched a performance from the first row of the orchestra, his mother and daughters sat directly behind him; his current lover (usually a serf actress) sat behind them wearing a large portrait of the count on her breast. If she was in disfavour, another portrait took its place – of the count's back.

Because serf actresses were chosen for their physical charms and commodified by their owners – whether for pleasure or profit – preparation for the stage did not require literacy. Although serf actresses usually received some kind of professional training and acquired certain technical skills, many were illiterate and learned their roles by coaching, routine and the whip.[33] Prince Gruzinskii's method of training serf girls for the stage exemplifies one popular approach. Because his actresses could not read, they learned their roles from a coach who spoke the lines aloud for the women to repeat. Frequent thrashings encouraged firmer memorisation and better understanding of the lines.[34] Gruzinskii's pedagogy was not unusual: corporal punishment was frequently employed to encourage artistry. A provincial priest recorded his impressions of serf performance on a local estate. 'In the evening, Sasha and Dasha, who had already been flogged earlier for singing off-tune, had to play princesses and countesses on the estate stage. During the intermission, the barin came backstage and said: "Sasha, your performance is unsatisfactory: countess N.N. must behave with great dignity." And during the fifteen or twenty minute intermission, Sasha caught it dearly from the coachman, who flogged her with all his might. Then Sasha had to perform again with the full dignity of a countess or act in a vaudeville or dance in the ballet.' The priest continued: 'However you struggle, however you try, you cannot imagine how people – especially young girls – could forget the pain and humiliation of the coachman's whip and transform themselves at a moment's notice into dignified countesses, or jump, laugh with all their soul, flirt, and fly in the ballet. But they had to do it. They did it because they knew by experience that if they didn't emerge from the whip happy, laughing, twirling, and jumping, they would visit the coachman again.'[35]

Conditions of life and service for women in serf theatres were not, however, uniform; the situation of actresses varied in proportion to the wealth, education, and progressive tendencies of the owner. Two theatres were considered exemplary with regard to the education, training and humane treatment of serf actresses: Count Nikolai Petrovich Sheremetev's in Moscow and Prince Nikolai Grigorevich Shakhovskoi's in Nizhnii Novgorod.

Apologists for serf theatre invariably cite N. P. Sheremetev's practice as an exemplary model of high art and humane treatment – especially of women. One of the oldest members of the Moscow nobility, the Sheremetev family enjoyed tremendous wealth and favour throughout much of the eighteenth century. Although largely indifferent to theatre except as a necessary *accoutrement* for a nobleman, Petr Borisovich Sheremetev, Nikolai's father, built the family's first theatre on the grounds of their suburban Moscow estate, Kuskovo.[36] Upon his return from abroad in 1773, Nikolai, whose genuine enthusiasm for music, theatre and art distinguished him from many of his contemporaries, assumed responsibility for the theatre. N. P. Sheremetev's advantage lay in his education: while abroad, he studied music and absorbed European culture. For that reason, when he returned to Russia, he had all of the necessary qualifications to produce theatre of the highest calibre: wealth, leisure, knowledge and taste. Sheremetev hired the best native and foreign actors, dancers and musicians to train his serf performers and ordered sketches from Paris for his serf designers to copy. His productions were of such high quality that the manager of Moscow's commercial theatre began to complain of unfair competition.[37]

Sheremetev's practice provides the principal evidence for serf theatre as a benignly paternalistic institution devoted to the cause of instruction and tasteful amusement. The high quality of his productions as well as his enlightened views on the education and training of serfs distinguished N. P. Sheremetev from most of his peers. At his home in Moscow, Sheremetev organised 'something like a theatre school for adult and adolescent serfs; boys and girls, men and women, lived there, each in separate groups'. Serf girls chosen for training were educated like boarding school girls (*institutki*): they studied French and Italian languages and needlework, and wore crinolines and corsets to achieve the bearing proper to a young lady.[38] Set against contemporary practice, Sheremetev's productions and pedagogy were remarkable. Ironically, however, his reputation – especially among apologists for serf theatre – rests primarily on his treatment of one woman: Parasha Kuznetsova, better known to her contemporaries as Zhemchugova.[39]

Rescued from poverty and ignorance by the wealthy, urbane, thoroughly Europeanised Nikolai Sheremetev, Kuznetsova represented a sort of fairy-tale princess – the exemplary issue of a benign, increasingly progressive serf system. Thanks to Sheremetev, she received the best theatrical training available as well as an excellent liberal education. Brilliantly clothed, decorated and set in a theatrical frame designed by European artists, Kutnetsova graced the Kuskovo stage for many years. She was also Sheremetev's mistress and, after 1801, his wife. Kuznetsova's great beauty, intelligence and talent were the purchase price of freedom and marriage with a prosperous, progressive and apparently loving nobleman. Contending that Kuznetsova was not unique, some historians generalised her case to the profession: although she was one of only two serf actresses to marry above her class, Kuznetsova was proof that acting offered women unprecedented opportunities for self-advancement.[40]

Although the artistic quality of Prince Shakhovskoi's theatre was less impressive than Sheremetev's, he was distinguished from most of his contemporaries by the rigid standards of private and public morality he imposed on his troupe. One of the few primary accounts by a serf actress of life in the theatre is of Shakhovskoi's practice. Nastasia Ivanovna Piunova, who performed on both serf and free stages, told her story to her granddaughter, who published it in 1889.[41] Her memoir offers a vivid picture of the treatment of serf actresses in one of the theatres considered most humane for the period. In certain respects Piunova's experience was better than most; in others, it was typical.

Like most serf actresses, Piunova did not choose her vocation. By her own account, she was taken 'in best sandals' from the village to Shakhovskoi's estate. There she was washed, dressed and placed in the *devich'ia* – a wing of the prince's house reserved for the girls in his troupe. The wing was crowded with girls who performed in his dramatic, ballet and opera troupes. Kept under lock and key, the girls were supervised by *mamushki* – middle-aged women who were, in Shakhovskoi's opinion, completely reliable. Special carriages conveyed the girls to rehearsals and performances; when they arrived at the theatre, new *mamushki* shepherded them to private dressing rooms. The *regisseur* called the girls to the stage as needed where they rehearsed under the vigilant eye of yet another *mamushka*. Casual conversation with men was strictly forbidden; touching between the sexes was prohibited on or off stage. When an actress celebrated her twenty-fifth birthday, the prince arranged her marriage. He accomplished this by summoning all of the single male actors to his office in order to discover which of them was willing to marry the actress in question. Having arranged the marriage, the prince blessed the couple, provided a dowry and often gave the newly-weds a special salary.

Education for Shakhovskoi's actors consisted of learning to read and write in Russian; 'in the interests of morality', actresses were taught only to read – a policy which prevented improper correspondence with men before marriage. So that they could learn by example how to conduct themselves with the proper decorum on stage, actresses were also required to spend time with the prince's wife. Their time together was passed in reading, conversation and handwork. When the prince organised balls, his actors and actresses often attended. Although actors were forbidden to dance with society women, actresses danced freely with men far above their social class. Finally, in the interests of their training, the prince frequently took his leading serf performers with him to Moscow to see productions at the Imperial theatres and to watch balls given by prominent representatives of the Moscow nobility.

Although entirely without freedom of choice or action, Piunova considered herself fortunate to have learned a craft under Shakhovskoi's tutelage. And by early nineteenth-century standards, perhaps she was: judged within his own context, Shakhovskoi was well-educated, humane and progressive. Many serf actresses were less fortunate than Piunova.

Submerged rocks of the Russian stage: the post-emancipation context

The enthusiasm for serf theatre abated by the early nineteenth century; although performances continued in reduced, and by many accounts, increasingly debased form until 1861, the emancipation suppressed serf theatre as a formal practice. Nonetheless, the effects of serf theatre were visible in Imperial and provincial theatre practice both before and after the emancipation. Indeed, evidence suggests that the autocratic paternalism of serf theatre was also the organising principle of free theatre in Russia.

The practices and conventions of serf performance infiltrated free theatre from several directions. Ruined by the excesses of estate life, financial necessity compelled impoverished estate owners to sell individual performers as well as entire troupes to both Imperial and provincial theatres. Most historians agree that provincial theatre rose from the ashes of serf theatre, especially in cities where owners transformed their private troupes into commercial enterprises or resourceful merchants simply appropriated or purchased existing companies. By the middle of the nineteenth century, serf performers were predominant in provincial theatres and most acting companies included three categories of people: serfs working under the *obrok* system for their impoverished masters; children of serf actors; and children of free actors.

The tendency towards autocratic paternalism was further reinforced in the Imperial theatres by the fact that some nobles who owned and managed serf theatres often occupied powerful positions in the Imperial bureaucracy. Because these aristocratic bureaucrats did not distinguish clearly between the Imperial troupes and their own serf companies, paid professionals in the Imperial theatres were treated like serfs. Ironically, they often were serfs; because the Imperial directorate purchased talented serf actors, dancers and singers for the Imperial companies, serf performers proliferated in the Imperial theatres.[42] Commercial trade in serf actresses was particularly important for staffing the Imperial troupes because, as one bureaucrat noted, free women rarely enter the acting professional voluntarily.[43]

The insinuation of the serf mentality into provincial and Imperial theatres had enormous consequences for free actresses. Unlike their European colleagues, Russian actresses bore the stigma of recent slavery; although their desire for recognition as free citizens and skilled professionals was great, their debasement under serfdom kept them from achieving respectability. Before and after the emancipation, Imperial and provincial theatres appropriated many practices and conventions of serf theatre. Provincial entrepreneurs, for example, required actresses to entertain male spectators after performances and encouraged liaisons with wealthy patrons so that they could pay the women lower wages.[44] In the Imperial theatres, the directorate recruited female students from the theatre schools to entertain influential state and city officials.[45]

Although not unique to Imperial Russia, irrational prejudice against theatre and its practitioners was sustained longer and more energetically there than in those Western and Northern European countries considered exemplary by educated Russians. Many factors peculiar to Imperial society and culture contributed to the debasement of Russian theatre, including autocracy, Orthodoxy, geographical isolation and xenophobia. The most powerful institution for producing and fuelling extreme attitudes as well as genuine debasement was, however, serfdom. The serf system gave rise to both a type of audience and a genre of performance not seen in the West since the Roman empire. While not innovative with respect to repertoire or production practice, serf theatre and performance were unique in the modern European context. In the eighteenth and nineteenth centuries, Russian actors and audiences learned their craft and acquired their taste for, and expectations of, theatre within the serf context – a context that presumed the debasement of the serf girls and women compelled to perform on public and private stages. Long after the emancipation, the tastes and conventions established under serfdom continued to affect the status and treatment of actresses in Russia.

Notes

1 N. V. Rodevich, 'Nashe akterstvo', *Russkaia stsena*, No. 11 (1864), p. 140. For additional views on actors and actresses in the immediate post-emancipation period, see Viktor Aleksandrov, 'Prichiny sovremennykh vozzrenii publikii na stsenicheskoe iskusstvo i akterov', *Russkaia stsena*, 1 (1864), pp. 1–29 and idem, 'Podvodnye kamni russkoi stseny', *Russkaia stsena*, 11 (1864), pp. 1–23.

2 Information for this section is drawn primarily from Jerome Blum, *Lord and Peasant in Russia from the Ninth to the Nineteenth Century* (Princeton, NJ, Princeton University Press, 1961); Isabel De Madariaga, *Politics and Culture in Eighteenth Century Russia* (London, Longman, 1998); Vasilii Semevskii, 'Krepostnye krest'iane pri Ekaterine II', *Russkaia starina* (Noiabr' 1876), pp. 579–618 and (Dekabr' 1876), pp. 653–690.

3 *Ibid.*, p. 587 and E. Letkova, 'Krepostnaia intelligentsiia', *Otechestvennyia zapiski*, 11 (1883), p. 171.

4 According to Semevskii, *Krepostnya*, p. 661, the estate owner was not only 'the lawgiver, judge, and executor of his own decisions', but also 'the plaintiff against whom the defendant had no defense'. Isabel De Madariaga counters that serfs did have legal recourse against excessive abuse: see De Madariaga, *Politics and Culture*, pp. 124–49.

5 *Ibid.*, p. 142.

6 Abby M. Schrader, 'Containing the Spectacle of Punishment: The Russian Autocracy and the Abolition of the Knout, 1817–1845', *Slavic Review*, 4 (1997), p. 618.

7 *Ibid.*, p. 626.

8 Liubov Gurevich, *Istoriia russkogo teatral'nogo byta*, Vol. 1 (Moscow-Leningrad, Iskusstvo, 1939), p. 209; A. B. Kosterina, 'Krepostnoi teatr na urale', in *Iskusstvo teatra: voprosy, teorii i praktiki* (Sverdlovsk, Izdatel'stvo ural'skogo universiteta, 1989), p. 4. Primary documentation of early serf theatre and performance can be located in fonds 17, 139, 248 and 1239 at the Arkhiv drevnikh aktov in Moscow.

9 Nikolai Evreinov, *Krepostnye aktery* (St Petersburg, Izdanie direktsii imperatorskykh teatrov, 1912), p. 5.

10 V. Ulanov, 'Krepostnoi teatre, stat'ia', unpublished manuscript, Bakhrushin Museum, Moscow, fond 532, d. 82, p. 1. For information on the Cadet Corps and the eighteenth-century context, see also, N. V. Drizen, *Materialy k istorii russkogo teatra* (Moscow, Izdanie A. A. Bakhrushina, 1905) and M. I. Pyliaev, *Staraia moskva* (St Petersburg, Izdanie A. S. Suvorina, 1891).

11 See Drizen, *Materialy k istorii russkogo teatra*, pp. 56–60, for information about theatre at the Smolnyi Institute. The rage for amateur theatricals among the aristocracy was fuelled during Catherine's reign by increased use of theatre as a pedagogical tool at the Smolnyi Institute and at Moscow University as well. Because Catherine supported women's education, during her reign young men *and* women acquired a taste for theatre, as well as the skills to produce it.

12 Ulanov, 'Krepostnoi teatre', p. 2. Echoing Ulanov, Letkova wrote,' The empress had only to show that she loved art for society to love it straightaway': 'Krepostnaia intelligentsiia', p. 160.

13 *Ibid.*, p. 161.

14 M. I. Pyliaev, 'Polubarskiia zatei', *Istoricheskii vestnik*, 9 (1886), p. 549. Estimates of the number of serf theatres vary. Located in Moscow, St Petersburg and the provinces, by one estimate, at the peak of their existence, there were at least 150 serf theatres. Perhaps because it was the seat of government, St Petersburg had fewer theatres than Moscow, which was home to at least twenty serf troupes. Although fewer in number and generally of lesser quality, serf theatres were found even in the most distant provinces. See, for example, Kosterina's discussion of serf theatre in the Ural mountains in 'Krepostnoi teatr na urale', pp. 4–19.

15 See, among others, Gurevich, *Istoriia misskogo teatral'nogo byta*, pp. 209–10; Ulanov, 'Krepostnoi teatre', 4; Letkova, 'Krepostnaia intelligentsiia', pp. 163–5.

16 A. Ivanovskii, 'Krepostnye aktery i aktrisy', *Kolols'ia*, 11 (1886), p. 254.

17 Ulanov, "Krepostnoi teatre', 9.

18 M. D. Kurmacheva, *Krepostnaia intelligentsiia Rossii: vtoraia polovina XVII – nachalo XIX veka* (Moscow, Nauka, 1983).

19 Letkova, 'Krepostnaia intelligentsiia', p. 159.

20 Semevskii, Noiabr', pp. 595–7; Dekabr', pp. 654–5; Blum, *Lord and Peasant in Russia*, p. 426. According to Semevskii, in the 1760s, men aged between 15 and 60 were worth on average thirty rubles; women with their belongings went for ten. Semevskii also notes that literacy was largely the privilege of male serf children, which would have increased their value.

21 Evreinov, *Krepostnye aktery*, pp. 78–9.

22 Letkova, 'Krepostnaia intelligentsiia', p. 172.

23 *Ibid.*, p. 165. For a moving depiction of the imprisonment of serf actresses, see Aleksandr Herzen's short story *The Thieving Magpie (Soroka vorovka)*.

24 I do not, however, intend to oversimplify the situation. Although formal schooling was encouraged by Catherine, finding competent teachers, persuading owners to build schools and convincing serf parents to send their male children was no easy task. See L. A. Lepskaia, 'Novoe o krepostnykh shkolakh-nachala XIX veka v votchinakh Sheremetevykh', in idem, *Pamiatniki kul'tury. Novye otkrytiia, Ezhegodnik 1987* (Moscow, Nauka, 1988).

25 Kurmacheva, *Krepostnaia intelligentsiia Rossii*, p. 79.

26 Although the reluctance of free women to join the ranks of professional acting is not unique to Russia, it was particularly strong there. For information on the practice of purchasing women and orphaned children for the theatre, see V. P. Pogozhev, *Stoletie organizatsii imperatorskikh teatrov*, kn. 1 (St Petersburg, n.p., 1906), p. 99 and 'Dogovory K. Knippera s Peterburgskim vospitatel'nim domom o soderzhdanii teatra', RGADA, fond 1261, op. 1, d. 3014.

27 Mikhail Shchepkin, *Zapiski aktera Shchepkina* (Moscow, Iskusstvo,1988), p. 51.

28 Letkova, 'Krepostnaia intelligentsiia', p. 161; N. Negorev, 'Krepostnoi teatr', *Teatr i iskusstvo*, 6 (1911), p. 133; A. M. Brianskii, 'Eshche o krepostnom teatre', *Stolytsa i usad'ba*, 50 (1916), p. 12.

29 F. F. Vigel, *Zapiski* (Moscow, Artel' pisatelei krug, 1928), pp. 235–6; Ivanovskii, 'Krepostnye aktery I aktrisy', p. 264; Pyliaev, 'Polubarskiia zatei', p. 541.

30 Evgenii Opochinin, 'Rasprostranennia krepostnykh pevcheskikh khorov, orkestorov i teatrov v Rossii v 18–19 stoleletiakh. Novye dokumenty o zhenskom sostave truppy riazanskogo pomeshchika Chulkova', unpublished manuscript, Bakhrushin Museum, Moscow, fond 196, d. 3., p. 6.

31 Kamenskii's practices are described in many secondary and primary sources. See, for example, Evreinov, *Krepostnye aktery*, pp. 63–5; Pyliaev, 'Polubarskii zatei', pp. 543–6; Ivanovskii, Krepostnye aktery i aktrisy', p. 264; Kurmacheva, *Krepostnaia intelligentsiia Rossii*, p. 118. According to legend, Kamenskii and one of his actresses were the subjects of Herzen's *The Thieving Magpie* (*Soroka-vorovka* in *Povesti i rasskazy* (Moscow, Gosudarstvennoe izdatel'stvo khudozhestvennoi literatury, 1962), pp. 264–86.)

32 Gurii Ertaulov, 'Vospominiia o nekogda zhamenitom teatre grafa S.M. Kamenskago v g. Orle', *Delo*, (Iun' 1873), p. 211. According to Ertaulov, Kamenskii's efforts to isolate his actresses simply fuelled the desire of fashionable young men to reach the forbidden women – often with great success.

33 Negorev, 'Krepostnoi teatr', p. 134.

34 Pyliaev, 'Polubarskii', p. 540.

35 'Zapiski sel'skogo sviashchennika', *Russkaia starina*, (Ianvarzatei'), pp. 67–8.

36 Vladimir Staniukovich, *Domashnii krepostnoi teatr Sheremetevykh XVIII veka* (Leningrad, Izdanie gosudarstvennogo russkogo museia, 1927), p. 9.

37 Pyliaev, 'Polubarskiia zatei', p. 533.

38 *Ibid.*, pp. 214–16.

39 Sheremetev's actresses and dancers were given new theatrical surnames from precious stones. Thus Parasha Kuznetsova became Zhemchugova (pearl). In

order to conceal her serf origins, Sheremetev later changed her name to Praskov'ia Kovaleva: Staniukovich, *Domashnii* Krepostnoi teatr, p. 12; Gurevich, *Istoorii russkogo teatral' nogo byta*, pp. 218–20.

40 Evreinov, *Krerpostnye aktery*, pp. 39 and 78–9. Most historians, however, acknowledge the uniqueness of Kuznetsova's situation. After all, why should owners marry their serf actresses when they could take what they wanted free of charge or obligation.

41 N. F. Iushkov, *K istorii russkoi stseny. Ekaterina Borisovna Piunova-Shmidgov, v svoikh i chuzhikh vospominaniiakh* (Kazan, Tipografiia gubernkogo pravleniia, 1889). The following account is drawn entirely from Piunova's memoir. Readers requiring confirmation from secondary sources can find it in, among others, Nicolai Evreinov, E. Letkova, Liubov Gurevich, Pyliaev, and N. Negoreview

42 Negorev, 'Krepostnoi teatr', p. 153. See also, Pogozhev, *Stoletie organizatsii imperatorskikh teatrov*, kn. 1, p. 167 and Gurevich, *Istoriia russkogo teatral'nogo byta*, p. 252, who argue that the Moscow Imperials were particularly dependent on serf performers.

43 Pogozhev, *Stoletie organizatsii imperatorskikh teatrov*, kn. 1, p. 99. Attempting to persuade Aleksandr I to buy an entire serf troupe for 42,000 rubles, the director of the Moscow theatres argued that this was a small price to pay for people who knew their craft. He was particularly concerned to keep the serf actresses because actresses '*nikogda s storony ne postupaiushchikh*' (never refuse to take direction).

44 For a more thorough treatment of actresses in the late Imperial period, see Catherine Schuler, *Women in Russian Theatre: The Actress in the Silver Age* (London, Routledge, 1996).

45 A. Vol'f, Khronika Peterburgskikh teatrov s kontsa 1826 do nachala 1855 goda (St Petersburg, n.p., 1877), pp. 1–2.

Index